Charleston in Black and White

CHARLESTON IN
Black and White

Race and Power in the South

after the Civil Rights Movement

Steve Estes

The University of North Carolina Press Chapel Hill

Published with the assistance of the Fred W. Morrison Fund
of the University of North Carolina Press

Set in Miller by Westchester Publishing Services
Manufactured in the United States of America

The paper in this book meets the guidelines for permanence and durability
of the Committee on Production Guidelines for Book Longevity of the Council on
Library Resources. The University of North Carolina Press has been a member
of the Green Press Initiative since 2003.

Jacket illustrations: "Hospital Workers on Strike" and "Joe Riley Inauguration"
(Courtesy of *The Post and Courier*, Charleston, S.C.)

Library of Congress Cataloging-in-Publication Data

Estes, Steve, 1972–
   Charleston in black and white : Race and power in the south after the civil rights
movement / Steve Estes.
        pages cm
   Includes bibliographical references and index.
   ISBN 978-1-4696-2232-3 (cloth : alk. paper) — ISBN 978-1-4696-2233-0 (ebook)
   1. Charleston (S.C.)—Race relations—History—20th century.
2. Charleston (S.C.)—Race relations—History—21st century.   3. Civil rights—
South Carolina—Charleston—History—20th century.   4. Civil rights—South
Carolina—Charleston—History—21st century.   5. Civil rights movements—
South Carolina—Charleston—History.   I. Title.
   F279.C49E87 2015
   305.8009757'915—dc23
                                                                                2014040785

Portions of chapter 2 were previously published in a somewhat different
form in "'I Am Somebody': The Charleston Hospital Strike of 1969," *The Avery
Review* 3:2 (Spring 2000): 8–32. Portions of chapter 5 were previously published in
a somewhat different form in "The Long Gay Line: Gender and Sexual Orientation at
the Citadel," *Southern Cultures* 16:1 (Spring 2010): 46–64. Used with permission.

Contents

Illustrations

Charleston in Black and White

TOO PROUD TO WHITEWASH

I was born in Charlotte, North Carolina. In Charleston, that makes me a Yankee. Well, not exactly a Yankee, but as Charlestonians of a certain generation would say, I'm "from off." My parents, my brother, and I moved to Charleston in 1977 when I was five years old, and I grew up surrounded by native Charlestonians. Still, as I grew up, I felt like something of an outsider. When I left Charleston in 1990 to study history in college and then graduate school, I focused on the civil rights movement, not the Civil War. I returned to the Lowcountry as a visiting assistant professor of history at the College of Charleston in 2001. The city had changed so much since I had first arrived more than two decades earlier that I truly felt like a tourist in my own hometown, so I did what any newcomer would do. I went to the visitor center.

The Charleston visitor center sits between King and Meeting Streets, two major commercial thoroughfares that run through the city's historic downtown and up the peninsula. The center's grounds are gracefully manicured, with fountains and iron gates. The building, a renovated nineteenth-century train depot, is well appointed, befitting the vital role of tourism in one of the oldest cities in America. Entering the visitor center, the first person I saw was a young white woman in her early twenties wearing an elaborate hoopskirt, the kind popular during Charleston's antebellum heyday. This image was a bit jarring next to the garish pamphlets advertising all-you-can-eat shrimp dinners and Day-Glo flyers for beach rentals, but the young lady seemed just as at home as if she had been on a plantation veranda in 1850. As a history professor, I knew that it was rare to hear the authentic voice of the past, so I approached with a mix of scholarly skepticism and tourist enthusiasm. I introduced myself to this iconic belle and asked where she was from. She replied in a charming, unmistakable accent: "New Jersey."

The South has long been a fixed star in the constellation of American popular culture. This mythic South allows Americans to navigate the dangerous shoals of racial politics. We can measure our progress as a people by how far we have moved beyond where the South was and still appears to be. Some southern historians have responded to this caricature of the region by showing how "American" it has become since the civil rights movement and/or how "southern" America has become since that tumultuous era. While there is undoubtedly truth in both of these propositions, there is something unique about the South that makes understanding it imperative if we are going to understand what has happened in the United States since the civil rights movement.[1]

Charleston may not be "the most southern place on earth," as Mississippians claim of their home, or the "heart of Dixie," as Alabamans boast, but its history contains many of the contradictions that drive the story of the modern South. Once, Charleston was a booming, cosmopolitan metropolis. On the eve of the American Revolution, it was the fourth largest city in what would soon become the United States, comparable in size and influence to Philadelphia, New York, and Boston. In the 1770s, according to a leading economic historian, the Lowcountry was "by many standards of measurement the wealthiest area in British North America, if not the entire world." Half of this wealth was held in human beings—slaves. In fact, Charleston is considered the African American "Ellis Island" as over 40 percent of the slaves brought to North America from 1700 to 1776 passed through the port. Charleston's power, wealth, and centrality in American life had faded completely by the early twentieth century, when it was one of the poorest towns in the poorest region in the United States. Fallen aristocrats clung to their historic but dilapidated mansions where it was said they were "too poor to paint, but too proud to whitewash." By then, Charleston had become at best a quaint but sad vision of a paradise lost and at worst a tragic lesson of the ways slavery and racism had nearly destroyed the country.[2]

Historical complexities and contradictions are still present in Charleston. In fact, they may be more easily visible there than anywhere else in America. This is why I decided to investigate the post–civil rights era in the city. With this book, I explore the ways that Charleston and the rest of the South have changed as a result of the social movements of the 1960s and, just as important, the ways that the city and region have *not* changed as much as civil rights activists once hoped and dreamed. While race is central to this story given Charleston's history, location, and people, this book also considers questions about politics, criminal justice, education, tourism, class, gender, and sexuality to understand larger trends in recent southern and American history. From beautifully restored colonial homes to cutting-edge Internet companies and medical research facilities, Charleston is no longer "too poor to paint." But the city has a long memory. Charlestonians cannot avoid the past. It is everywhere. In this way, Charleston is unlike Atlanta or Charlotte, Jacksonville or even New Orleans, where development and boosterism have often obscured the ways that these places continue to wrestle with vestiges of their troubled histories. Despite all of the advances and opportunities that have come in the years since the civil rights movement, Charlestonians are too proud to whitewash the ways that the past continues to define the city's present and future.[3]

This history of Charleston since the civil rights movement is informed by four strands of recent historical scholarship. First, since the 1990s, civil rights historians have written local histories to revise the national narrative of the movement that had dominated both popular and scholarly accounts since the 1970s. From the Mississippi Delta to Birmingham, Alabama, from Oakland, California, to Newark, New Jersey, these local stories have expanded our definition and understanding of the movement.[4] With a narrow geographic scope, local movement histories tackled a longer period of time, often bringing the story of race relations into the 1980s or 1990s. As much as these studies told us about the parallel stories of local movements in the 1950s and 1960s, there was little consensus about whether these movements bent toward or away from justice in the post–civil rights era. The history of Charleston suggests that this is because race relations took two divergent trajectories in the post–civil rights era, with growing opportunities for the black middle class and elite, accompanied by increased segregation and disempowerment of lower-income African Americans.

The second, related strain of scholarship that informs the book is a question about periodizing the "long civil rights movement."[5] There has been some debate about whether we must lengthen our narrative of the movement to encompass earlier and later struggles for rights or whether such expansion actually distorts beyond recognition the original movement, doing injustice to the activists of the classic civil rights era in the 1950s and 60s.[6] There are undoubtedly continuities between the struggles for justice in the 1950s and 60s and those in the years since. As in the classic phase of the movement, the struggle for equality after the 1960s continued in classrooms and courtrooms, dormitory halls and city hall. Post–civil rights era campaigns borrowed from the tactics, philosophies, and language of the movement. They sought to defend the legacies of that movement and continue the fight in an era when many Americans seemed to believe that the battle for racial equality—or at least, equal opportunity—had already been won. As a result, the campaigns for racial justice in the post–civil rights era faced subtler and often more effective opposition than those in the 1950s and 60s. There was less grassroots activism for southern civil rights and simultaneously less national support for the cause from the 1970s to the 2000s. This did not mean, however, that Charlestonians, and other Americans, stopped struggling with the relationships between race and rights or power and democracy that underpinned the campaigns of the civil rights era.

The third body of scholarship addressed by this book concerns urban and/or suburban studies of the conservative backlash to the civil rights movement. Many, though not all, of these books focus on the South, and they tend to echo the themes of Republican campaigns from the late 1960s and 70s that called on the "silent majority" and "southern strategy" to roll back liberalism.[7] These works argue compellingly that a grassroots, conservative backlash to the civil rights movement, particularly in the South, facilitated the Republican revolution for the next forty years. Still, local politics—even in cities like Atlanta and Charlotte, which were the focus of two books on the New Right—were much more complicated in the post–civil rights era than the simple backlash thesis would suggest. An examination of postmovement politics in Charleston highlights these complications and revises the master narrative of the period in two ways. First, it reveals that a biracial, progressive coalition in the Democratic Party did work in southern urban areas. Second, and perhaps more surprising, some of the most impressive black electoral victories came not from this Democratic coalition, but from an unlikely alliance of liberal, black Democrats and conservative, white Republicans.

The final strand of scholarship that informs this book consists of works on the post–civil rights era that look at the ways the civil rights movement influenced subsequent movements for women's rights, gay rights, and workers' rights. Scholars who have drawn direct parallels between these movements and the black freedom struggle have been criticized for comparing apples to oranges or distorting the earlier movement story to score political victories for other oppressed groups. Yet these subsequent movements clearly borrowed from the rhetoric and strategies of the civil rights movement, and though it is often forgotten, African Americans played integral roles in the later struggles even when these movements did not focus explicitly on race or racism.[8] As a result, this book explores the way gender integration at the Citadel, labor struggles in Charleston, and conflict over urban gentrification carried the fight for equality into the twenty-first century. In some ways, these more recent struggles would have sounded very familiar to civil rights activists of the 1960s, and in other ways, they struck dissonant chords with the earlier movement. Just as the post–civil rights era witnessed divergent paths for different groups of African Americans, other movements for equality saw mixed, often contradictory, results. Women gained admission to all-male universities and joined the former "good ole boy" club of southern politics, but they did so as decidedly unequal partners. Workers defended hard-won gains through organized labor in places like the Charleston docks, but they did so as the city, region, and nation shifted to a service economy that was much harder to organize than an industrial one, especially in right-to-work states like South Carolina. In all of these struggles, economic class became an increasingly important (but not the only) factor determining victory or defeat during the post–civil rights era.

Fifty years after civil rights activists conducted sit-ins in downtown restaurants as part of the Charleston Movement, the struggle for civil rights had reshaped politics, policing, education, housing, jobs, and everyday life in the city. By the twenty-first century, African Americans represented the Lowcountry in the city and county councils, the state house and senate, the U.S. Congress, and even the U.S. Senate. An African American police chief had protected the city for half of the post–civil rights era. There were African American doctors at the Medical University and professors at the College of Charleston and the Citadel. Many of the sons and daughters of these professionals went to integrated suburban schools and lived in integrated suburban neighborhoods. A black candidate had won the South Carolina Democratic primary with massive Lowcountry support on his way to a historic election as president of the United States. Despite these accomplishments, most of them unimaginable to the activists who risked life and limb simply for service at downtown businesses in the 1960s, some aspects of Charleston had not changed nearly as much as civil rights leaders hoped. Downtown public schools were segregated not only by race but also by class. Residential neighborhoods on the East Side and the Neck were likewise segregated by race and class. Many of the residents of these neighborhoods lucky enough to have employment held the same types of low-paying jobs that their grandparents once worked. This book looks at how the civil rights movement could have changed a southern town like Charleston so much and yet left other parts of the city nearly untouched or perhaps even worse off than in the Jim Crow era.

To chronicle this relatively recent historical era, I relied heavily on oral interviews with the people who made this history. I had to. The archival collections for this period remain limited. Many of the people who wrote the letters, speeches, meeting minutes, and other primary documents of the late twentieth century still have them. Those who documented the early years of the twenty-first century have often done so digitally. On the one hand, then, the great challenge of writing recent history is that a historian must rely (ironically) on a *smaller* base of archival material. On the other hand, historians of the recent past have enviable access to the people we are writing about. This, too, is a blessing and a curse, because unlike other historians who toil exclusively in dusty archives, our sources talk back and sometimes fight back. Their memories and opinions are vital to understanding the past, but none of them are complete or completely accurate on their own. They must be compared with other perspectives and the documentary evidence available from the period. This book collects the stories of more than fifty Charlestonians who shared their life stories and local perspectives with me. Although this is not the story any one of them would tell, I hope that each will see his or her influence in the narrative and analysis, just as I hope readers from outside of Charleston will see the value of including the memories and opinions (however faulty and contradictory) of the people who lived through this particular time in this particular place.

By weaving together a diverse collection of Charlestonians' stories into this narrative, I also hope that I have illuminated more than simply the last fifty years of my hometown's history. In researching and writing the book, I have tried to choose topics, people, and events from Charleston's recent past that have national significance, shedding light on major trends and themes in the modern South and modern America. Questions about the legacies of the social movements of the 1950s and 60s have defined our recent past, affecting decisions about where we send children to school, how we fight crime, whom we elect, where we work, and where we live. In other words, this book focuses on a small place to answer big questions about the modern history of the United States. It seeks to address questions that Martin Luther King Jr. asked at the end of his life: where have we gone since the civil rights movement, and where do we go from here?

There was one final question that I sought to answer when I set out to write this book, a far more personal one. Where am I from? I began asking that question many years ago, but the inquiry gained more urgency at the end of my one-year teaching gig at the College of Charleston in 2002. Leaving Charleston for the second time was bittersweet. I was moving to the San Francisco Bay Area to take a permanent job teaching history. The night before I left Charleston, I stood at the kitchen sink peeling shrimp with my mom. We were making shrimp and grits, one of the simplest and best Lowcountry dishes. "I am just afraid that I won't get to see my grandchild grow up," my mom explained, using a time-honored parental guilt trip. Never mind that there was no grandchild yet. The grits boiled. The shrimp cooked. I stewed.

A few years later, there was a grandchild, one who didn't see her grandmama nearly as much as she should have. I started to work on this book. Research trips and family vacations became attempts to bridge the thousands of miles between San Francisco and Charleston. They gave my daughter and her grandmama a chance to get to know each other. After these visits to the Lowcountry, my daughter would come back to California with just the hint of a southern accent, a genteel Charleston one, of course.

On one trip to visit us in California, my mom seemed tired. It was more than just jet lag. She had a persistent cough, and she napped more than her granddaughter. Not long after she got back to Charleston, doctors gave my mom the bad news. She had stage-four cancer. The rest of her life would be measured in months, not decades. On one of my visits home to help care for my mom, she asked if I would make shrimp and grits for dinner. It had been almost exactly ten years since we stood at her kitchen sink, peeling shrimp together the night before I moved away. This time, however, my mom was too weak to get out of bed to help. Cancer, chemo, and radiation had taken their toll. I stood at the sink, peeling the shrimp, angry and alone. That night, after my mom fell asleep and I cleaned up from dinner, I went to work on this book.

The Lowcountry

If there was ever a place that was both godforsaken and God's country, the Carolina colony was it. After a few failed attempts to settle a colony between Virginia and Spanish Florida, a wealthy group of British investors—the Lords Proprietors—financed a voyage that left England in August 1669. After stops in Ireland and Barbados, the *Carolina* deposited ninety-three passengers on the southeast coast of North America in April 1670. The Lowcountry must have looked beautiful that spring. Palmetto trees and sea grasses swayed in warm breezes. Fauna was plentiful and potable water not far away. Two broad rivers forked around a picturesque peninsula that would ultimately become the site of Charlestown. Promotional literature later claimed that the healthful Carolina air gave settlers "a strong appetite," making men in the colony "more lightsome" and women "very Fruitful."[1]

As spring turned to summer and summer to fall, however, some of the less pleasant aspects of the Carolina Lowcountry emerged. The stifling heat and humidity were bearable until an armada of insects arose from the surrounding wetlands. Settlers complained of "pestiferous gnats, called moschetoes" that bedeviled the colony. Unbeknownst to the colonists, these mosquitoes often carried deadly strains of malaria and yellow fever—diseases that would decimate populations in the Carolina Lowcountry for more than two centuries. The sea breezes that blew over Charlestown offered some small protection but certainly not immunity to the mosquito-borne plagues. The rest of the Lowcountry was more vulnerable. In one rural county during the mid-1700s, eighty-six of every hundred white residents died before the age of twenty. Africans and later

African Americans proved more resistant to malaria than white settlers, but a punishing slave labor regime led to mortality rates so high that the black population grew only because white planters purchased thousands of new slaves from Africa and the Caribbean each year. The Native American population of the Lowcountry, already devastated by European diseases contracted from contact with early explorers, plummeted after the permanent settlement of Charlestown.[2]

Still, despite the disease and death that marked many early adventures in Carolina, settlers continued to arrive. Most of the early colonists came from England or the British colony of Barbados. Barbados had seen such phenomenal economic growth from its sugar plantations that little free land remained on the island by the 1670s. The number of Barbadian planters who moved their families and slaves to Carolina in the late 1600s led one historian to call the Low Country the "colony of a colony." Barbadian and British migrants wagered their lives on what they hoped would be fortunes from Lowcountry plantations. Though many individuals lost this wager, families survived. Allstons, Fenwicks, Gibbes, Logans, Bulls, Middletons, and other families who came to the colony in this first generation acquired the richest land and dominated the Lowcountry for centuries to come.[3]

As with much of the South, the contradictory relationship between freedom and slavery dominated the history of the Carolina colony. The liberal political philosopher John Locke worked with Lord Ashley Cooper, one of the colony's original Lords Proprietors, to craft a colonial constitution. Enlightenment ideals influenced that document, but it was also infused by the era's nearly unchallenged support of chattel slavery. The constitution protected the rights of the aristocracy, providing absolute power for colonial nobility over servants and slaves. Yet true to his ideals that would inspire the Declaration of Independence and the American Revolution, John Locke had crafted a political framework for the Carolina colony that gave almost all men with even minimal property the right to vote. Locke's constitution guaranteed trials by juries and even mandated religious tolerance of "Jews, heathens, and other dissenters," including slaves. The colony never fully ratified Locke's charter, but its principles had an enduring influence on the paradoxical commitments to both slavery and freedom in the Lowcountry.[4]

Charlestown would later be nicknamed the "Holy City" because of its numerous and varied religious meeting houses, but the city's elite were as devoted to their fields as to their faiths. Over the course of the eighteenth century, Charlestown planters settled on two dominant cash crops: rice and indigo. Dubbed "Carolina gold," rice made Lowcountry planters rich. By the 1770s, Charlestown was one of the wealthiest cities in North America with more than 20 percent of the city's estates valued at over £2,000 sterling. Half of that wealth consisted of property in the form of human beings—slaves.[5]

By 1708, the Carolina colony had a black majority. Charlestown and its neighboring plantations looked "more like a negro country" than a European one to visitors in the colonial period. The presence of so many Africans and African Americans in bondage made white visitors and residents alike anxious. Fear of slave insurrection was ever present in the colony. Colonists must have asked themselves if rumors of rebellion were like harmless heat lightning that danced along the Carolina coast every summer or if they were fearsome storms just over the horizon.[6]

In September 1739, white fears became a reality as about twenty slaves gathered on a plantation near the Stono River just south of Charlestown with a plan to kill white masters and escape to freedom in Spanish Florida. An Angolan man named Jemmy led the rebels to a country store, where they took guns and ammunition. The white shopkeepers were killed and decapitated during the assault, their heads left on the store's front steps. As the slaves moved south on the road between Charlestown and Savannah, they burned and looted four plantations, killing the white inhabitants and growing to a band of nearly 100 rebels. The killing was not indiscriminate, however. The rebels spared the life of a white innkeeper, "for he was a good man and kind to his slaves." By sheer coincidence, the lieutenant governor of the colony was traveling northward toward Charlestown when he met the approaching rebels. Fleeing on horseback, the lieutenant governor called up the white militia. It took almost a month before the whites captured and killed the last of the rebel slaves.[7]

In the decades after the Stono Rebellion, white South Carolinians took greater legal control of their slaves, even as they began to chafe at the increasing regulations imposed on them by the British government. Christopher Gadsden, a white seaman and merchant, came of age in Charlestown during this era. Schooled in England and a veteran of the British navy, Gadsden became one of the most ardent patriots in South Carolina. A close friend of Bostonian Samuel Adams, he founded the South Carolina branch of the Sons of Liberty in the 1760s and in the 1770s designed an iconic flag featuring a coiled rattlesnake representing the American colonies and the motto "Don't Tread on Me." Yet as the American Revolution began, Gadsden and other Charlestown elites did their best to control the passions for liberty that they aroused in the Lowcountry. When white workingmen formed a mob to punish local Tory elites, Gadsden quickly quelled the riot. When northern patriots suggested arming slaves to fight the British, Gadsden expressed "great resentment" at the "dangerous and impolitic step." Few would have questioned Christopher Gadsden's patriotism or his commitment to the Revolution. The South Carolinian who became a general in the Continental Army spent nearly a year as a British prisoner of war in the old Spanish fort at St. Augustine. Still, his was a complicated devotion to liberty. Like fellow revolutionaries slave merchant Henry Laurens and plantation masters Thomas Jefferson and George Washington, Gadsden valued freedom and independence precisely because he well understood the meaning of slavery. In South Carolina and other colonies, the American Revolution meant liberty for some and continued enslavement for many others.[8]

Incorporated and renamed in 1783, Charleston was approaching its historical zenith. Millions of pounds of rice shipped out of the port city annually, and cotton further enriched the Lowcountry's already booming agricultural economy. The famed Charleston single houses with side porches or piazzas bustled with growing families. Charleston's elite built even grander mansions as they amassed great wealth. They continued to dominate South Carolina politics and to play a leading role in national politics. Though Charlestonians could not have known it at the time, the clock was already beginning to tick toward the end of this golden age. By the 1820s, international competition undermined the market for Carolina rice. Plantations in the southern hinterland and Gulf Coast regions rivaled producers of Lowcountry cotton as well.[9]

Whether they sensed the turning point or not, black Charlestonians chose this historical moment to challenge white control of the city. Their leader was a man named Denmark Vesey. Born in the 1760s either in Africa or the Caribbean, Vesey had come to Charleston owned by an American sea captain and slaver. When Vesey arrived in the city in the 1780s, Charleston had more black residents than Boston, New York, and Philadelphia combined. The vast majority of these black residents were enslaved. Charleston was a place ripe for revolution, though Vesey seemed, on the surface, an unlikely revolutionary. After winning $1,500 in a lottery in 1800, Vesey bought his freedom and started a carpentry shop. For the next fifteen years, he lived a relatively quiet middle-class life.[10]

There was a strong black middle class in Charleston in the antebellum period. Many of these men and women were, in fact, of mixed racial ancestry. Called mulattoes in the parlance of the day, they were the sons and daughters of white planters and black slave mistresses. Such unions had long been an open secret in the city, as in other parts of the South. In the 1730s, an anonymous writer had expounded on the merits of such relationships in the Charleston newspaper, rhetorically asking, "Kiss black or white, why need it trouble you?" A century later, the white diarist Mary Boykin Chesnut explained, "Any lady is ready to tell you who the father is of all the mulatto children in everybody's household but her own." This mixed-race community of free men and women made up between 5 and 10 percent of the city's population in the antebellum period, living parallel lives to the city's white elite. They owned homes and businesses. Many of them owned their own slaves. They founded exclusive social and mutual aid organizations, such as Brown Fellowship and Friendly Moralist Society. They attended the city's elite churches, sitting not far from some of their white relatives every Sunday at St. Philip's, St. Michael's, and St. John's.[11]

Despite his relatively dark skin and African lineage, as a skilled craftsman living just three blocks from the South Carolina governor and the Charleston mayor, Denmark Vesey could have lived the rest of his days without much trouble. He did not. After first joining the Second Presbyterian Church, Vesey left the predominantly white church for Charleston's first African Methodist Episcopal church. Another free black man, Morris Brown, had founded the AME church in 1815. Inspired by the new theology of the black church, Vesey began to plan an uprising in Charleston. Black informants and white court officials documented Vesey's plot, though their motives for accusing and convicting the rebels were far from pure. The AME church members supposedly formed the nucleus of the rebellion's supporters. With the help of several lieutenants and perhaps hundreds of slave supporters, Vesey planned to torch parts of the city, assassinate its political leaders, and storm the local arsenals for weapons. Once in control of Charleston, Vesey hoped to commandeer ships from the local wharves and make an escape to Haiti. But the plot was discovered in the summer of 1822. Turned in by a few slaves and free blacks, Vesey and other ringleaders were arrested. "Die like a man!" one of the rebels supposedly urged a coconspirator in prison that summer. Thirty-five of them did, hanged to death after brief trials. The AME church founder Morris Brown, who had not been privy to the plot, was deported, along with nearly thirty others. Whites in the city burned their church to the ground.[12]

In the decades that followed the aborted insurrection, attitudes toward slavery hardened not only in the city, but around the country. A political impasse emerged between North and South. To white South Carolinians, the election of Abraham Lincoln as president in 1860 seemed to leave few options but secession from a country that appeared hell-bent on abolition. In December of that year at a meeting in Charleston, South Carolina leaders voted unanimously to leave the United States. "The Union is dissolved!" cheered the Charleston *Mercury*. The lone remaining garrison of federal troops in the Lowcountry took up a defensive position on an unfinished island fortress in Charleston harbor. In April 1861, Charleston's batteries opened fire on the Union troops at Fort Sumter. The Civil War had begun. "We will be in Washington in less than a month," boasted one Charleston soldier, who foresaw a quick southern victory.[13]

"A city of ruins, of desolation, of vacant houses, of widowed women, of rotting wharves, of deserted warehouses, of weed-wild gardens . . . that is Charleston." So wrote a northern journalist who traveled to the city in 1865. Two fires and a Union bombardment had destroyed a third of the city, even though many colonial and antebellum buildings had been spared. Black Charlestonians, understandably jubilant at the prospect of freedom, paraded through the city in 1865 with signs that read: "Slavery is Dead." Just as understandably, formerly wealthy whites in the city believed "the war has ruined us." Both assessments proved somewhat premature.[14]

Reconstruction completely upended Charleston society, but as radical as it was, this revolution also proved ephemeral. African Americans gained a political voice, economic opportunities, and religious freedom undreamed of before the war. Black Charlestonians served in the city government, made up half of the police force, and rode on integrated streetcars. By the late 1870s and 80s, however, conservative whites had regained political control of the city and state. White South Carolinians disfranchised African Americans through discriminatory voter registration laws and further stifled black political dissent with lynching. In Charleston, many of the same white families who had come to the city two hundred years earlier regained their unquestioned status as community leaders, but the community they led was in trouble.[15]

Through all of the social and political changes that followed the Civil War, no one found a way to halt Charleston's economic decline, which the war had only accelerated. The Chamber of Commerce wrote optimistically in 1873 "to dispel the opinion, entertained in some quarters abroad, that this city is losing its commercial status." Notwithstanding such sunny promotional literature, Charleston's exalted commercial status was already history. Fertilizer (in the form of phosphate) became one of the most valuable exports from the Lowcountry at the end of the nineteenth century. Needless to say, fertilizer was not "Carolina gold."[16]

A "golden haze of memory" was one of the most precious commodities in Charleston for the first half of the twentieth century, when the wealth of the past seemed a panacea for the poverty of the present. The nostalgia and romantic myths of the Old South sustained white Charlestonians in an era when even the city's elite quietly counted every penny. As the rest of the country boomed economically and embraced modern progress in the 1920s, a national market emerged for art that capitalized on the image of Charleston as a repository of white gentility and black primitivism. A 1920s dance craze that originated in Charleston's black community catapulted the city into the national consciousness. One 1928 Chicago newspaper article on the "Renaissance in the South" claimed that artists were setting up easels on nearly every block depicting Charleston's picturesque street scenes. The most famous of these scenes was the fictional Catfish Row, imagined by Charleston novelist DuBose Heyward and immortalized in George and Ira Gershwin's 1935 opera *Porgy and Bess*. Despite the artistic renaissance of the 1920s and 30s, the reality of life for most black and white Charlestonians remained hard. Even as Heyward and the Gershwins were romanticizing black life in Charleston, African Americans were leaving the Lowcountry in droves to join the Great Migration north. Though he remained an eloquent spokesperson for the city, Heyward himself joined the exodus, departing in the mid-1920s.[17]

Only when federal money poured into the city during World War II and the Cold War did Charleston finally began to regain some of its former luster. Population growth during and after the war, along with the presence of relatively high-paying government jobs for both black and white workers, laid the foundations for dramatic social movements in the coming years. Throughout the 1950s, a relatively placid and prosperous decade in Charleston, few of the city's residents foresaw the dramatic social changes coming just over the horizon. Some of the first folks who saw the changes coming were those who lived farthest from the stately homes of downtown Charleston, the people of the Sea Islands.[18]

CHAPTER ONE

Pater Familias

Historically somewhat isolated from metropolitan Charleston, residents of the Sea Islands along the Lowcountry coastline were in the vanguard of numerous eras in the region's storied past. Plantations on the islands and up the coastal waterways were the foundation of Charleston's wealth and power before the Civil War. During the war, the Sea Islands were some of the first places that the Union Army captured from the Confederacy, setting up what one historian called a "rehearsal for Reconstruction." The geographic isolation of these islands and their large black majorities allowed African cultural influences to survive well into the twentieth century. The best example of this was Gullah—a mix of African, European, and American influences that produced a unique creole language and culture. Yet the isolation that protected this vibrant Gullah culture also consigned most Sea Island natives to grinding poverty. Many black Charlestonians had new economic opportunities during and after World War II, and the city's paternalistic race relations seemed to ameliorate some of the worst excesses of Jim Crow. In the Sea Islands, however, the combination of extreme poverty and virulent racism from white property owners circumscribed black life as much as the water and wetlands surrounding the islands. A combination of this rich cultural heritage and impoverished economy on the Sea Islands inspired a local civil rights movement that would ultimately feed into the struggle for racial equality in Charleston. That movement culminated in a 1969 hospital workers' strike, one of the last major direct action campaigns of the civil rights era.[1]

We could understand the Charleston movement and the hospital strike as simply community activism and a labor struggle, but it is also important to view these campaigns in the broader context of the fight against pater- nalistic racism. The idea of paternalism goes back to the Roman era, when the *pater familias* was the head of the household and estate owner. Though the term has come to mean a domineering father figure, it was once applied simply to upstanding Roman citizens who owned property. The Roman *pater familias* had a responsibility to protect his dependents— wife, children, and slaves—but he also had the power of life and death over them. In the antebellum South, southern planters cultivated a pater- nalistic relationship with their slaves based on this Roman model. In their eyes, this was a mutually beneficial and relatively benign master- slave relationship. Yet it was clearly not a democratic one. Although the Civil War destroyed slavery, paternalism survived. Unlike overtly racist demagogues in places like the Mississippi Delta or the Alabama Black Belt, paternalists in Charleston well into the twentieth century took pride in their "moderate" vision of race relations, which saw black workers as de- pendents or children. As long as workers did not challenge this hierarchy, paternalists treated them as inferiors, but with civility rather than vio- lent repression. To be sure, there was more than a hint of paternalism in race relations across the South (and perhaps much of the country) during the Jim Crow era, but while rural whites resorted to the rope or bullet to suppress black dissent, leaders of many southern cities wielded subtler pa- ternalism to ward off both internal protests and external pressure to alter the racial and economic status quo. In a study of Greensboro, North Carolina, historian William Chafe first argued that the paternalistic ideal of civility was "a way of dealing with people and problems that made good manners more important than substantial action." This genteel and patronizing approach to race relations allowed white leaders in Charles- ton and many other southern cities to avoid early civil rights protests, but a reckoning would come in time.[2]

If you take a long view of the Lowcountry civil rights movement, you might say that the story started at the Promise Land School on Johns Island in the 1910s. Unfortunately, there was not much promising about the Promise Land School in those years. The two-room building made of logs and clay housed more than 130 black students on the rare occasions when fieldwork did not take priority over schoolwork. The two teachers at Prom- ise Land each made $35 a month at the end of the 1910s. Across the road, the white school had three students with a teacher who made $85 a month. Promise Land School may have seemed an unlikely incubator for the civil rights movement, but two local leaders got their start at the school. One was a teacher, and the other a student.[3]

Septima Clark was eighteen when she left her Charleston home to take her first teaching job on Johns Island in 1916. The daughter of a former slave and a washerwoman, Clark was no stranger to the economic privations that many Lowcountry African Americans faced, but she had grown up in the city and attended the private black high school, so the abject poverty and racism on Johns Island was a shock. "The rankest discrimination" existed on the island and in its schools, according to Clark. Another black teacher who came from Charleston to Johns Island a few years before Clark described the impoverished and isolated community as "a place behind God's back." During Clark's tenure, Promise Land School served both elementary and middle school students. There would be no high school for black students on the Sea Islands for another half century. The challenges at Promise Land School pushed Clark further down the path to becoming a lifelong educator and activist. Like many young teachers, Clark left the island after a short tenure, teaching for most of her career in other South Carolina public schools, but fate brought her back to Johns Island in the 1950s to work with a Promise Land dropout at the dawn of the civil rights movement.[4]

Esau Jenkins left Promise Land School after the fourth grade to get a job. He had to choose between helping his family make ends meet and furthering his own education. It wasn't long, however, before Jenkins realized that a lack of education would hold back both his entrepreneurial and civic ambitions, so he sought out education at night from community leaders. When he exhausted the island's resources, he took night classes at the black public high school in Charleston. Esau Jenkins never went to college, and he never formally taught school. But like Septima Clark, Jenkins dedicated much of his life to advancing the education and civil rights of African Americans in the Sea Islands and Charleston.[5]

Whites on Johns Island may have been somewhat paternalistic toward black tenant farmers and sharecroppers for much of the Jim Crow era, but they were not above using violence to keep black residents in line. In the 1930s and 1940s, white islanders shot black residents with impunity for the smallest infractions of the social order. One of these shootings in the 1940s took place after a black resident's dog got into a fight with the dog of a white resident. White authorities did not even investigate the incident. "We can't afford to let things like that go on," Esau Jenkins realized. "We as people, who know better, should make it better and make race relations better." Inspired by this incident, Jenkins founded the Progressive Club in 1949 to raise civic awareness on Johns Island and channel the frustrations of the black community into social action. Jenkins's motto was simple: "Hate is expensive; love is progress." The Progressive Club served as a legal aid society for victims of racial violence and the home of a co-operative store where black residents could buy and sell goods relatively cheaply. The club would also become home to a citizenship school that served as a model for grassroots civil rights activism throughout the rural South.[6]

The idea for the citizenship schools emerged from discussions between Septima Clark and Esau Jenkins in the 1950s at the Highlander Folk School in the mountains of Tennessee. Run by an old lefty named Miles Horton, Highlander was like an adult summer camp for union and civil rights activists. Highlander gave Clark employment and direction after she was fired from her teaching position in Charleston County because she was an active member of the NAACP. During a 1955 summer workshop at Highlander, Septima Clark struck up a friendship with a fellow southern activist who wanted to challenge Jim Crow in her hometown of Montgomery, Alabama. That young woman, Rosa Parks, would later introduce Clark to a minister named Martin Luther King Jr. at Highlander. Inspired by activists like these, Esau Jenkins pitched the idea of a citizenship school for adults on Johns Island, where nine out of ten black adults could not read well enough to pass the literacy test required for voting in South Carolina. With advice and support from Highlander staff, the first citizenship school opened in the back of the Johns Island Progressive Club in 1957. The school taught adults the basics of reading and writing, as well as the requirements for voter registration and civic participation. Eight of the fourteen participants in that first class registered to vote in 1957. "I've never seen Negroes standing up for their rights as now," a jubilant Clark wrote to friends the following year, but she was not the only one to note the potential of the citizenship school. "There's a school on the island," the Charleston *News and Courier* reported. "Not a White Citizens' Council, not a Ku Klux Klan, none of us knew about this school. They're teaching Negroes to read, and teaching them to register and vote." Highlander supported extension of the citizen school program to other parts of the Lowcountry, and Jenkins set up a voter registration drive in Charleston in the late 1950s. Clark explained that there was still resistance even in the black community because many black Charlestonians had bought into the "paternalistic doctrine" of race relations. "I'm trying to tear that down and teach by example," she wrote in 1960, but replacing the mind-set of paternalism with equality was no easy job. In 1961, the Johns Island citizenship school became a model for a series of schools set up across the South by Martin Luther King's organization, the

Southern Christian Leadership Conference (SCLC). With King's support, Clark was hired to direct the program. She had become, according to one biographer, "freedom's teacher."[7]

As African Americans began to challenge Charleston's system of paternalistic race relations in the 1940s and 50s, they found few local white allies. After all, it seemed foolish for white men and women to undercut a system that privileged them, and white people who did challenge this system became pariahs. The experience of a federal judge named J. Waties Waring became a case in point. Waring was from one of the oldest white families in the Lowcountry. His father and two uncles had fought for the Confederacy. In the 1920s, he lived in a large old house on Meeting Street, not far from his law office on Broad Street. Black Charlestonians were Waring's employees, not friends. "Most of the Negroes I knew were exslaves," he recalled years later, "and you loved them and were good to them. We didn't give them any rights, but they never asked for any rights." Born into a paternalistic system, he did not question it. As Waring explained, he "was raised in the atmosphere that we ought to take care of these people." Politically connected, the Charleston attorney was appointed to the federal bench by President Franklin Roosevelt in 1942. Nothing in his history suggested that he would be a radical jurist, but civil rights historian Steve O'Neill argued that is exactly what he became. "Waring not only distinguished himself with several landmark decisions," O'Neill observed, "but he also shattered the comfortable existence that his aristocratic birthright had provided him." In 1944, Waring issued a decision forcing Charleston schools to pay black and white teachers equally. That ruling ruffled a few feathers. A year later, he divorced his first wife, a native Charlestonian, and shortly thereafter married an outspoken liberal divorcée from New York. The scandal began a process of social ostracism from elite white society in Charleston that would be complete after two more controversial decisions.[8]

In the late 1940s and early 1950s, black activists in South Carolina with the support of the NAACP legal defense fund began to challenge racial segregation in politics and schools. In 1947, black South Carolinians challenged the all-white Democratic Party primary that basically decided the state's elections. The Supreme Court ruled racially exclusive primaries unconstitutional in 1944. South Carolina tried to skirt the decision by making political parties private clubs. After hearing the arguments of the NAACP's lead counsel, Thurgood Marshall, Waring held that the South Carolina political clubs were unconstitutional. "It is time for South Carolina to rejoin the Union," he wrote. "Racial distinctions cannot exist in the machinery that selects the officers and lawmakers of the United States." The decision garnered Waring national attention. *Colliers* and *Time* ran feature stories on him. But the more famous Waring became nationally for his liberal rulings, the more infamous he became in Charleston. The *Colliers* piece dubbed him "the loneliest man in town." After lightning struck Waring's neighbor's house, someone nailed a sign in the yard: "Dear God, He Lives Next Door." In 1951, Waring had one last chance to weigh in on the legalities of segregation in South Carolina. Thurgood Marshall argued in front of Waring and two other federal judges that segregation in the state's public schools was unconstitutional. The other two judges on the panel ruled against the NAACP position in *Briggs v. Elliot*, deciding— as the Supreme Court had more than fifty years earlier in *Plessy v. Ferguson*—that segregation was constitutional. Waring dissented. He began by applauding the "unexampled courage" of the plaintiffs in challenging "the false doctrine and patter called 'separate but equal.'" He then traced the long history of race and the law with a detailed analysis of the Fourteenth Amendment and the increasingly progressive interpretations of that amendment by the Supreme Court. "Segregation is *per se* inequality," he reasoned. "And if the courts of this land are to render justice under the laws without fear or favor," Waring concluded, "the time to do it is now." The Supreme Court echoed much of Waring's dissent when it addressed *Briggs* as part of its *Brown v. Board of Education* decision in 1954. By then, Waring was no longer in South Carolina to relish his vindication by the high court. He retired in 1952 and immediately moved to New York, having been all but run out of Charleston. Judgments were one thing. Enforcing civil rights and changing mind-sets were different animals entirely.[9]

For better and worse, paternalism allowed Charleston to avoid much of the cinematic drama that provided reels of film for national news broadcasts in the 1950s and 60s. "We didn't have Little Rock, Arkansas. We didn't have Mississippi. We didn't have Bull Connor. We didn't have police dogs," recalled one white attorney who represented Charleston in the state legislature during the 1960s. Dramatic confrontations between police and protestors in other southern cities called on the collective conscience of America, leading to expansions of civil rights and voting rights. The Charleston Movement, which saw demonstrations spike in the summer of 1963 and again in 1969, was a much more controlled, local affair. One could expect nothing less (or more) from a city that prized politeness and order above nearly all else.[10]

In the summer of 1963, as Martin Luther King Jr. articulated his dream of racial progress in the March on Washington, mass demonstrations came to Charleston. Young people marched down King Street and up Broad. They rallied outside the steps of city hall. They sat in the whites-only section of movie theaters. They swam at whites-only pools and beaches. They laid themselves down in the road in front of the offices of the *News and Courier* to halt delivery of the conservative paper and rebut its antimovement editorials. In one of the more memorable contests between activists and the establishment, the executive director of the state NAACP attempted to dine at a racially restricted restaurant in the upscale Fort Sumter Hotel. The lawyer for the restaurant later harangued the man in court, "You knew when you went down [there] that they didn't serve colored people, didn't you?" The NAACP activist just smiled. "Counselor," he responded, "we didn't go to the Fort Sumter Hotel to *eat* any colored people." Laughter pealed across the courtroom. Even the attorney from the white-shoe law firm on Broad Street knew he had been bested.[11]

Worried about the impact of demonstrations on the local economy, particularly on tourism, white business leaders crafted a compromise with movement activists. That compromise ultimately included a pledge from more than 100 white businesses to hire and promote employees and serve customers without regard to race. A biracial committee of community leaders was formed to talk about racial issues in the city. It was not a total victory for civil rights activists, but it seemed a harbinger of Jim Crow's demise in Charleston. Most important for city leaders and many residents, the end of the summer saw a return to order in the city.[12]

One person who was not happy about the compromise or the end to demonstrations was a militant activist from Johns Island named Bill Saunders. Saunders was one of a number of bright young people on the Sea Islands who got an education because of Esau Jenkins. Since there was no black high school on the islands when Saunders was growing up, his only option was to catch a ride with Jenkins as he drove into the city for work. Jenkins gave youngsters like Bill Saunders more than a ride to school; he gave them an education in how to be a community leader and an activist. Like his mentor, however, Saunders felt that he could learn more in the real world than in the classroom. He dropped out of school in 1951 and joined the military. If Saunders had hoped to find a haven from discrimination in the recently integrated U.S. military, he was out of luck. "That's the place I first really think I encountered racism, racism that was really, really bad," he later said. From combat in Korea to the home front, Saunders felt that black soldiers got the short end of the stick. There were five black soldiers in his company in Korea. With white casualties, the wounded or killed would be taken from the field of battle as soon as combat ended, but when North Korean bullets felled one of the black machine gunners, Saunders recalled, "he laid right on the hill there until he stunk." Finally, the other black soldiers found a body bag and went to retrieve their dead comrade. When Saunders was later wounded by a booby trap, he walked on a broken foot to see the medic rather than wait for assistance. Returning home on leave after the war, Saunders entered a bus station to buy a ticket home. "Boy, you know you don't belong in here," a white policeman told him. The man motioned with his gun for Saunders to exit the station and go to the "colored" ticket window around back. The policeman's actions did not surprise Saunders. It was the reactions of the other soldiers in the station that truly saddened him. "All the white guys that I fought with for that year," Saunders recalled bitterly, "all of them just dropped their heads. . . . Nobody said nothing." It was, he said, "the sin of omission, not commission, because they didn't do anything to me, but they could have helped me."[13]

When Saunders returned to the Lowcountry after the war, he got involved with grassroots activism for civil rights. In the late 1950s, he signed on as the business manager of the Johns Island Progressive Club, where he worked with Esau Jenkins, Septima Clark, and others on literacy and voter education. Like Jenkins and Clark, Saunders would spend time at Highlander honing his skills as a community activist. Unlike his older mentors, Saunders took an increasingly militant approach to civil rights. He was a foot soldier in the Charleston Movement of the early 1960s. By the late 1960s, he aligned with more radical factions of the movement, founding a militant newsletter and an armed self-defense group. He had had enough of the nonviolent philosophy, which asked activists to turn the other cheek. "I only got one cheek," Saunders said, half-joking. "You hit me on that one; I'll knock your ass back." For younger black activists in the late 1960s, Bill Saunders became the go-to guy in confrontations with the city's white power structure. With an unquestioned commitment to civil rights activism, Saunders took on a crucial role as a local advisor and negotiator in the conflict at the climax of the Charleston Movement, a hospital workers' strike at the Medical College of South Carolina.[14]

Three black nursing assistants and two licensed practical nurses (LPNs) at the Medical College walked off the job in February 1967 after a white registered nurse denied them access to patient medical records. When the Medical College fired the five workers, one outspoken hospital worker named Mary Moultrie asked Bill Saunders to help organize a union. Saunders brought in Isaiah Bennett, an experienced union man who worked for the American Tobacco Company. As Moultrie remembers, at the begin-

ning, there were "about five or six of us, and it kept growing. We organized, and it was about a year before we even said anything to the administration. . . . We just asked everybody that would come to join: 'We got
to keep it a secret and next week, when you come, you bring your best
friend.'" Within a year, there were hundreds of hospital workers interested
in the fledgling group.[15]

At the beginning, the hospital workers met at Reginald Barrett's house
in Charleston. Barrett was a member of the local advisory group to the U.S.
Department of Health, Education, and Welfare (HEW), and he looked
into the matter of the fired black employees. In 1965, HEW had investigated the Medical College on complaints of racial discrimination and requested a report on its hiring and admissions practices. At that time, no
black students, faculty, or professional staff worked there, and little had
changed over the following few years. Pressure from Barrett and HEW
led to the reinstatement of the five workers, but this was only the beginning of problems at the Medical College.[16]

When the black LPNs, aides, orderlies, and kitchen workers met with
Mary Moultrie and Bill Saunders to discuss their individual problems at
the Medical College, they realized that they shared many of the same
grievances. White doctors and nurses openly referred to black hospital
workers as "monkey grunts" and "niggers," and the hospital administrators paid white staff more for the same jobs done by their black cowork-
ers. Employee break rooms were segregated by race as well. One organizer
characterized conditions at the hospital as a "plantation overseer-slave
relationship." Conditions like these led the workers to consider action
against the Medical College. In September 1968, they requested that New
York Local 1199 (a union affiliated with the AFL-CIO) send a representative to help the hospital workers formally organize. The local union became 1199B, and the workers voted overwhelmingly to elect Mary Moultrie president. The union then requested recognition from the Medical
College in February 1969. Medical College President Dr. William McCord
agreed to meet with the hospital workers to discuss their grievances, but
when the union representatives arrived, McCord was nowhere to be found.
The workers staged a protest in the president's office, and the administration responded by firing twelve of the union leaders.[17]

To the hospital workers, Medical College President William McCord
represented everything that was wrong with race relations in Charleston.
There was some irony in this, because McCord was a relative newcomer
to the Lowcountry. McCord's parents were Southern Baptist missionaries
in what is today South Africa. He was born in Durban in 1907. His father

constructed one of the first accredited hospitals in sub-Saharan Africa, and McCord taught chemistry at a Zulu school as a teenager. McCord came to the United States for college, ultimately earning a PhD in chemistry at Yale and an MD at Louisiana State University, where he taught for a decade before serving in the U.S. military during World War II. After the war, he took an appointment teaching chemistry and toxicology at the Medical College of South Carolina. In Charleston, students nicknamed McCord "The Whip," because his classes were so demanding. As a practical joke, one student hung a bullwhip in his classroom. Not without a sense of humor, McCord let the whip hang there for years. In 1964, he became the interim president for the Medical College and soon after won the permanent position. McCord was aware of racial problems at the Medical College. He would later take credit for ending the practice of segregating patients into different wings of the hospital. "When I became president," he said, "I made it my objective to raise the pay of blacks to equal that of whites. That was not easy at that time, because of state policy and because of available money. I was doing it, but it couldn't be done overnight." In 1969, some black workers at the Medical College were making $1.30 an hour, thirty cents less than the federal minimum wage. When McCord refused to meet with the hospital workers' representatives and fired twelve leaders of their fledgling union, the workers felt that they had no choice but to strike.[18]

More than 300 members of Local 1199B from the Medical College walked off the job on March 19, 1969. The strikers demanded that hospital administrators officially recognize 1199B, create a fair-minded grievance procedure, and raise the facility's minimum wage up to the federal standard. In addition, they insisted that the hospital rehire the twelve union leaders. Mary Moultrie stated the union position: "We are contending that the racist attitude exhibited today by the administration staff of the Medical College hospital was a discriminatory act and duly unjustified." When McCord did not respond to their demands, union members began picketing the Medical College.[19]

On the strike's first day, a small but determined nurse's aide, Naomi White, stalked the picket lines. In her zeal, she exchanged insults and blows with strikebreakers until a police officer grabbed her. As the officer gripped her arm, he said, "Sweetheart, you're going to jail." White pushed him back against the patrol car and chided, "The chief shouldn't send a boy to do a man's job." When asked about the incident years later, White said that if "somebody rough you up and hit you, you [are] not just going to stand there and take it—you know. You will retaliate." White and several other protestors were arrested for disorderly conduct. The Medical College won a court injunction limiting the picket line to ten demonstrators at a time. A frustrated Mary Moultrie observed, "You could drive about three buses through how they wanted us to picket, so that wasn't going to be effective at all. We just did what we had to do."[20]

Striking workers ignored the injunction against picketing at the Medical College, extended their protests to other parts of the city, and hammered McCord with negative publicity. Pickets went up around the Old Slave Market Museum a few days after the strike to juxtapose the plight of the hospital workers with the long history of slavery and racism in Charleston and to catch the eyes of curious tourists who might not have wandered past the Medical College itself. Just in case the tourists missed the symbolism, picket signs read: "In Memory of the Old Slave Tradition, Consult Dr. McCord." Over the course of the strike, McCord came to personify the paternalistic attitudes held by many of Charleston's city fathers toward black residents. Despite his efforts to address some of the worst aspects of segregation at the Medical College, the president had a reputation, even among his friends and colleagues, for troubling racial views. "He had an attitude about blacks," recalled one colleague years later. "He didn't like them." McCord told the press that he was not about to "turn a $25 million complex over to a bunch of people who don't have a grammar school education." The president saw no need for a union, because he felt that he knew what was best for *his* employees. The workers disagreed. They felt that the only way to break out of the paternalistic relationship with white officials was through the solidarity of a union. The workers also realized that they could not tackle the state of South Carolina and the Medical College alone, so they called in national civil rights and labor organizations to bring additional publicity and support.[21]

The strikers' best hope for outside assistance seemed to be from Martin Luther King's organization, the SCLC. Septima Clark connected the national civil rights organization to the Lowcountry, and King had been shifting the group's focus to address racial *and* economic inequality since the mid-1960s. But King had been assassinated during a 1968 sanitation workers' strike in Memphis, and after his death, the SCLC had struggled to organize an ill-fated Poor People's Campaign in Washington, D.C. At the end of the 1960s, the SCLC saw its nonviolent approach to civil rights and its role at the forefront of the movement slipping away. Reverend Ralph Abernathy, King's longtime friend and the new president of the SCLC, was wary of getting involved in another local struggle far from the group's Atlanta headquarters. Still, Abernathy had to weigh the risk of losing in Charleston against the risk that the SCLC might fold if it did not find a cause around which the organization could rally. The organization needed a successful campaign, Abernathy realized, "something we had not won in Washington . . . something big in order to reestablish the credibility of nonviolence." Gradually, Abernathy and other SCLC leaders began to see Charleston as a chance to work with union officials in a concrete fight against poverty and racism that offered the possibility to honor Dr. King's legacy and, just as important, get a clear-cut victory with national publicity.[22]

At the same time that the SCLC was considering support of the Charleston hospital workers, state officials began throwing their weight behind McCord. On the advice of the state attorney general, McCord argued that state institutions could not officially recognize or bargain with a union. Like many southern states, South Carolina prided itself on its right-to-work laws, which thwarted most union organizing drives and strike attempts while bolstering state efforts to entice outside industrial and commercial investment. Just a year before the hospital workers went on strike, the state had weathered a longshoremen's strike with similar legal stonewalling. Medical College administrators relied on the right-to-work laws to reject official union negotiations or recognition throughout the hospital strike.[23]

While state and union officials remained at an impasse, the picketers kept up demonstrations around the Medical College, and rumors flew about the strike spreading to other area hospitals. Mary Moultrie told the press that the union would continue to organize "until every hospital and nursing home worker in Charleston is earning a living wage and is rid of the yoke of discrimination." Just over a week after the Medical College workers struck, more than a third of the "nonprofessional" workers at Charleston County Hospital walked off the job. All of the striking workers at the county hospital were black, and, as at the Medical College, the majority of them were women.[24]

Black women have always played a large part in the civil rights movement, often participating in greater numbers than the men who dominated the headlines and the leadership ranks of movement organizations. The mostly female hospital workers in Charleston quickly garnered support from many of the women in the black community, but it was sometimes more difficult to recruit local men. "You could very easily get a woman and her children to come out to a rally quicker than you could get the male support," Mary Moultrie observed. "I would say that women outnumbered the men all around." There were male orderlies, custodians, and others who went on strike and struggled alongside the women. Still, the dominant role of black women both behind the scenes and in public leadership roles was a unique aspect of the hospital strike. Historians have long understood that women were the "backbone" of the movement. Some scholars have suggested that female civil rights workers were more active than men because white police officers were less likely to use physical violence on women. This assumes that white officials viewed black female protestors as "ladies" who deserved chivalrous treatment. The history of sexual oppression of black women that dates back to the era of slavery and violent white resistance to both women and men active in the civil rights movement suggests that this was not the case. "I think [if police] really wanted to be violent, they would," Moultrie noted. "If they wanted to put the fire hose on us, they would have cared less if we were women or men." Disregarding the risk of violent reprisal, many women from Charleston's black community marched with the strikers, and the public support eventually prodded more men to get involved. "Here [were] all these women out here struggling like this," Moultrie remembered proudly, "and it brought in a lot of men who felt that they had to . . . lend their strength."[25]

As the president of Local 1199B and the leading spokesperson for the hospital workers, Mary Moultrie became a symbol of newly empowered black womanhood during the strike. Moultrie followed in the footsteps of an earlier generation of South Carolina activists like Septima Clark, but it was Esau Jenkins who first inspired her. Born in Charleston in 1942, Moultrie was still in high school when she got a job at a restaurant that Jenkins owned in the late 1950s. Her first introduction to politics and community activism was working alongside Jenkins in voter registration drives around the Lowcountry. After high school, Moultrie went to New York to work and study nursing. She returned to Charleston in 1967 and got a job at the Medical College. Having worked in New York where she was treated fairly well, Moultrie was particularly struck by the racism and discrimination at the Medical College. Opponents of the hospital strike suggested that she might have been a plant from the New York union, but Moultrie strongly denied this, saying that she only wanted to get respect for herself and the other hospital workers. An outspoken critic of the problems at the Medical College, she was an obvious choice for president of Local 1199B. Moultrie traveled around the country, raising money to replace the lost wages for her fellow workers. She literally wore holes in her shoes walking the picket lines and marching with Coretta Scott King in Charleston. Years later, her friend and fellow activist Bill Saunders recalled a time when Moultrie almost single-handedly kept the strike going.

Three Charleston hospital workers sing jubilantly at a demonstration during the 1969 strike. They are (left to right): Charlotte Venning, Anabelle Green Brown, and Diane Flemming. Courtesy of the Post and Courier.

"That girl was so dynamic," he said, remembering a mass meeting at Morris Brown AME Church during the strike "when things were going so bad." At the podium that night, Moultrie acknowledged that the strikers were really struggling to make ends meet and to bring the Medical College to the negotiating table. Then she broke into "Only the Strong Survive," Jerry Butler's hit song in the spring of 1969. A song about lost love, Butler's lyrics also seemed to speak to a civil rights movement that had begun to stall. "You gotta be strong. You gotta hold on. You gotta keep going on. Only the strong survive!" When Moultrie came to that chorus, Saunders said, "The church just went mad!"[26]

Although Mary Moultrie and the other strikers were not consciously waging a battle against sexism in Charleston, their public struggle against discrimination undermined both racist and sexist stereotypes of black women. When Moultrie called for a living wage for the women workers, she challenged traditional gender assumptions in two ways. As a spokesperson rather than a spokesman, she played an unconventional role in the arenas of civil rights, labor organizing, and politics. As Moultrie's public role grew during the strike, it opened some Charlestonians' eyes to a possible future for women in power. One striker's protest sign demanded

"Moultrie for Mayor"—an extraordinarily radical idea for a city where neither an African American nor a woman had ever led the city government. Moultrie's call for a living wage for black women was a demand for acknowledgment of their equal status in households and society at large. These women were mothers and wage earners, often heads of households, who needed a "family wage" to take care of their children as much as union men ever did. "I had [five] children to take care of," one striker remembered. "I was head of the household even then." With both the Medical College and county hospital workers striking, these women felt that they had the power to win a living wage.[27]

After the county hospital workers struck, the Concerned Clergy Committee formed in Charleston and released a "Peace with Justice Proposal," calling for the reinstatement of the dozen union leaders and for suspension of demonstrations if meetings could be arranged between workers and hospital administrators. Charleston clergy were not the only pastors whose concern grew after the walkout of county workers. At this point, Ralph Abernathy decided that the SCLC should lend more than moral support to the strike. After many invitations, Abernathy flew to Charleston on March 31. Preaching to a crowd of 1,500 supporters at the Fourth Baptist Church, Abernathy said that the SCLC had come to help the striking workers "sock it to" Charleston. National media attention following the SCLC president's visit underscored the potential negative effects of the strike on Charleston's tourist economy.[28]

On an institutional level, the hospitals felt the economic impact of the strike almost immediately. By early April, the county and Medical College hospitals had to reduce patient admissions. County administrators announced that they were operating at half of normal capacity, even though they had already begun hiring replacements for unskilled positions. Despite the pressure, Medical College President McCord rejected the Concerned Clergy Committee's proposal, saying he could not "sanction lawlessness" by rehiring the twelve workers. McCord believed that he could outlast the strikers with state support. Former faculty members remember that the Medical College president did everything he could to keep business as usual at the Medical College hospital.[29]

Business was anything but usual on the streets of Charleston during the strike. Realizing that they needed to bring more pressure on the hospital, leaders of 1199B requested more help from New York Local 1199 and the SCLC. Together the union and the civil rights group organized the first of several large marches in early April to honor the late Dr. Martin Luther King Jr. Approximately 450 marchers listened with heads bowed as a local minister prayed, "May we never sully the name of Jesus Christ by resorting to violence." Reiterating the message of nonviolence, one marcher carried a sign saying, "There will not be any Orangeburg here." The sign referred to the "Orangeburg Massacre," in which several people were killed when authorities opened fire on demonstrators at South Carolina State College the year before. Throughout the strike, the majority of union members remained true to the nonviolent spirit of King and the SCLC, but not all of the strikers and their supporters wanted to turn the other cheek. On April 10, one striker threw pepper into the eyes of a policeman, and onlookers threw bottles and bricks at officers. "The crowds of young blacks were becoming more unruly," Abernathy remembered. "There were times when we weren't quite in control." People on both sides of the strike were threatened with violence. State law enforcement had a twenty-four-hour guard on President McCord and his wife. Mary Moultrie and Rosetta Simmons, the leader of the county hospital workers, had a female bodyguard named Eva Alston. "This sister was bad," Bill Saunders said, "but she loved Ms. Moultrie and Ms. Simmons. She would do anything. She would die for any one of them." The state authorities that protected President McCord were armed with guns. Eva Alston was armed with a bottle of battery acid.[30]

Union and civil rights leaders had mixed emotions about violence and threats of violence. There were news reports of vandals throwing Molotov cocktails and shooting out store windows. These were minor disturbances compared to the full-scale riots in cities across the country during the late 1960s, but the sporadic acts of violence in Charleston were lumped into the general unrest associated with the strike. Hospital worker Naomi White believed that it was unfair that "some people that weren't even connected with the strike [gave] us a bad name because that was an opportunity for them to get their revenge on certain merchants." Bill Saunders was not worried about the violence. He felt that it pressured whites in positions of authority to come to the bargaining table. Abernathy and many older black leaders in Charleston did not share Saunders's view. They preached against all forms of violence, believing that the loss of the moral high ground far outweighed the potential benefits. But preaching seemed to do no good. By the late 1960s, expectations of a better life had been raised, but not always met, by more than a decade of nonviolent protest. Violence was "more a sign of the times than any deliberate change in style of SCLC," Abernathy explained in his autobiography. "Young people in Charleston were watching [riot footage] every night before joining us for what was supposed to be a peaceful march," he wrote. "The results were predictable." If the resulting violence was predictable, it nonetheless jeopardized the nonviolent strategy that had been so successful in earlier campaigns, and it also elicited a crackdown by state law enforcement. After several nights of police reports of fires and rock throwing, South Carolina Governor Robert McNair placed Charleston under a curfew from 9 P.M. to 5 A.M.[31]

As the strike continued throughout the spring, it crippled the local economy. The SCLC staffer—and later U.S. ambassador to the United Nations—Reverend Andrew Young organized an economic boycott of Charleston businesses to build on this economic pressure. "I don't think anything [can] be accomplished by destroying people and property," Young said. "The only way to make [white leaders] respect the color of black is to deprive them of the power of green." Along with the curfew and unrest, the boycott did bring added pressure on local business leaders. "I'm losing my shirt," one Charleston businessman complained, and the manager of the city's Francis Marion Hotel said that they had lost $30,000 to $40,000 of convention business. Business leaders began to feel that a strike settlement might be in the best interests of the city and their bottom lines. This was part of the SCLC's boycott strategy, which was meant to "force the economic power structure to keep the political structure in line."[32]

One place where Charlestonians could find unwavering support for the state and opposition to the strike was in the pages of the Charleston *News and Courier*. One of the most conservative papers in the South, the *News and Courier* published editorials likening the Governor McNair's resistance to union organizers in the 1960s to Confederate General Robert E. Lee's defense against the invasion of the Union Army in the 1860s. The paper also became a forum for hashing out the loyalty of black Charlestonians, who were presumed by white leaders to be pawns of national civil rights organizations and labor unions. Reverend Leon J. Hubacz, the pastor of Blessed Sacrament Church, published an open letter blaming the strike on outside "rabble rousers." Responding to the strike's rallying cry, "I Am Somebody," Hubacz wrote as if he had slept through the decade of civil rights unrest. "What of the colored Mammy?" he asked. "Could all of your speeches and marches ever replace the glow of pride in her face as she watches, day after day, as her little charge grows into a man of importance in the world? . . . You claim you want to make her 'somebody,' and she knows she is SOMEBODY." For the white pastor, the paternalistic ideal of a black woman was someone whose identity and pride were wrapped up not in her own accomplishments, but in those of the white family for whom she worked.[33]

Strikers reminded Charlestonians that they had their own families and their own dreams by scheduling their largest march on Mother's Day. More than a symbolic protest, the Mother's Day march brought additional national support and attention to the Charleston strike. Walter Reuther, the head of the United Auto Workers' union, walked arm-in-arm with Mary Moultrie and the SCLC's Ralph Abernathy as they led 5,000 people through the streets of Charleston. Reuther cut Local 1199B a check for $10,000 to cover the growing cost of the strike. "We're going to have the governor of this state jacked up into the twentieth century," the union president shouted. In addition to Reuther, five U.S. Congressmen from New York and Michigan joined the Mother's Day march. Even with all of the national luminaries, however, Mary Moultrie stole the show. "You thought we'd say, 'Sorry, boss,' and put those handkerchiefs back on our heads," she said, before offering a mock apology. "Sorry about that, governor, but we just had to disappoint you."[34]

Echoes of the hospital workers' marching feet reached even Washington, where President Richard Nixon agreed to meet with Abernathy and other civil rights leaders. Abernathy left the Mother's Day march early to see Nixon, but nothing substantial came out of their conversation. In public, Nixon remained reticent about the strike, electing to leave the final decisions of mediation in the hands of state and local officials. Although Nixon decided to stay out of the strike, other federal officials did not. Led by Minnesota Senator Walter Mondale and New York Senator Jacob Javits, a bipartisan group of seventeen U.S. senators signed a petition urging the president to send a federal mediator to Charleston. The senators observed, "The strike is a test of nonviolence when many in this country are turning to violence as a means of achieving social change." Senator Strom Thurmond of South Carolina, a staunch opponent of organized labor and civil rights, denounced the petition drawn up by his colleagues as blackmail. This was a states'-rights issue, according to Thurmond, and the federal government should not dictate South Carolina policy. When Bill Saunders and Mary Moultrie asked their connections in the Department of Health, Education, and Welfare to put pressure on the Medical College hospital by threatening to withhold federal funds, Senator Thurmond intervened to protect the hospital.[35]

Surprisingly, signs of change came from the state, not the federal government. In June, the South Carolina General Assembly voted to raise pay scales for all state employees from the governor to the hospital workers. The new pay scale at the Medical College brought the hospital workers' wages up to a minimum of $1.60 per hour, the wage they had been demanding since the beginning of the strike. Perhaps feeling more magnanimous after receiving his own pay raise, Governor McNair lifted the evening curfew in Charleston that had lasted thirty-two days. He also publicly stated that the decision whether to rehire the twelve union members was up to Medical College administrators. At this time, Bill Saunders arranged a secret meeting outside Charleston between the Medical College Board of Trustees and a small group of strikers to see if they could iron out their differences. Saunders would never forget the meeting. It was the first time that he saw white leaders treat the hospital workers with the respect they deserved. "These black women and these white men got together," Saunders remembered. "The men held out their chairs and stuff like that." It was the beginning of the end of the hospital strike.[36]

The vigilance and determination of the strikers and pressure from local business leaders finally wore down the resolve of President McCord and other Medical College administrators. After ninety-nine days of protest, Medical College administrators finally agreed to rehire the twelve union organizers. The Medical College created a credit union for hospital employees and instituted a six-point grievance system. Though the hospital workers won the pay raise from the state, they did not get official union recognition or any system of collective bargaining. Even without union recognition, the workers felt they had won a great victory. Tangible concessions were important, but the most salient change at the Medical College was increased respect for the workers. When the county hospital strike finally ended a few weeks later, the leader of the county workers, Rosetta Simmons, told reporters, "We will return to work in a new relationship of mutual respect and dignity."[37]

The strike left a mixed legacy for race relations in Charleston hospitals and the rest of the city. Without official recognition or collective bargaining power, Local 1199B struggled to survive. The union folded in 1972. Mary Moultrie went back to work at the Medical College, but she struggled to find a department that would take her. Ultimately, she spent five years in the psychology department. The department chairman later admitted that the administration was "watching her like a hawk." Dr. McCord remained president of the Medical College, overseeing its transition into the Medical University of South Carolina. When he was eased out of the position in 1975, McCord left Charleston. Bill Saunders was a little sad to see him go. McCord was the very embodiment of the *pater familias*.

A rigid determination to control "his" workers revealed the racism just under the placid surface of Charleston's paternalistic system of race relations. As Bill Saunders later said, one of the great ironies of the hospital strike was that McCord did more to organize black Charlestonians into a movement than nearly anyone else, black or white. Despite the fact that Mary Moultrie had to brave a hostile work environment for years, she was proud of the strike's effect on the black community. It was "certainly an awakening" for a lot of people, she said. "People woke up to the fact that they needed to get out and vote."[38]

A new political consciousness and empowerment for black Charlestonians were the immediate legacies of both the hospital strike and the larger civil rights movement in the Lowcountry. The strike was merely the culmination of this movement that had begun decades before and would be felt for decades to come. That movement reached far beyond Charleston hospitals to influence education, housing, policing, and, of course, politics. Like many places in the South, the first chapter of Charleston's post–civil rights era would be written in the ballot box. By 1975, half of the seats on Charleston City Council were held by African Americans, and the city would elect its first "black" mayor—a man who was born white.

CHAPTER TWO

Little Black Joe

They nicknamed him "Little Black Joe." He was short of stature—
"altitudinally challenged," one supporter joked. But that was not the main
point of the nickname. More than anything else, of course, the pejorative
moniker boiled down to race. Joseph P. Riley Jr. shocked his fellow white
Charlestonians and even a few black residents when he turned out to be
far more liberal on racial issues than any of them expected, perhaps more
of a racial liberal than any white Charleston politician had been since
Reconstruction. Riley was not just liberal in comparison to the Charleston establishment, which had raised and supported him. No, Riley was
lauded as a "progressive" in both local and national media, touted as one
of the Young Turks with limitless political possibilities in the post–civil
rights era South. Over time, his commitment to affirmative action
would reshape local government, bringing more minorities and women
into executive and administrative positions than most had dared to dream
in the civil rights era. This dedication to multiculturalism and affirmative action was sincere, but Riley was no civil rights activist. He was a
savvy strategist who welded together diverse constituencies to undergird
his own political career. A deep "blue" Democrat in a very "red" state, Riley
forged a local version of the biracial coalition that the Democratic Party
hoped to build across the South in the wake of the Voting Rights Act of
1965. As those hopes dwindled in the 1970s and 80s, the region became
the base for a national Republican revolution. Urban politics produced
an interesting counterpoint to this regional and national story line. The
biracial political machine that Joe Riley built serves as an important

corrective to the seemingly monolithic nature of southern political conservatism.[1]

Joe Riley's life and career suggest that the popular narrative of the Republican revolution conquering the American South in the post–civil rights era does not capture the whole story of the region's political trajectory. By exploring Riley's life, we come to see an alternative history of white southerners' evolution from the era of segregation and black political disfranchisement through the civil rights movement and beyond. Previous scholarship on white southern politics in the wake of the civil rights movement focused on suburban flight and the resulting shift toward the Republican Party. "White flight," according to historian Kevin Kruse, "was more than a physical relocation. It was a political revolution." Kruse analyzed Atlanta politics, but Matthew Lassiter found much the same story in Charlotte and Richmond, where conservative grassroots politics was "produced by residential segregation and suburban sprawl," as well as the increasing popularity of the Republican Party nationwide.[2] The conservatism of Charleston's growing suburbs mirrored these trends in other southern metropolitan areas. Yet the focus on conservative suburban politics in the historical literature has hidden a fascinating history of urban and liberal southern politics in this era, a strain of politics that led to the election of left-of-center black and white officials across the South, men and women like Harvey Gantt, Maynard Jackson, Barbara Jordan, Jimmy Carter, Bill Clinton, and Joe Riley.

Joseph Patrick Riley Jr. was born in Charleston on January 19, 1943. With the nation mobilized for war, defense industries were slowly awakening the southern port city from a deep economic slumber that had begun with the Civil War. One Charlestonian, who grew up in the Great Depression and had little nostalgia for that era, painted a drab picture of the town from his distant memories. "I think of it as being grays and blacks and whites," he recalled, as if describing a faded picture from a dusty photo album. Color cameras would have been unnecessary to capture Charleston of the 1930s and early 1940s. Soft pastels and gentle pigments would not wash over the old southern city until decades later. In the war years, the antebellum mansions and colonial houses were in disrepair. Tenements still dotted the cityscape, and they quickly filled up with country folk, streaming into the Lowcountry for defense work.[3]

The expansion of the city's economy and the growing Lowcountry population enriched the lives of the Riley family. Joseph Riley Sr.—later nicknamed "Big Joe" to differentiate him from his son—had lost his own father at a young age. Before he died, Big Joe's father, who had served as a Charleston alderman for more than two decades, instilled in his son a deep commitment to public service, a commitment that Big Joe would pass on to his own son. Big Joe dropped out of college after one year to work in the local cigar factory owned by the American Tobacco Company. Losing his job during the Depression, he joined the Civilian Conservation Corps after hearing rumors that the CCC might take him to California. The adventurous trip west that Big Joe had envisioned ended in rural Round O, South Carolina, less than fifty miles from the city where he grew up. Big Joe returned to Charleston and founded a real estate and insurance business in 1937, just before the wartime and postwar booms that resuscitated the local housing market and economy.[4]

After coming home to Charleston, Big Joe met and married Helen Schachte. Growing up, Helen had always dreamed of becoming a doctor. Much to the horror of her parents, she dissected runaway cats in the attic of their Beaufain Street house. Helen had graduated second in her class at the College of Charleston with a double major in biology and chemistry. In another era, she would have undoubtedly gone on to study at the Medical College of South Carolina, located just blocks from where she grew up. But that was not to be her path. Helen's father informed her that becoming a doctor was not appropriate for a lady. Though she did graduate work as a medical technician in Philadelphia, once she had a family of her own, she focused her energies on them, particularly their education and spiritual life.[5]

Joseph Riley Sr. and his wife, Helen, were devout Catholics, dedicated to the local diocese and the city's Catholic community. Their children attended parochial schools that were racially segregated much like the public school system. As Irish American Catholics, the Rileys lacked the ancestral pedigree of older Charleston families, but with Big Joe's business success, few doors were closed to the family.[6]

When Little Joe was born in 1943, the family lived in a small home on Gibbes Street. It was a duplex, and they rented out the other half to bring in extra income. Over the next twelve years, Big Joe's real estate business grew. The Charleston Chamber of Commerce elected him president in 1949, and he later became president of the state chamber, as well as a board member of the U.S. Chamber of Commerce. Big Joe's business acumen and financial success allowed the family to move to a much bigger house on Murray Boulevard in the mid-1950s. What really mattered in Charleston was that both of these homes were south of Broad Street, the line demarcating the most historic part of the city, where scions of the oldest families lived. The Riley's address left little doubt that they had made it. Overlooking the water at the very southern tip of the city peninsula, the Murray Boulevard home was stately and beautifully situated. Little Joe could walk out of his front door and down the steps to play on Charleston's picturesque promenade that ran along the Battery. More often than not, however, he ran to the nearby "Horse Lot" for a game of baseball or to a neighbor's backyard for a little basketball.[7]

Little Joe was not simply junior to his father. Big Joe stood over six feet tall, and though he had been a thin man in his younger years, he was beginning to wear the weight of success by the 1950s. He was a gregarious, larger-than-life character, "a big, red-faced Irishman," in the words of one of Little Joe's childhood friends, a "charmer" and a "great man." As a child, Little Joe literally stood in his father's shadow. With a lean frame that he would keep all of his life, Little Joe would grow to only five feet, nine inches tall. He had blue eyes, a ready smile, and an affable manner that put friends at ease, but he was quieter than his father, more thoughtful and precise, like his mother. Despite his relatively small physical stature, Joe loved sports. He made his closest friends on the ball fields and courts of the city. He played baseball, basketball, and football, though he readily admitted that he was not particularly good at any of them.[8]

As a spectator, Little Joe gravitated toward major league baseball. The 1950s was an exciting time to be a baseball fan. Big changes in the game mirrored changes in society. When Jackie Robinson burst onto the national scene as the first black player to break into the major leagues in the twentieth century, Little Joe was only four years old. But as the young white Charlestonian grew, he came to love the iconic black player and his Brooklyn team. Little Joe collected the team's baseball cards and fanatically memorized rosters and stats.[9]

Little Joe gradually realized that his devotion to Robinson and the integrated Brooklyn Dodgers did not jibe with the racial segregation defended by his father and most other white Charlestonians. "I was wrestling with these people who I loved and who gave me so much happiness," he said. "If [black players] came to my community, they wouldn't be able to drink at the same water fountain [as me]." Decades later, he reserved a special place in his office for a picture of Robinson and the 1955 Dodger team that won the World Series. That team had won the hearts and minds of young boys like Joe Riley across America, even in the South.[10]

Like many white Charleston families of their social standing, the Rileys hired African American housekeepers and handymen. In the wake of the civil rights movement, wealthy white baby boomers struggled to express their love and gratitude for black employees without sounding naively nostalgic. Susanne Emge, the eldest of the Riley children, was willing to try. "I would feel a little awkward using the word 'maid,'" she said, "but that's how we were all raised. I mean we had somebody in the house that helped do the cooking and the cleaning and helped raise us up." For Little Joe's formative years, that person was Estelle Fickling. The Riley children were taught to love and respect her. Despite their different backgrounds and stations in life, it is hard to think that they did not. Little Joe later served as a pallbearer at Estelle Fickling's funeral. She was "very much a part of our family," Emge remembered, as was the black handyman who was nearly inseparable from her father. Big Joe helped find jobs for the relatives of the black men and women who worked for the family. In the paternalistic parlance of the day, he "looked out for" their children, their grands, and great-grands.[11]

Even with these deep personal connections between black and white families in Charleston, there was little doubt about the proper social order during the era of segregation. Little Joe learned the etiquette of Jim Crow from his father one night at a local restaurant when he unintentionally challenged Charleston's racial hierarchy. That night, an African American waiter asked Little Joe if he liked his meal. The man was older, well dressed, and polite, so Little Joe responded, "Yes, sir." "After he was out of earshot," Riley later remembered his father correcting him. "You didn't say 'Sir' to an African American. I said 'Yes ma'am' and 'Yes sir' to everyone . . . and so I just couldn't quite figure that out."[12]

As vital as such racial lessons were for young white children in Charleston, they were not the kinds of things that most dwelled on. They did not have to. Their world was both intimately influenced by race and completely separate from its concerns. The Rileys provided a comfortable and loving home for their children—three girls and one boy. The Riley children's fondest memories were of annual trips to the sun-drenched barrier islands near Charleston. In the mornings, the children raced over the dunes to play in the waves until the noon heat and hunger sent them to the shade of the house. In the afternoon, the children might go fishing or crabbing, with chicken necks tied to strings and rusty old traps. For the kids, the summers always ended too soon as the new school year inevitably approached.[13]

When Little Joe thought about where he wanted to go to college, there were really only two options—the same two options that nearly every college-bound white Charleston boy considered: the University of South Carolina and the Citadel. Leaving town or the state for school may have been an option financially, but in the small world of Charleston society, few young men saw any need to look beyond even the city's boundaries. The Citadel, the state's all-white, all-male military college, was right in town, and it was an obvious choice. The school virtually minted distinguished graduates and connected them to a powerful alumni network. When Little Joe made his decision about schools, a Citadel alumnus and fellow Charlestonian, Fritz Hollings, had just been elected governor of South Carolina. Little Joe knew where he wanted to go.[14]

The Citadel has long been known for its brutal initiation of freshmen, who are welcomed to the school in the stifling heat of August by a cadre of upperclassmen for what is known as "Hell Week." When Joe Riley entered the gates of the military campus in August 1960, he understood what was coming. The yelling and screaming began almost immediately. The gray uniform pants and white shirts molded to the young cadet's thin frame with his sweat. Knowing full well how to take advantage of Charleston's inhospitable August climate, upperclassmen ordered new cadets to put on every uniform they had at once. Then they corralled Riley and his classmates into a single communal shower room and cranked on the hot water. This seemed to accomplish the impossible task of raising the humidity above 100 percent and the temperature over 100 degrees. Like most of the hazing that week, it wasn't life-threatening, but it was ingenious in its sadism. Riley's head was shaved—a blessing because of the heat, a curse because it was a sure sign that he was a "knob" in constant need of "training" by upperclassmen. "I was certain that some of those people who were yelling at me and being unfair—I felt that I would detest them until the day I died," Riley remembered. But he never considered quitting. Even decades later, he could still taste the ice-cold Coca-Cola that he tipped up to his lips at the end of Hell Week. It was just about the best thing he had ever had in his life. At that moment, he knew that he would one day wear the ring that marked him as a Citadel man.[15]

Riley majored in political science at the Citadel. The dedication to public service his father instilled in him led him to seek opportunities and mentors in the political realm. As the civil rights movement came to Charleston in the summer of 1963, Joe Riley set off for an internship in the nation's capital. That year, President John F. Kennedy had finally begun to make good on his commitment to civil rights. It is hard not to draw parallels between the idealistic Charlestonian and the youthful president from Boston. Both were from Irish Catholic families with fathers whose successes buoyed them above the Brahmans that dominated their respective cities. The fathers had achieved much, but they hoped for even more from their sons. Riley never met Kennedy, of course, but there is little doubt that the president had a deep impact on the younger man. Years later on an anniversary of Kennedy's assassination, Riley eulogized the fallen president. "We have lost a thousand speeches never given, programs never enacted, decisions never made. . . . His torch has become ours and in time, we will pass it on as well. But before we do, there is much to be done."[16]

Kennedy inspired Riley, but a more pragmatic southern politician guided him through the world of politics. Lucius Mendel Rivers had represented the Lowcountry in Congress since before Joe Riley Jr. was born. In 1963, Rivers was approaching the zenith of his political career. His seniority and the Democrats' control of Congress gave him an important position on the powerful House Armed Services Committee. He would become chairman of the committee two years later. From this position, Rivers channeled millions of dollars in defense spending to his Lowcountry district. He had both philosophical and political reasons for doing so.

Like many congressmen in the 1950s and 60s, Mendel Rivers believed that the Cold War was the biggest threat that his generation faced. The Cuban Revolution and subsequent missile crisis brought the reality of this contest dangerously close to home. "If we don't have the courage to eliminate communism at our backdoor, by one means or another," Rivers opined in a speech on Cuba, "then it is time for us to stop claiming a role in world leadership." The Charleston congressman likened communism to a rattlesnake. Some American peaceniks wanted to coddle the venomous serpent. He wanted to crush it. A hawk on national defense from the Korean War through the Vietnam conflict, Rivers consistently voted to expand American military forces.[17]

The Cold War military buildup almost single-handedly revived the Lowcountry economy. Rivers beamed with pride when he spoke of this on the stump. In a speech titled "What the Military Means to the Lowcountry in Dollars and Cents," the congressman ticked off all the bases he had built or expanded in his district: an "enormous" shipyard and naval base, an Air Force base, mine sweeper facility, Polaris missile base, naval ammunition depot, Coast Guard base, and an army transportation depot. The Sixth Naval District Headquarters was located in the Lowcountry, and a large Veterans Administration hospital was also in the works for Charleston. One of Rivers's colleagues in Congress ribbed him in the 1960s, saying, "You put anything else down there in your district, Mendel, it's going to sink."[18]

Perhaps President Dwight Eisenhower had congressmen like Rivers in mind when he warned in his 1961 farewell address that the Cold War was creating a "military-industrial complex" in the United States—a combination of defense industries and weapons manufacturers that had a vested interest in expansion of federal military budgets and expenditures. "In the councils of government, we must guard against the acquisition of unwarranted influence, whether sought or unsought, by the military-industrial complex," Eisenhower warned. "We must never let the weight of this combination endanger our liberties or democratic process."[19]

As the treasurer of Mendel Rivers's campaigns in the 1960s, Big Joe Riley saw the influence of defense industries on the democratic process firsthand. Rivers's correspondence files are full of letters between Riley, Rivers, and defense industry executives like W. F. "Red" Raborn, vice president of Aerojet-General Corporation, and Harvey P. Jolly, vice president of United Aircraft International, extolling the virtues of "our good friend, Mendel." Big Joe organized luncheons in Charleston, and Rivers hosted them in Washington, serving quail, she-crab soup, "and other delectable morsels only found in our native state" to industry executives. Many of the executives helped to underwrite Rivers's campaigns.[20]

Big Joe was not worried about these relationships, and neither were most Charlestonians. Coming out of decades of poverty, Lowcountry residents were far more concerned about bread-and-butter issues than fears of defense industry lobbyists and influence peddling. With more than 22,000 employees (nearly 10 percent of the region's population), federal military facilities were by far the biggest employer in the Lowcountry. The military pumped $133 million directly into the local economy every year in the mid-1960s, while other sources (tourism, agriculture, industry, and shipping) combined for only $90 million. Mendel Rivers had made it all happen. He was a hero, a political genius, someone to be lauded and reelected, not feared. As Joe Riley Jr. ran errands and answered mail in Rivers's office in 1963, he found much to admire about the congressman who served his district so well.[21]

There was one matter, however, that the young intern and the congressman disagreed upon: race. Like most white southerners of his generation, Rivers strongly believed in racial segregation. In the late 1940s, he revolted against the Democratic Party with other "Dixiecrats" to support presidential candidate Strom Thurmond. Rivers was a proud member of the Citizens' Council, a segregationist organization mocked by critics as the "white-collar Klan" in the 1950s. He remained a staunch segregationist in the early 1960s. "Avoidance of Negroes by whites is not based on skin color," Rivers explained in a 1962 speech. "It is because so many of the Negroes are backward, improvident, undisciplined, [and] disorderly."

The Charleston congressman fought against civil rights bills, believing that change could not be "legislated or brought through racists like Reverend Martin Luther King."[22]

Martin Luther King came to the nation's capital in the summer of 1963 to join the March on Washington and lobby for the passage of Kennedy's proposed civil rights bill. King did much more than that, of course. With his "I Have a Dream" speech on the steps of the Lincoln Memorial that summer, King inspired a generation. "What Martin Luther King did for white people, white people of good will," Riley later said, was that "he exposed them to their consciences." Riley had missed the March on Washington because he had to report back to the Citadel for the start of his senior year at the end of August. Five hundred miles to the south, he had still heard King's message.[23]

In his final year at the Citadel, Riley began to rethink the lessons of southern history. Through the early 1960s, southern schools related the history of Reconstruction as a morality tale. It had been a period of chaos after the devastation of the War between the States. Corrupt, carpetbagger Republicans and their incompetent, even dangerous, southern black allies only made matters worse as they ran southern states and cities into the ground in the decade after the war. In this telling, segregation and disfranchisement of black southerners were necessary remedies for the sick, utopian dreams of racial equality that racked the South in the late 1860s. A century after the war, Riley sat in his Citadel dorm room, wrestling with a different story, a revision of that history. In this new version, Reconstruction had been an opportunity lost, a chance for whites and blacks to work together to build a truly "new" South. Perhaps, he thought, the opportunity had come again.[24]

Local politics in Charleston during the 1950s and 1960s did not look all that much different from a century before. The Democratic Party continued to dominate the city, state, and region so extensively that its primaries basically decided general elections. Old Charleston families, most of whom lived south of Broad Street, continued to win or strongly influence elections. Palmer Gaillard, a candidate for mayor in 1959, exemplified the city's traditional leadership class.

The Gaillards had a long history of civic and political involvement in Charleston. Peter C. Gaillard, a colonel in the Confederate Army, returned to his home in the city in 1865, seeking to minimize the changes that the war had wrought. He ran for mayor with an all-white city council slate that, in the words of one historian, "set out to restore white rule." Since black Charlestonians, many of them newly freed slaves, could still not vote in the first few years after the war, Gaillard won. Under his leadership, the city enforced South Carolina's Black Codes, which restricted black mobility and banned interracial marriage and black gun ownership. When military reconstruction began in 1868, the Union Army unceremoniously ended Mayor Gaillard's term and put a northern white officer in charge of the city. For the remainder of Reconstruction, half of the aldermen on the city council were African Americans, but that biracial coalition lost power in the late 1870s. There were no black aldermen in the city for the first fifty years of the twentieth century.[25]

When Palmer Gaillard ran for mayor in 1959, he campaigned on the slogan "We Need a Change." Gaillard wanted to modernize and expand the city to build on the postwar economic boom, but he did not want to change the social status quo. A navy pilot during World War II, Gaillard had come home from the war to establish a lumber business. He also won a seat on city council. When he ran for mayor, like his ancestor a century before, Gaillard ran with an all-white city council slate. In part to minimize the impact of newly enfranchised black voters in the 1950s, Charleston had switched from a ward system of elections for city council, where neighborhoods voted specifically for their representatives, to at-large council voting. This enabled the mayor to choose a slate of candidates from any part of the city. Many of the candidates on Gaillard's slate came from below Broad Street. Despite receiving little support from African American voters in the city's northern neighborhoods, Gaillard won.[26]

Mayor Gaillard had the unenviable task of presiding over the city during the height of the civil rights movement, as black Charlestonians began to chip away at the walls of segregation that divided the races in the city and in the rest of the South. When lunch counter sit-ins began in the city in 1960, the conservative *News and Courier* urged police to "use the whip, the rope, the knout, the gun or anything else" to subdue the protests, but Charleston police offered a more moderate response to the demonstrations. From his office in city hall, Palmer Gaillard had a unique vantage point on the civil rights movement. Facing few real electoral challenges during the 1960s, Gaillard worried little about political fallout from civil rights protests. The mayor was, however, anxious about the mounting racial tension and the potential for violence in the city. A "law-and-order" man years before Richard Nixon took up that mantle, Gaillard said, "I could not change state law and I would not tell people how to run their private businesses, except for to conform to the laws." Gaillard sought court injunctions against demonstrations, but at the same time, he quietly supported moderate business leaders who ultimately crafted a compromise with movement activists in 1963. During the 1969 hospital strike, Gaillard once again opposed civil rights demonstrations. "We were determined to meet any unlawful force with overwhelming lawful force," Gaillard later wrote. Though he remained largely in the background during the hospital strike, the mayor's distaste for civil rights activism was widely known. It would open the door for potential rivals and a new generation of political leadership.[27]

Joseph Riley Jr. was neither a civil rights activist nor even a movement ally in the mid-1960s. After graduating from the Citadel, Riley had wanted to go into the army. Hearing loss that had plagued him since childhood disqualified the proud Citadel graduate. Despite pulling strings with Mendel Rivers, Fritz Hollings, and other South Carolina political luminaries, Riley was unable to challenge the military's 4-F classification in 1964. If he had, Riley might have become one of the sixty-seven Citadel alumni who died fighting in Vietnam. As some of his friends and thousands of other recruits trained to fight in Southeast Asia, Riley went to law school at the University of South Carolina.[28]

On weekends when he wasn't studying, Riley returned to Charleston for family gatherings and other social obligations. On one such trip to see a friend graduate from the Citadel, a particular young lady caught Riley's attention. After the graduation ceremony, visitors, alumni, and graduates all mingled, seeking shade from the sun and heat. The men who weren't in uniform wore summer suits. The women wore light, cotton sundresses. Riley ran into some young women he knew from Charleston, and they introduced the young law student to their new roommate. It was, of course, a set-up. "One of the first things I learned was that she had a good sense of humor, that she could laugh easily," Riley later recalled. It certainly did not hurt that Charlotte De Loach was also pretty and petite. Riley noticed that, too.[29]

A bright, quiet young woman, known as "Boo" to friends and family, Charlotte had the itinerant childhood shared by most military kids. After her father left the army, the family settled for good in the small town of Camden, South Carolina. Charlotte's lithe frame lent itself to the ballet classes that consumed her teenage years, but by the time she went to college, ballet had given way to the wanderlust of young adulthood. She went to St. Mary's College in Raleigh for a few years and then traveled to Austria to complete a degree in German at the Institute for European Studies. Returning to South Carolina, she settled in Charleston, hoping to find work as a translator for an international shipping company in the port city. Compared to Camden, Charleston may have seemed cosmopolitan and full of opportunities, but it was no Vienna. Instead of international business, Charlotte found work in mortgage banking. She discovered that she thrived in the real estate business, and she immediately fell in love with the city of Charleston. It took a little longer, but eventually she fell for Joe Riley as well.[30]

After Riley graduated from USC and passed the bar, he and Charlotte began to build a life together in Charleston. He started a law practice and ran for a seat in the state legislature. Given his future career trajectory, it is tempting to explain this campaign as a result of youthful impatience and unbridled political ambition. There is undoubtedly truth in this, but Riley was also moving along the well-worn path for Lowcountry lawyers from elite families. In those days, a young attorney from south of Broad raised his profile by joining certain social clubs and running for the legislature. It was just something one did.[31]

With his father's connections, Riley embraced the establishment, and the establishment embraced him. As an Irish Catholic, there was no better place to network than the Hibernian Society. An Irish benevolent organization founded in 1801, the group's historic hall had housed the ill-fated Democratic National Convention of 1860 that helped precipitate the Civil War. In the modern era, the Hibernian Hall hosted annual balls where Big Joe Riley held forth before throngs of friends and admirers. For real establishment connections, Joe Riley Jr. ultimately joined the exclusive Carolina Yacht Club. True membership was reserved for men, though spouses were welcome. The Yacht Club barred African Americans and Jews as a matter of course. Yacht Club membership was a vital strand in the aristocratic web connecting elite Charleston families. Given this network, Riley's campaign for the legislature in 1968 could not fail. He became the chamber's youngest member at the tender age of twenty-five.[32]

Though his legislative class would be known as the "Young Turks," Riley's campaign agenda was anything but radical. Increased teacher pay, a new bridge in the Lowcountry, and the dredging of Charleston harbor offended few and pleased many by bringing state funds to the district. Riley had learned well from Mendel Rivers. Once in the legislature, however, the young lawmaker did ruffle a few feathers. The most controversial bill that Riley introduced was a day to honor the memory of recently slain civil rights leader, Martin Luther King Jr. "I always suspected you were a communist," one angry constituent wrote, "but now I know!"[33]

A communist he was not. Riley stumped for the reelection of Mayor Palmer Gaillard in 1971. Though the two men belonged to different generations, they traveled in many of the same social circles, and in the wake

A "Young Turk" in the South Carolina House of Representatives, Joseph P. Riley Jr. rides his bike through downtown Charleston in 1973. A few years later, Riley would run for mayor. He would govern the city for the next four decades. Photo by J. R. Burbage. Courtesy of the Post and Courier.

of the hospital strike, the mayor needed all the help he could get. This would be the city's most bruising political contest in a generation, revealing a racial divide that had widened with the civil rights movement. Still, the competitive race caught Gaillard by surprise. He had encouraged the police department to hire more African Americans and had built more public housing for working-class white and black residents. In 1967, the mayor had even supported the candidacy of a conservative black businessman, who became the first African American to serve on city council since Reconstruction. But resentment in the black community ran much deeper than Gaillard realized. His opponents understood this. It was the Achilles' heel of the otherwise popular three-term mayor.[34]

To add insult to injury, it was a Jewish lawyer "from off" who challenged Gaillard in the Democratic primary. Bill Ackerman may not have been a native Charlestonian or member of the Carolina Yacht Club, but the successful attorney and real estate developer still rubbed shoulders with high-society swells in Charleston as the executive director of the Charleston Symphony Orchestra. Gaillard viewed Ackerman's candidacy with bitter disdain. More than thirty years later, the former mayor still could not bring himself to write the name "Ackerman" in his self-published memoirs. "My enemies from way back," Gaillard explained, "believed that I had been politically wounded and [that] they could, with the support of the Blacks, get rid of me. They soon came at me with a vengeance!"[35]

Regardless of whether vengeance accurately describes Ackerman's campaign, emotions did run high among his many black supporters in the 1971 primary election. The vote broke down along racial lines. The bulldozing of black neighborhoods for the crosstown expressway and municipal auditorium, as well as the mayor's opposition to the hospital strike, weighed heavily on the minds of black voters. Gaillard had African American allies, but they were a tiny, elite group. "There were certain blacks that had access to him," community activist Bill Saunders remembered, and "they said, 'We the only ones that can talk to the mayor.'" The vast majority of the black community cast their ballots for Ackerman, and when he lost by a mere ninety-one votes, black Charlestonians backed the socially conservative Republican candidate Arthur Ravenel, who, like Gaillard, came from one of the oldest Charleston families. The general election was decided by less than 850 votes. A Gaillard defeated a Ravenel. With the blue-blood names on the ballot, it could have been the 1800s, but the nail-biting primary and surprisingly close general election pointed to two trends that would dominate the future of Lowcountry politics. The growing importance of African American votes in Democratic politics and the movement of conservative white voters toward the Republican Party anticipated major changes in the southern political landscape after the civil rights movement.[36]

Joe Riley Jr. may not have understood exactly how these trends would play out in 1971, but he was painfully aware of the anger reflected by black opposition to Gaillard. He also believed that a successful southern politician (black or white) in the post–civil rights era would have to bridge the political chasm that had separated the races since Reconstruction. After the election, Riley wrote Mayor Gaillard a heartfelt, idealistic letter about the need for real change in Charleston politics and race relations. "It was a letter of a young man in anguish," recalled Peter McGee, a Gaillard supporter in the early 1970s. "You're the winner," Riley wrote, "and I support you. But I hope you will do what you can to bring [the city] back together." Now is the time for "reaching out, to those people whose homes are hot in the summer and cold in the winter." It was long past time, Riley argued, for the mayor to work for all Charlestonians: black and white, rich and poor. Gaillard seemed little moved by the impassioned letter. The bitterness of the campaign still nagged at him. He was a moderate, not a radical opponent of civil rights. Yet he was, even in the view of his supporters, stuck in another time. Gaillard had grudgingly moved beyond public segregation, but his vision of leadership was one in which white paternalists did things *for* African Americans, not *with* them.[37]

Joe Riley wanted to be a different kind of southern politician. Jackie Robinson, Martin Luther King Jr., Septima Clark, and other black pioneers and activists had taught him about the need for civil rights, integration, and social justice. When Riley returned to Charleston after six years in the state legislature, he said that it was simply to be with his growing family. He and Charlotte already had one son, Joe III, and they would soon have another. Still, the 1971 mayor's race and the suspicion that Gaillard might be leaving city hall must have been in the back of Riley's mind. When Gaillard accepted a position in Washington arranged for him by his friend, Senator Strom Thurmond, the contest for mayor in 1975 became wide open. Few could have known it at the time, but the outcome of that race would decide the city's future for the next four decades.[38]

Riley appeared to be a shoo-in. He had the blessing of former mayor Gaillard, the supporters of Gaillard's rival Bill Ackerman, and the backing of most Catholic voters, who still represented a solid bloc in city politics during the mid-1970s. The main platform of his campaign was racial reconciliation through affirmative action and expanded access to city offices for black Charlestonians. "In the city of Charleston," he said bluntly in the jargon of 1970s urban politics, "black people have never had a piece of the action." He hoped to win the support of young African Americans, who saw "most vividly the cruel contrast of our dual society." Comments like these won Riley black support that helped him coast to an easy victory in the Democratic primary. A decade earlier, that would have been the election. By 1975, however, despite the disaster of Watergate and Nixon's resignation on the national level, the Republicans' "southern strategy" was beginning to make headway in state and local races.[39]

Charleston Republicans nominated Nancy Hawk to challenge Joe Riley in the 1975 mayor's race. It was only the second time a woman had run for mayor in the city's long history. Since Lowcountry residents might not have heard of the first-time candidate, the local paper always added the descriptor "physician's wife" in articles about Hawk. That annoyed the Republican candidate. She did not consider herself a feminist like Bella Abzug, Billie Jean King, or Gloria Steinem. She had no use for the title "Ms." No, the mother of nine children—who had even won United States Mother of the Year—was proud to be *Mrs.* Nancy Hawk. Yet she was just as proud of her own accomplishments.[40]

Nancy Hawk had relocated in Charleston in 1951, when her husband was offered a position as a surgeon at the cancer clinic affiliated with the Medical College of South Carolina. Originally from Virginia—the only place "from off" that was acceptable in Charleston society—Hawk was not initially impressed with the city. "I'll never forget," she recalled fifty years later, "we drove all the way through town and we got to the Battery, and I said, 'Where was the downtown?'" There was more than a little irony in the joke. Nancy Hawk, a relative newcomer by Charleston standards, would make it her life's work to preserve the architecture, scale, character, and feel of the city that became her home. She came to love every crumbling brick, fallen shutter, leaky roof, and broken flagstone that made the place unique. Hawk would play a key role in the historic preservation movement in her adopted city.[41]

Sometimes derided by locals as "hysterical" rather than "historical" societies, Charleston had not one, but two formal preservation organizations and a bevy of informal grassroots groups that reined in development when it threatened the historic character of the city. The Society for Preservation of Old Dwellings (later the Preservation Society) was the first group, founded in 1920. Historic Charleston Foundation became the second in 1947. Preservationists in the city created one of the first historic districts in America with a 1931 zoning ordinance that restricted demolition, renovation, and remodeling of structures in an area south of Broad Street that contained homes from the colonial and antebellum eras. The Board of Architectural Review created by that ordinance would eventually have veto power over proposed changes to buildings in large sections of the peninsula city.[42]

By the time that Nancy Hawk arrived in town, the city was just coming out of the decades of poverty that had actually saved it from redevelopment and the wrecking ball. In the 1950s, preservationists began to take an increasingly active role in saving historic structures from postwar development. Hawk and others recognized early on that a holistic plan to preserve entire neighborhoods would be more effective than a scattershot approach to saving individual structures. They set their sights on neighborhoods that had fallen into severe disrepair, neighborhoods that the preservationists described as ghettos and slums. As laudable as the preservationists' goals were from a historical perspective, the contemporary repercussions of their movement were not always beneficial for all Charlestonians, particularly for the city's working-class African American residents.[43]

Unlike other cities, where roads and rails visibly demarcated the "other side of the tracks" as the "Negro" side of town in the late nineteenth century, Charleston housing remained integrated well into the twentieth century. Some of this integration was due to African Americans living in close proximity to the wealthy white families for whom they worked, but there were also apartments and small homes in the shadows of the mansions in the historic downtown. Though this was the historical reality of the city, and even the romanticized vision of Charleston popularized by the opera *Porgy and Bess*, the residence of working-class African Americans south of Broad did not jibe with the idealized vision of many white preservationists. Starting in the 1930s, the preservationists worked to get public housing funds to relocate black renters north of downtown, in the words of one historian, "ironically beginning the erasure of Charleston's historically integrated streets and neighborhoods."[44]

Like many wealthy white preservationists, Nancy Hawk believed that historic preservation's side effects of gentrification and segregation were far less worrisome than the alternatives. She feared the prospect of historic homes deteriorating beyond repair, historical neighborhoods remaining blighted by poverty, or, perhaps worst of all, redevelopment done merely for shortsighted profit. These possibilities had inspired preservationists to battle developers and the politicians who supported them since the 1920s. In the early 1970s, Hawk had fought off two initiatives that she believed would have ultimately destroyed the historic character of the city. She campaigned against the completion of a bridge from James Island, a dream of Joe Riley's, as long as the terminus was planned anywhere near south of Broad. Hawk also waged and won a war against high-rise condominiums in the historic city. Beating back avaricious developers had given Hawk a reputation as a gadfly who got things done, albeit one whose stately 1 Meeting Street address still bespoke wealth and class. Like many southern women reformers in earlier eras, Nancy Hawk channeled her energies and activism into an area that was appropriate for a southern lady. When she entered politics and later the law, however, she was much more in step with the feminist pioneers of her time than even she wanted to acknowledge.[45]

Joe Riley understood this. His rhetoric about affirmative action in city hiring began to include women as well as African Americans. It was the right thing to do, he realized, but it was also politically savvy. In an era when both women and Republicans were coming into their own, Riley's race against Nancy Hawk would not be the cakewalk many had predicted.

According to Hawk, Big Joe put his thumb on the political scale as the election approached. The political connections Big Joe had made as Mendel Rivers's campaign treasurer surely helped the younger Riley's fundraising efforts. But Hawk believed there were more insidious ways that Big Joe influenced the race. "He went around and he left notes in everybody's mailbox that rented from him," she remembered bitterly. "If Joe Riley doesn't win the mayorship, your rent will go up." Big Joe supposedly went to the places where workingmen bought lunch in the city and paid for everyone to eat during the weeks before the election. Hawk could not or, perhaps more tellingly, did not do these things. Whether Riley needed such tactics or not, the election certainly taught Hawk a lesson in the rough-and-tumble of urban politics. To her, it felt like an Irish Catholic conspiracy. To Riley, it was simply a victory.[46]

When Charlestonians pulled back the curtains from the voting booths on Election Day, Riley had won the support of many wealthy whites south of Broad and most African Americans in neighborhoods far to the north of that historic dividing line. He had forged the kind of interracial coalition that had not been seen in Charleston since Reconstruction. As a result of a federal lawsuit that brought ward elections back to the Lowcountry, the city council elected with Riley included six African Americans and six whites. There were two Republicans, and there were councilwomen as well. Riley would have to hold this diverse coalition together as he governed the city. Nancy Hawk would not have to worry about that. But she did not simply go back to having afternoon tea and playing bridge with other "physicians' wives" south of Broad. Instead, Hawk went to law school, at the age of fifty-six. It was not the last time Riley would hear from her.[47]

Big Joe held the Bible. Bishop D. Ward Nichols of the local district of the African Methodist Episcopal church gave the invocation. A Navy band in white dress uniforms and the predominantly black Burke High School band battled one another in rousing marches and patriotic musical numbers. On a sunny and unseasonably warm mid-December day in 1975, Joe Riley Jr. took the oath of office as mayor.[48]

"Fundamentally, we are but one people," Riley said in his inaugural address. Noting that some still believed that the city should simply live with segregation, Riley said that it was too late for that. "I reject, and I believe our community in this past election rejected, that approach," he said. "We are but one community and those things that affect one segment directly [or] indirectly affect us all." Connecting two themes that had divided the electorate, Riley tackled race and redevelopment. "The bulldozer and insensitive development is as inappropriate in our historic district as it is on the East Side," he said. Yet even while he recognized development's downsides, he knew that it could also deliver the city from many of its problems. Just as he sought reconciliation between black and white Charlestonians, Riley also hoped to forge compromises between preservationists and developers. "Progress and preservation are not mutually exclusive terms," he explained. "We cannot let [the city] become a museum, for it will surely die; but we must insure that development be done in balance with the surroundings."[49]

The substance of Riley's address and what he hoped would be the substance of his administration consisted of bread-and-butter issues that faced not just Charlestonians, but people in cities across America. Crime, economic development, and expansion of the city and its services were central themes of the speech. They were the themes that crackled through aging public address systems from the steps of nearly every city hall in the country during the 1970s. From Baltimore to Birmingham, from New York to Los Angeles, cities were dealing with the same issues. They saw middle-class flight to suburbs drawing not only residents but also businesses out of the city centers. Urban tax bases shrank, and city coffers rang hollow. To make matters worse, simultaneous economic stagnation and inflation crippled the national economy and kept the wallets and pocketbooks of average citizens clamped tight. These were the problems faced by all mayors and cities in the mid-1970s. Riley had to deal with them while also addressing the city's racial divisions and protecting its historic character. "Yet we cannot allow the difficulties of the times," Riley concluded, "to cause us to withdraw from responsibility and creativity." It was a tall order to live up to the hopes and expectations shared by many of the onlookers that sunny December day.[50]

Riley truly believed in civil rights and in making a biracial coalition work, but this was also a political necessity in the wake of the movement. When Riley was first elected mayor, there were 125 African American mayors in the United States. Fifteen years later, there would be 313 black mayors across the country, with black executives having run southern cities like Atlanta, New Orleans, and Charlotte. This explosion of black city leaders took place for three reasons: (1) black political empowerment as a result of the Voting Rights Act of 1965, (2) the growing percentage of black urban residents due to white suburban flight, and (3) the coming of age of a generation of African American activists who cut their teeth in the movement and transitioned into electoral politics in the 1970s and 80s. White mayors like Joe Riley had to understand this political reality if they wanted to remain in office. Looking back, critics of the mayor suggested that he

For his second inauguration in 1980, Joe Riley asked to be sworn in by
local civil rights icon Septima P. Clark (far left), reflecting his debt to the civil rights
movement and to the biracial political coalition that swept him into office.
Photograph by Tom Spain. Courtesy of the Post and Courier.

could not have continued to win unless he changed the rules of the game
by leading an annexation campaign to incorporate nearby suburbs that had
larger white populations than the Charleston peninsula. Riley did oversee an impressive suburban annexation campaign, arguing that city hall
could serve these unincorporated areas better than the county or
smaller municipalities. Annexation meant that as middle-class residents
left the city, the city, in some sense, followed them, protecting its tax base
and Riley's moderately liberal interracial coalition. In this light, perhaps
Riley's commitment to civil rights should be seen as the shrewd political
maneuver of a white mayor swimming with the current of increasing black
urban political power. It may have been. But with Riley, this was also a
personal commitment to racial progress.[51]

It began with affirmative action. This was the guiding philosophy for
hiring and promotion at Charleston City Hall through the late 1970s and
into the 1980s. For a city that had few black or female professional

employees in the 1960s, the change was dramatic. As white male depart-ment heads left or retired, Riley sought to replace them with African Americans and/or women. The mayor, a southern gentleman who literally opened doors for ladies visiting or working in city hall, opened them figu-ratively as well. The chivalrous progressive managed to change the faces of city government without altering its graces. By the early 1990s, there were about a dozen black department heads and an equal number of women running major city departments, from the police to public works. In fact, women and minorities outnumbered white men in comparable positions. Though there was much grumbling, white leaders from across the politi-cal spectrum recognized the change as a good thing for a city with such a troubled past.[52]

The past and its symbolism offered the first test of Riley's biracial co-alition. In the wake of the civil rights movement, the 1960s and 70s saw a renaissance of black history. African Americans and their white allies looked to commemorate ancestors and historical antecedents to twentieth-century social movements. In Charleston, they needed look no further than Denmark Vesey. The African American community saw the free black man who tried to lead a slave insurrection in the 1820s as a hero and a martyr. Many in the white community saw him as a dangerous megalo-maniac. With the naming of the municipal auditorium after former mayor Palmer Gaillard, Riley and African Americans on city council also hoped to recognize the sacrifices and contributions of the black commu-nity. The city commissioned a portrait of Vesey for the auditorium in 1976. Since no likenesses of Vesey survived, the artist depicted the lay preacher from behind, speaking to African American congregants in the old AME church. The painting was tame by the standards of the day. There were no raised fists, broken shackles, or drawn weapons. Still, the symbolism of Vesey remained powerful 150 years after his execution.[53]

"It is important that all of us have the opportunity to consider our her-itage and those who came before us," Riley said at the unveiling of the por-trait. He believed that the city needed to recognized Vesey as "a man who was interested in righting the wrongs [of slavery] . . . a hero, who gave his life so that man may be free." An AME bishop echoed Riley's praise of Vesey: "He was not a black against white people. He was a liberator who God had sent to set the people free from oppression." The 250 black Charlestonians at the unveiling ceremony heartily agreed.[54]

Some white Charlestonians begged to differ. "If black leaders in Charles-ton had searched for a thousand years," opined the local columnist who wrote under the pen name Ashley Cooper, "they could not have found a local black whose portrait would have been more offensive to many white people." Others wrote to the newspaper comparing Vesey to Hitler and Attila the Hun. Despite the white backlash, Riley stuck by the painting and supported the creation of a National Historic Landmark at a house where Denmark Vesey had once lived, acknowledging that the heroes of black Charlestonians deserved just as much recognition as the Gadsdens, Calhouns, Hamptons, Ravenels, and Gaillards.[55]

The Vesey painting, the affirmative action hires and appointments at City Hall—all of it rankled older, conservative white Charlestonians. They knew Big Joe; they had watched Little Joe grow up. They had assumed that Mayor Riley's rhetoric about racial reconciliation was just talk, the kind of paternalistic noblesse oblige that elite Charlestonians were used to. The more politically savvy among them must have recognized that governing a city that was 45 percent black in the post–civil rights era required a more even hand than previous administrations had shown. Still, Riley seemed to go too far. The whispers began.

This was when "Little Black Joe" became the mayor's nickname, a derisive remark that tied the mayor to a long line of race traitors and scalawags from the southern past. Riley embraced the moniker as a badge of honor. It connected him to liberal southern white politicians, from Lyndon Johnson to Jimmy Carter, who had racial epiphanies on the road to Damascus. Political pragmatism, idealism, or both led these white southerners, raised in the Jim Crow era, to become vocal supporters of civil rights and racial equality. "I was called 'LBJ' behind my back, 'Little Black Joe,'" Riley said, remembering when the rumors first got back to him: "All he cares about is black people." Even African American allies began to warn the mayor that a white backlash might torpedo his career and scuttle the changes he had begun to make. "Joe, I'm concerned you're doing too much in the black community," a black lawyer and NAACP activist told Riley in his first term. "I'm afraid it's hurting you politically." The mayor could imagine no higher praise for his commitment to racial progress in the face of resistance.[56]

Resistance to change was strongest among white Charlestonians who had initially been staunch supporters of the mayor. Riley's membership in the Irish Hibernian Society had given him a strong political base in all of his campaigns. Yet it bothered him that the Hibernian Society, St. Cecilia Society, Carolina Yacht Club, and the like stubbornly clung to segregationist attitudes. Of course, there were African Americans who attended the ostensibly all-white black-tie affairs sponsored by such groups. Many even wore tuxedos. Black staff had to look nice to serve food or play in the band for the parties that quickly filled up the white elite's social calendars.

Given his background, Riley could not do much about the more exclusive WASPy societies, but he could do something about the Hibernians. When the mayor found out that the Hibernian Society was not going to extend a traditional invitation to the Charleston County Council chairman for its St. Patrick's Day party in 1977, he dared to ask why. Because, a Hibernian elder explained bluntly, the new chairman was black. The following year, Riley skipped the society's signature event, snubbing old family friends and political allies. Media coverage of the flap caused only a minor disturbance in Charleston social circles, but it was enough. The Hibernian Society president went on the record to say that the group had no official discrimination policy and that members were welcome to bring black guests to events, even the St. Patrick's Day celebration.[57]

In 1979, Riley decided to test the society's newfound racial tolerance. He invited A. J. Clement, a prominent black businessman, as his guest for St. Patrick's Day. Just before the celebration, a friend called up the mayor. "I hear you are taking that nigger to the Hibernian," said the older man. Feigning concern, the man added, "Somebody might kill you." It was hyperbole, but the conversation spoke to the hard death of segregation in the minds and institutions of the old city. On the night of the banquet, Riley walked up the street with Clement and other friends, including the governor of South Carolina. A tourist stopped them to ask for directions. After finding out where he needed to go, the tourist thanked the formally dressed, racially integrated entourage and then asked, "Are y'all members of some kind of band?"[58]

As important as such symbolic gestures of progress were, they did not put food on the table, pay taxes, or fund city services. With the recessions of the 1970s and early 1980s, Riley understood that nothing could bring together Charlestonians of all races, colors, and creeds like a stronger local economy. The middle class, particularly middle-class white residents, had begun fleeing the city of Charleston in the 1950s. Fewer people lived in the city in 1970 than in 1940, though Charleston County's population more than doubled over those three decades. When Riley took office in the mid-1970s, the peninsula was shedding more than 10 percent of its population per year, and city revenues had fallen by 12 percent since 1970. More than a quarter of city residents lived below the poverty line. Boards covered windows and dust draped displays in shuttered businesses downtown. Meanwhile, malls and suburban developments sprang up like mushrooms in a ring around the old city. During the 1940s, 90 percent of the county's retail commerce took place in the city; by the late 1970s, less than half of it did. "We were dying," recalled one small-business owner. "Downtown was really kind of a no-man's land."[59]

Downtown Charleston was certainly not alone in this misery, but the company of cities like Charlotte and Atlanta provided small solace. The skyscrapers that emerged as the saviors of those cities may have attracted business to their downtowns, but at night and on the weekends, their high-rise office towers became hollow, glass obelisks—monuments to the soul-lessness of development in the "new" New South. Even if it had been possible in the Lowcountry, such development did not fit with the pace and character of Charleston. The historic southern city would have to find its own solutions to the problems posed by suburban flight.[60]

Conservative critics later said that Riley tried to build "Atlanta by the sea." That was not the mayor's vision, but he did want to spur downtown development. "People [are] leaving the city physically and emotionally," he said. "It's a very bad thing to happen, because we need people to be emotionally oriented toward the center city." Riley pursued two parallel strategies to reorient Lowcountry life toward downtown Charleston. He brought people into the city with arts and commerce and brought the city to the people through aggressive annexation of unincorporated rural and suburban areas.[61]

The Spoleto Festival USA became the first step in that emotional reorientation of the Lowcountry. Founded in 1977, Spoleto USA was half of the Italian Festival dei Due Mondi (Festival of Two Worlds). The brain-child of composer Gian Carlo Menotti, the festival took place annually in Spoleto, Italy, and Charleston. Charlotte Riley was an early and avid supporter. "It was absolutely magic," the mayor's wife said of the first time she saw the festival in Italy, "the closest thing I can imagine to heaven." Back at home, the festival brought in much-needed tourist revenue and encouraged middle-class suburbanites to return to the city, if only for two weeks every spring. In the words of a senior editor at *Newsweek*, the festival brought a "whirligig of opera, dance, chamber music, jazz, gospel singing, theater, and puppets"—not to mention national media attention—to the "sleepy" southern city. Though the art in Spoleto was rarely avant-garde, the presence of the festival did bring a new air of cosmopolitanism to the city that had been painfully provincial for so long. "It's so exhilarating . . . to have people from all over, strolling our streets, to hear all the fascinating, different languages and accents," Charlotte Riley said on the festival's twentieth anniversary. "It has added a whole new personality to the city."[62]

While Spoleto brought visitors for two weeks every spring, Charleston needed more substantive development to anchor the economy year-round. The mayor dreamed of a large hotel and convention center somewhere amid the picturesque but vacant storefronts and empty warehouses at the center of the downtown commercial district. A massive hotel and conference center sounded like a nightmare to Charleston preservationists. Chief among them was Riley's former political rival, Nancy Hawk.

The development had many names, some unprintable, but it would come to be called Charleston Place. Original plans envisioned a ten- to twelve-story building that would cover an entire square block of town. It would house a hotel with more than 400 rooms, a convention center, space for a high-end department store as well as other shops, and, of course, a parking garage. The plan called for the gutting of historic, but dilapidated buildings in the area, keeping only the quaint facades. Critics howled that this "facadism" was a travesty. Riley shot back that the empty warehouses were little more than "brick coffins," fit only for housing the memories of a dying city. Preservationists responded with a lawsuit to halt development in 1978. *Historic Preservation* likened the campaign to a "religious crusade," asking: "Should Charleston go New South?"[63]

The forces against Charleston Place seemed formidable and united. Preservationists from south of Broad created the "Save Historic Charleston Fund" specifically to lobby against Charleston Place. One of their broadsides included a drawing of the proposed development so out of scale that critics mocked the propaganda piece as "The Great Wall of Charleston." Nancy Hawk joined the preservationists' jeremiad, warning of impending tragedy. From her law office on Broad Street and her home on Meeting Street, she resolved to fight the developers and the mayor. "We thought Charleston Place was too large," she said simply. It would destroy some historic structures, eclipse others, and inundate the old city with a flood of tourists. Hawk and other preservationists saw the potential for developer profits, additional jobs, a boost to the local economy, and a higher profile for the city, but what was the price of "progress," they asked?[64]

Riley went to work, lobbying his allies south of Broad and trying to assuage the fears of the preservationists. "Preservation means many things," he said. "One of the things it means in a city like Charleston is keeping a central business district alive and helping it return to a degree of . . . economic health that is important to a city." The Historic Charleston Foundation, an occasional ally of the Preservation Society, ultimately sided with Riley. Its leaders suggested that Charleston Place was a "plausible answer" to downtown redevelopment. Hawk and others felt stabbed in the back by such fair-weather preservationists who supported the Disneyfication of the city, as long as it did not directly affect their neighborhoods. "Historic Charleston Foundation had made the decision that we could only save below Broad Street," Hawk said. "So we should just let [the rest] go." To the combatants, this was a battle for the heart and soul of the city.[65]

Nearly a decade after he first proposed Charleston Place, Riley saw the cornerstone laid and the first visitors arrive at the new hotel and conference center. Originally proposed for a price tag of $40 million, the final bill came in for twice that at over $85 million. That was on top of thousands of dollars in legal fees that the city shelled out to battle the preservationists in the courts. Two decades later, the hotel had still not repaid the multimillion-dollar loan from the city, but it employed 550 workers and housed more than 17,000 guests annually. As Riley had hoped, Charleston Place anchored redevelopment of the downtown, spinning off an estimated $70 million of additional development in the Sun Belt boom years of the late 1980s and 90s. Tourism became the horse that pulled the carriage economy of Charleston. In some ways that the preservationists had warned and in ways that even they did not foresee, tourism would be a mixed blessing for the Lowcountry.[66]

Riley's vision for Charleston had become the dominant one, and the mayor's star was rising fast. Yet on the national political scene and throughout the South, the Reagan revolution had begun an era of conservative ascendancy in the 1980s. Many white southern Democrats followed Strom Thurmond out of the party. In Charleston, however, the biracial Democratic coalition that Riley had forged in the mid-1970s still held. It had become a fine-tuned political machine by the 1980s, the envy of city leaders across the country. Riley's election as president of the U.S. Conference of Mayors in 1986 testified to that.

As powerful as Riley had become and as liberal as the city government was on racial issues, the growing Republican clout in the state and region did influence Charleston. Perhaps responding to this pressure, the city hired an outspoken, conservative police chief in the early 1980s, and the chief remained at his post for nearly twenty-five years. But this was no stereotypical southern lawman. The new chief was conservative to the core; he was also an African American Jew.

Race against Crime

Reuben Greenberg had led the Charleston police force for seven years when Hurricane Hugo slammed into the city in 1989. The first black and first Jewish police chief in Charleston's history, Greenberg had met and exceeded the expectations placed on him as a historic trailblazer. The mayor and most Charlestonians trusted Greenberg implicitly. Bigger cities tried to woo him away from the Lowcountry, and law enforcement agencies in other countries hired him as a consultant. As Hurricane Hugo approached, however, the chief knew that reputation alone would not keep law and order in the city.[1]

Greenberg gathered the senior officers of the force together to give them their marching orders: "Get your families out of town. You're gonna be in this thing for the duration." With his usual bluntness, the chief warned his senior staff: "You're not gonna leave this job unless you do it permanently once this hurricane hits." Everyone on the force was prepared for Greenberg's workaholic expectations. They were used to 3 A.M. calls from their boss when Charleston was quiet. Things would get worse in a natural disaster. Hugo would mean endless days and nights in uniform.[2]

Officers hunkered down in secure locations all over the city, but Greenberg and most of his command staff were at headquarters on the Ashley River outside the historic downtown. Herb Whetsell recalled standing in front of the station and watching transformers blow as the hurricane hit. Those flashes and explosions were nearly all that he could see in the pitch-black dark. As the storm's eye passed over the city, several officers took a bus to patrol the commercial district. They made it about a block from the station when the bus plowed into five feet of water from the storm surge and stalled. "Had they been able to go, they probably could have all been killed," Whetsell said. "They were lucky . . . just very lucky that that bus stalled out." As it was, the officers waded back to the station just as the second half of the storm struck. Hugo blew rocks and pieces of the building around like bullets in a shoot-out. One officer described the storm peeling back the station's roof "like a spatula." Then rain began to pour in on the dispatch consoles. Officers and staff were rattled. Greenberg went to the dispatch station himself, according to Whetsell. He "got on one of the switchboards and started talking to people in the public and stuff, and it just kind of calmed them back down."[3]

As dawn broke after the storm, the police surveyed a surreal cityscape. A crane mounted on a massive barge had been thrown out of the river into the middle of a residential neighborhood. A sailboat sat tilted on its keel in one of the city's main thoroughfares. Nearly every block exhibited evidence of water and wind damage with pieces of roofs, streetlights, signs, trees, bricks, and masonry strewn about the historic peninsula. Approximately one-third of the homes downtown had been seriously damaged by the storm. The scene was reminiscent of pictures after the bombardment and fires of the Civil War.[4]

Worried about the potential for looting, Greenberg sent his officers out to patrol the downtown disaster area with clear but controversial orders. "The jail will be full within the first hour [or] at least packed," the chief explained. "So I'm telling you right now, don't try to arrest anybody else." He distributed forty-eight-inch riot sticks to all of the officers. If they found looters, the chief told his officers, "Beat 'em and leave 'em." Ned Hethington rode along with Greenberg on a patrol after the hurricane to monitor an evening curfew. They came upon two young men on the street. When Greenberg asked why they were out, the young men struggled for an answer. "Well, goddamnit, don't you know there's a goddamn curfew?" One of the young men started to run, and Greenberg swung his riot stick. He missed, but seeing the stick in action made the other man think twice about being out after curfew. He ran, too. "I don't think [Greenberg] was trying to hit the guy, really," Hethington said. "I don't think he was trying to hurt anyone. . . . It was a lesson."[5]

There were no reports of police brutality after the storm, and Greenberg heard few complaints from Charleston residents. Merchants and political leaders were quick to praise the chief for maintaining order in the city. There was very little looting. Whenever he was asked about the orders to beat looters, Greenberg was not sorry that he issued them. "I wanted to make sure that we didn't have a black-white thing," Greenberg explained, "you know blacks attacking whites or whites attacking blacks, or blacks looting people's shops and all of that. That wasn't going to do anybody any good. And I said, 'We can stop that.'" Greenberg also confiscated the trucks of out-of-state contractors who gouged Charleston residents on repairs after the storm. As Ned Hethington recalled, this was part of the chief's philosophy about right and wrong. Even if he didn't always follow the proper protocols, Hethington recalled of his former boss admiringly, he always did the right thing. Reuben Greenberg idolized the Lone Ranger, so much so that the license plate on his car read "Kemo Sabe"—referring to the iconic western hero's sidekick. "He told me one time," Hethington said, "I'm the guy in the white hat. I'm the good guy."[6]

Through much of the twentieth century, the archetypal southern lawman was a potbellied sheriff. His ruddy neck accentuated an otherwise pale complexion. In the 1950s and 60s, he unleashed dogs on violent criminals and nonviolent protestors alike. The civil rights movement and professionalization of law enforcement gradually changed policing in the South, a transformation dramatized by the 1967 film *In the Heat of the Night*. From the 1970s to the 1990s, southern law enforcement became more "community oriented," addressing institutional racism and police brutality. Sun Belt cities from Houston to Miami, New Orleans to Atlanta, hired pioneering black police chiefs. Historian Marvin Dulaney, who first examined the rise of African American police administrators in this era, argued that black chiefs accelerated the professional reforms that improved law enforcement effectiveness and fairness. Similarly, sociologists Kenneth Bolton and Joe Feagin interviewed black policemen and women who sought to reduce "overt racial hostility and discrimination within their law enforcement agency" and improve community relations. At the same time that Sun Belt cities were hiring more black officers and chiefs, however, elected officials warned of an urban crime wave and drug epidemic unparalleled in modern American history. A chorus of politicians, pundits, and police called for cities to get "tough on crime," yielding mandatory minimum sentences, three-strikes laws, and a local prison-industrial complex. This confluence of historical forces put black cops, particularly African American police chiefs, in a difficult position, one that would help to define the post–civil rights era.[7]

As the Charleston police chief for nearly a quarter of a century, Reuben Greenberg came to embody both the promise and the problems of policing the South in the post–civil rights era. Greenberg's professionalism and racial identity shielded him from the kinds of allegations that had historically plagued southern lawmen, but he worked in a political environment in which coded rhetoric linked "law and order" with control and containment of minority communities. By exploring the dilemmas faced by southern lawmen like Greenberg in communities like Charleston, we can better understand the ways the civil rights movement succeeded and failed in altering power relations in the South.

Reuben Greenberg was born in 1943, the same year as Joe Riley, but the two men who would later work together to police and govern Charleston were born into very different circumstances. Unlike Riley's patrician upbringing south of Broad Street in Charleston, Greenberg was born into a working-class family on the wrong side of the tracks in one of the segregated black neighborhoods of Houston, Texas.

Greenberg's paternal grandfather, Sol Greenberg, had fled the Jewish pogroms in the Ukraine and migrated to the United States in 1898. He ended up in Texas, where he fell in love with an African American woman. Their mixed-race son, Reuben's father, disavowed his Jewish heritage and shortened his name to Green. His children grew up attending the black Methodist church in which their mother had been raised. In the Jim Crow South, Reuben's father decided, a black Jewish identity was neither possible nor desirable.[8]

When Reuben was born, his father was working as a machinist in the Houston shipyard, cranking out vessels that saw action in World War II. After the war, when white veterans returned looking for work, Reuben's father lost his shipyard job and briefly shined shoes in a white barbershop. Servile work did not suit him. He left the barbershop for a job at a black-owned insurance company. Working for a black company may have insulated Reuben's father from racism, but it did not provide enough income to support the family. Reuben's mother, who had picked cotton as a child, worked as a maid for white families for much of her adult life.[9]

With six children, the Greens' two-bedroom house felt cramped, but it was all Reuben and his siblings knew. When his parents were at work, Reuben was the boss. An autocrat like his father, Reuben demanded that his sisters set the table and bring him meals. His sisters, who shared their father's relatively light skin, would mock Reuben's dark complexion. Regardless of their coloring, the Green children were all quite familiar with racial segregation. They attended all-black schools in Houston, rode in the back of city buses, drank from "colored" water fountains, and sat in the hot, stuffy balconies of movie theaters.[10]

Reuben Green knew from an early age that segregation was wrong, but he did not take action against racial injustice until he left the South. After graduating from high school in 1962, the bright, bookish young man had the academic aptitude to go to college, but not the money. A childless uncle and aunt offered free rent and help with tuition if their promising nephew came to live with them in California. In San Francisco, Reuben recalled years later, "a whole new world exploded before my eyes." "It was inevitable," he added, "that I would be attracted to the civil rights movement." During his first two years at San Francisco State University, Reuben Green majored in demonstrations. He picketed Bank of America, Cadillac, Foley's, the Emporium, and other businesses that served black customers but refused to hire or promote "Negro" employees. Reuben never laid his life on the line in these protests, and he did not portray his activism as particularly heroic in later years. It was just something he felt that he had to do.[11]

At demonstrations, Reuben began to notice that many of the white students he met were Jewish. Unlike the South, where most mass meetings were held in black churches, in the urban North and West, synagogues were just as likely to be the epicenters of movement activities. Inspired by Jewish friends and several mentors who happened to be rabbis, Reuben began to explore Judaism, and he talked about reclaiming his grandfather's surname. When Reuben told his family about his interest in his Jewish roots, he got little support. One brother who briefly followed the Nation of Islam agreed that Reuben should change his last name but said it should be to "X," not Greenberg. Reuben's parents, particularly his father, were embarrassed that their son was reopening this old chapter in the family's history. Despite such reactions, Reuben formally changed his name and converted to Reform Judaism in 1965.[12]

As the civil rights movement grew more militant, Reuben Greenberg found himself frequently face-to-face with Bay Area police officers. Reuben and his friends called the cops "pigs" and "fascists"—agents of oppression, not public servants. Then, during one demonstration on a rainy winter day in San Francisco, Reuben sought shelter from the downpour under an awning and found himself next to a cop. The idealistic young protestor confronted the policeman, challenging him to defend his profession. The officer responded, "If you don't like what we're doing, why not join the police?" That question changed Reuben Greenberg's life.[13]

For the next decade, Greenberg followed parallel career paths in academia and law enforcement. After graduating from San Francisco State in 1967, Greenberg went to graduate school at Berkeley. He earned two master's degrees, one in public administration and one in urban planning. As he studied and later taught, he also began building his résumé in law enforcement, working as a corrections officer in Marin County, a community liaison officer in Berkeley, and finally undersheriff of San Francisco. By the late 1970s, Greenberg had moved back to the South, where he began to focus on criminal justice. After working as an assistant to the chief of police in Savannah, Georgia, he took a job as the chief of the tiny town of Opa-Locka, Florida. He moved from there to Tallahassee, where he worked for the Florida Department of Law Enforcement. The Tallahassee position paid well, but state bureaucracy held little romance for a man who had fallen in love with local police work. When Greenberg saw the opening for the chief's job in Charleston, he threw his hat in the ring.[14]

The history of the Charleston Police Department is inextricably linked to race relations in the city. With a black majority for much of its antebellum history, the all-white force before the Civil War spent as much time controlling slaves as fighting crime. During Reconstruction, Republican political leaders created a truly biracial police force. Black Charlestonians joined the department and rose through the ranks. By 1870, more than 40 percent of the force was African American in a city that was 54 percent black. After southern white Democrats "redeemed" the city from Republicans in the late 1870s, however, the number of black officers declined precipitously. African Americans made up less than 5 percent of the force by the 1890s. No black policemen were hired for permanent positions between 1896 and 1950.[15]

Change came gradually to southern police departments in the second half of the twentieth century. After petitions and lobbying from the black community, the Charleston PD hired a handful of black officers in the 1950s. The local paper supported the change, blithely noting, "Negro police are nothing new in the South, but for some reason there was a long period when they were not used." The black officers hired in the 1950s patrolled black neighborhoods and "Negro trouble spots" like the infamous "Do as You Choose Alley," where white police rarely ventured. The newspaper applauded the African American patrolmen for exercising "tact and discretion" when dealing with white residents—as much a warning as a compliment. So while black officers had returned to Charleston, they were part of a segregated force, policing a segregated city.[16]

Beat cops, white and black, who joined the Charleston Police Department in the 1960s and early 70s saw the mundane reality that belied the gritty glamour of the era's cinematic crime dramas. These were not the "Streets of San Francisco" policed by valiant vigilantes like Dirty Harry. Charleston police were poorly paid. Some had high school diplomas, but many did not. Only a few had gone to college. In the summers, they sweated through baby blue uniform shirts with cheap patches sewn onto the short sleeves. If they were lucky, they got to ride in patrol cars, and if they were really lucky, the cars had working air conditioning. Without a walkie-talkie system, foot patrols had to rely on call boxes every few blocks to request backup. In the late 1960s, members of the vice squad supplemented their meager official incomes with weekly payments and bottles of liquor from club owners in exchange for ignoring prostitution, illegal alcohol sales, and the like. The old station house, built in 1908 at the corner of St. Philips and Vanderhorst Streets, looked like a castle. Although imposing from the outside, the interior told a different story. Naked bulbs hung from wires in the jail, where walls were covered with the names of former prisoners—men like Al, Lefty, and Rudy, who had left their marks in the dank, dilapidated cells. A leaky ceiling welcomed visitors to the department's front desk. The signs of decline were hard to miss.[17]

Given the state of affairs in the department, Charleston was lucky that the civil rights movement had nearly bypassed the sleepy port city. The Charleston police force had not cracked down on nonviolent demonstrators the way that Bull Connor's men had in Birmingham or Jim Clark's deputies had in Selma, Alabama, but this may have been due to a lack of opportunity as much as reasoned strategy. By the time the national movement briefly came to Charleston in the 1969 hospital strike, there was a new lawman in the city and a surprisingly progressive attitude on the force.

Chief John F. Conroy was not a black Jew, but he was a Yankee. From New York, the chief hired in the late 1960s had already had a decorated career in the U.S. Marine Corps. His military bearing garnered respect among Charlestonians, and his unflappable, evenhanded approach to civil rights demonstrations won him admiration even from black activists who had little love for white lawmen. Conroy oversaw hiring the first female officers on the force in 1972, and he groomed African American officers for leadership positions. Ligure "Duke" Ellington, who joined the force in 1967 and walked segregated beats in his early years, came to admire and respect the northern-born chief. "John Conroy and I became pretty close," Ellington remembered. "He motivated me to go back to school. . . . He [said] to me, 'You can be the first black chief of police. I know you have the ability.'"[18]

Aware that community relations were still not what they should be, Conroy instituted the concept of "team policing" in the late 1970s to get officers out of their squad cars and into the community, where they could be a seen as a positive force. The teams were racially integrated. Ellington headed up the first team assigned to the East Side. Not long after they set up a satellite office in the predominantly black neighborhood, a disgruntled resident welcomed them with a Molotov cocktail. They cleaned up and re-opened the next day. Ellington and Conroy encouraged their officers to shoot pool in dive bars on the East Side so that they would get to know everyone, not just ministers and other community leaders. When "the community sees the same patrolmen and detectives and gets to know them," Conroy said, "it reduces alienation between the citizen and patrolmen."[19]

As hard as Conroy, Ellington, and others worked on community relations, there was a growing chorus of complaints about police brutality in Charleston. "There is hardly a week that passes," wrote a columnist for the black-owned Charleston *Chronicle* in 1981, "when [our paper] is not called by some citizen being accused or physically assaulted by police when their only crime is being black and defenseless." The paper detailed several examples of African Americans from all walks of life that were questioned or harassed by police.[20]

In one of the more dramatic confrontations, a police cruiser came upon a carload of young black men in their teens and twenties who were double-parked on the East Side. This was a late autumn evening in 1975. According to the driver, Frederick Bailey, the police pulled him and his friends out of the car and threw them to the ground. "Then they picked me up, and hit my head on the hood of my car," Bailey later told a reporter for the *Chronicle*. When the officers put Bailey into the back of their cruiser, he claimed that one of the men tried to ram his head into the door, saying, "Oops, I missed." Black residents gathered to see what was going on. The officers took the young men to the police station on charges of disorderly conduct and resisting arrest. Once at the station, one of the arresting officers told Bailey, "Get up SOB and show me some of the Black Power now! Your black people ain't here to interfere now; it's just you and me!" Bailey later described how police had whipped him, spit on him, and knocked him unconscious with a nightstick. The officers involved in the case never spoke publicly about it, and Chief Conroy told the paper that the case files had been turned over to the Federal Bureau of Investigation. But no formal action was ever reported in the case.[21]

The relationship between police and black Charlestonians was still tense in the fall of 1981 when Chief Conroy shocked friends, family, and the community at large by committing suicide. The chief left no note, but his death seemed unrelated to his job or the racial tensions with the department. In fact, black and white Charlestonians alike mourned the chief's death and wondered aloud who could replace him.[22]

Mayor Joe Riley oversaw the search for Conroy's successor. Black community activists urged the mayor to consider African American candidates, and this fit with Riley's own commitment to affirmative action. Yet the mayor also understood that hiring a black candidate simply because of his or her race would be disastrous if crime then rose. This was an era when conservatism was in ascendance, with both crime and affirmative action becoming wedge issues in national campaigns. Like many decisions about policing, this one was as much about politics as law enforcement.

Reducing crime had been a central tenet of Riley's administrations since he first took office in 1975. Though racial harmony had been one of the ideals that fueled his political career, he recognized that crime was one of the realities that could easily derail it. Nationally, crime rates had risen all but two years in the 1970s, as stagflation crippled the economy and unemployment seemed to drive desperate Americans to desperate measures. On the local level, Riley attempted to highlight the few areas where the police were making progress. He boasted about crime reduction in his annual state-of-the-city addresses, but such claims were based on only modest gains. There was a 1 percent reduction in serious crimes in 1977 and a 5 percent reduction in violent crimes in 1980, but that same year, property crimes also *rose* nearly 5 percent. In fact, according to the FBI, the Charleston metropolitan area had a higher per capita violent crime rate in 1980 than Chicago, Cleveland, and Charlotte.[23]

In the early 1980s, violent crime became something of an obsession for journalists. "If it bleeds it leads" has long been a moneymaking mantra for editors, but the aphorism rang particularly true in this era. *Time* and *Newsweek* ran sensational cover stories—respectively on "The Curse of Violent Crime" and "The Epidemic of Violent Crime"—during the same week in March 1981. *Newsweek* subscribers stared into the barrel of a gun on the cover, while a red-eyed villain with a metallic facemask and snub-nosed pistol menaced *Time* readers. Within a year, the Charleston *News and Courier* ran a similar feature, "Crime: It Can Strike Anyone, Anytime," which warned: "The truth is, statistics and analyses aside, we are all possible victims." The rash of stories chronicled a culture of fear apparently gripping the public.[24]

Reporting that citizens were organizing their own neighborhood patrols across the country, *Newsweek* cited a 1981 Gallup Poll showing that 58 percent of Americans thought crime was rising annually. *Time* acknowledged the possibility that "the fear of becoming a victim is greater than the actual risk." But then the magazine pointed out that even the police chief of Houston, Texas, slept with "several loaded guns in his bedroom." Seeing both a modest growth in real crime and a potential argument for more crime-fighting funds, police chiefs across the country chimed in. In Los Angeles, Daryl Gates called 1980 "the worst year ever in my 32 years as a police officer." In Atlanta, Chief George Napper joked, "When you're up to your ass in alligators, it's hard to remember your purpose is draining the swamp." Few of these chiefs and even fewer journalists explicitly addressed the effect that their sensational crime stories might have on public perceptions and fears.[25]

Politicians responded with tough new crime legislation in Washington, D.C., and even tougher talk. In a 1982 radio address to the nation, President Ronald Reagan spoke of the crime epidemic that left many Americans afraid "to walk the streets at night." He asked for average citizens to support "our war on crime" but closed with classic optimism about "working together . . . [to] make America safe again for all our people." Although he was a liberal Democrat, Charleston Mayor Joe Riley hit the same themes as the conservative Republican president in 1982. Like Reagan, Riley placed the blame for rising crime rates on "career criminals" who benefited from lenient sentencing and early parole in the criminal justice system.[26]

When Reuben Greenberg interviewed for the job in Charleston, he did not try to hide his strong opinions about law enforcement. He opposed parole and favored the death penalty. As Greenberg explained, when criminals murdered victims in cold blood, they should understand that with the death penalty they were also committing suicide. As tough as he was on criminals, Greenberg could be just as critical of his own officers. To curb police brutality, he ordered "use of force" reports whenever officers faced even the slightest resistance, and he gradually increased educational qualifications for new officers, ultimately requiring a four-year college degree.[27]

Perhaps even more than the institutional reforms, Greenberg's personal style of management and policing dramatically altered a departmental culture that by nature was resistant to change. Initially, there was disturbing grumbling from veterans. "Well, I ain't working for no nigger," a few unreconstructed old-timers groused. The new chief had no patience for either insubordination or racism in his ranks. "We are going to strap ourselves to this ship," Greenberg said in his first staff meeting, and "either we will all sink or we will all sail. But if it goes down, we're all going down." The staff learned quickly of the chief's volcanic temper. He was known to slam his fist on tables, walls, and doors for emphasis. During one particularly heated staff meeting, the chief worked himself into such a rage that blood shot from his nose. He backed up this bluster with a tireless, almost obsessive work ethic, and he demanded similar commitment from his officers. He ordered members of his command staff to take personal responsibility for fixing broken taillights on police cruisers. A micromanager, the chief made the final call on hiring decisions down to the lowest level beat cop and even directed street traffic in his suit and tie when he came upon an accident. He was such a stickler for rules that he even ticketed himself for parking and traffic violations.[28]

"Reuben was never off duty," his wife, Sara, recalled. "I knew I was marrying a dedicated police officer and not a man who would be home for dinner at 6 o'clock every night." Sara Horne met Reuben Greenberg on a train on January 1, 1980. The beautiful young graduate student had rung in the New Year with her family in Savannah the night before and was in no mood for chitchat when Greenberg asked if he could sit next to her. Horne grudgingly said that he could, even though she was initially wary of the man who appeared to be just another "young hotshot." Their romance blossomed from that encounter. Sara was as dedicated to her teaching career as Reuben was to police work, and they were both strong-willed, independent people. He was a Jew and she a Baptist, but they clicked. Coming home from a romantic dinner not long after they moved to Charleston, the police radio—which was always on—crackled to life. The dispatcher reported a crime in progress at a nearby drugstore. The chief flipped the blue light onto the top of his car and sped to the scene. "I want you to get down on the floor, and just lay there," he told his wife. "Don't say a word." Another day they were coming back from filing taxes when Reuben responded to a call. This one was going to be particularly dangerous, so the chief asked his wife to get out of the car. She had no money to call for a taxi. When she knocked on the door of a nearby house to ask for a ride, she remembered explaining, "'My husband put me out on the corner,' and they thought it was hilarious."[29]

Greenberg's race allowed him a public hearing in Charleston's black community, and his reforms ultimately paid dividends in better community relations. The local NAACP welcomed the hiring of the first black chief as a move that was "long past due." City Councilman Robert Ford put the matter more bluntly: "I like the fact that he's black and was the top applicant." Within days of becoming chief, Greenberg addressed African American protestors who were irate about police brutality. The chief's swift and judicious responses to protests and controversies early in his career won him praise in both the black and white communities.[30]

Community support also reflected the police department's stunning success in fighting crime. The violent crime rate in Charleston declined

Reuben Greenberg received his service revolver from Mayor Joe Riley as he took the reins of the Charleston Police Department in 1982. He was the first African American and first Jewish chief in the city's history. Photograph by Bill Jordan. Courtesy of the Post and Courier.

by more than 30 percent in Greenberg's first seven years on the job. Property crime dropped by nearly 40 percent. There were fifty-nine murders in the city between 1982 and 1987, and all but two of those cases were closed with arrests and convictions. Though the country did not see the "epidemic" of crime that *Time* and *Newsweek* warned about in 1981, national rates did inch upward over the course of the decade, making Greenberg's accomplishments in Charleston appear even more impressive by comparison.[31]

The national media smelled a story, and Greenberg was more than willing to give them one. In 1986, Morley Safer interviewed the Charleston chief for the weekly news show *60 Minutes*. Thus began Greenberg's fifteen minutes of fame. He appeared on *Larry King Live* and had profiles in the *New York Times, Christian Science Monitor, Los Angeles Times, Ebony, Newsweek*, and *Time*. There were other police chiefs with equally impressive crime-fighting records, and there were black chiefs in bigger cities who had addressed historic racial tensions. But Greenberg played the media like a maestro. His unique identity was the initial hook, but his tough talk and quirky persona added color to every story. He liked to show visiting reporters his Confederate cap and Confederate flag cigarette lighter that played "Dixie." He was more than happy to mug for the cameras while roller-skating around Charleston's historic Battery. An *Atlanta Journal Constitution* reporter described the chief as "black, Jewish and a tough talking conservative who appeals to gentrifying liberals." So he did. Charleston Mayor Joe Riley told the Atlanta reporter, "There is no liberal or conservative attitude about crime. Everybody wants people who break the law to be punished. Reuben delivers."[32]

Greenberg's religious faith got much less play than his race and politics in these stories, but Judaism was a significant part of his life and appeal. When Greenberg originally converted to Reform Judaism in 1965, black-Jewish relations were very close. Seeing parallels between their own oppression and racial prejudice, Jews supported the civil rights movement with activism and donations. Rabbis advised and marched with Martin Luther King Jr. His struggle became theirs. Like Greenberg, a small number of African Americans—most famously the entertainer Sammy Davis Jr. and activist-scholar Julius Lester—converted to Judaism. But a combination of factors, including the increasing popularity of Black Nationalism, the rise of Jewish neoconservatives, fallout from Arab-Israeli conflicts, and the growth of identity politics, corroded relations between African Americans and Jews from the late 1960s to the 1980s. Unlike his father, who felt that he had to choose one of his two identities during the Jim Crow era, Greenberg embraced both his race and his religious faith. He underwent the rigorous conversion process required by Conservative Judaism in 1982.[33]

When Greenberg arrived in Charleston, he joined a Jewish community that had a history nearly as long and storied as that of the city's black community. Charleston's reputation for religious tolerance and role as a trading center in the Atlantic World inspired Jewish immigration and settlement in the eighteenth century. There were more Jews in Charleston in 1800 than in any other city in North America, including New York. In the 1820s, one of the earliest Reform congregations was founded in the city as some Charleston Jews began to assimilate American religious practices (English-language prayers and even an organ) into their services. Charleston Jews had been slaveholders and supporters of the Confederacy, but their experience with prejudice also made at least some Lowcountry Jews quietly supportive of black civil rights. For much of the city's history, Jews inhabited a middle ground between black and white, though economic prosperity in the twentieth century placed them closer to Charleston's WASPy elite. As the civil rights activist Bill Saunders told a visiting writer in the early 1970s, "The Jews are not caught in the middle anymore. They're on their way." Both Jews and African Americans were still excluded from institutions like the Carolina Yacht Club, but Saunders joked, "It's the only place they can't go. And they can park their yachts someplace else."[34]

As a black Jew, Greenberg could tack back and forth between these two communities in Charleston, but his religious conversion as an adult did raise questions. When asked why Judaism, Greenberg placed his initial conversion in the context of his family history and the civil rights movement. But he explained that his deeper commitment emerged as he studied the faith. He liked that the religion was not evangelical and that it taught absolute equality and charity. He embraced Conservative Judaism because he saw it as the middle way between the liberal philosophies of Reform temples and the absolutist strictures of Orthodox synagogues. As he grew more politically conservative, he found support for this in his faith as well. "In Judaism, there is a great deal of emphasis on personal accountability," Greenberg explained to a reporter from the Jewish paper the *Forward*. "You have to account for your own misdeeds. You can't blame society or someone else for the things you do."[35]

Faith took a backseat to conservative politics in the book that Reuben Greenberg co-wrote with editor and freelance writer Arthur Gordon in 1989. *Let's Take Back Our Streets!* was both a memoir and a call to arms for everyday citizens to fight crime. The book hewed closely to the "law and order" philosophy of policing. Presidents Richard Nixon and Ronald Reagan articulated this view in the political arena, and the academics Edward Banfield and James Q. Wilson supported it with scholarship. "You may have the wistful notion that the criminal is the way he is because of poor environment, deprivation, [or] social disadvantages," Greenberg began, paraphrasing Wilson. "When you think this way, you rule out the critical factor of choice." For Greenberg, the reality of law enforcement did not square with the social theories of "wooly-minded liberals." Instead, left-leaning criminologists and policy makers were part of the problem, along with defense attorneys, liberal judges, and lenient parole boards. "A liberal," Greenberg quipped, "is a conservative who hasn't been mugged yet."[36]

Despite the occasional stabs at humor, Greenberg's tone in the book was angry, tapping into a deeper national sentiment of fear and frustration with urban crime in the 1980s. "Our first reaction [to crime] should be indignation, anger, and righteous wrath," Greenberg wrote. "Otherwise the barbarians will take over even more territory than they already have." On a national level, such sentiment crystallized around a 1984 incident in the New York City subway, when Bernard Goetz, a white man, shot four young black men who had demanded money from him. A New York jury ultimately acquitted the "subway vigilante" of nearly all charges. Greenberg sympathized with men like Goetz, who defended themselves when law

enforcement proved inadequate, but he struggled with the racial under-
tones of the Goetz case and the national reaction to it.[37]

Greenberg's mission since his early days in law enforcement had been
"deracializing the war against criminals." Having more minority police
was part of the answer to this problem. Acknowledging the devastating
extent of black-on-black crime was also vital. But just as important as
these steps was recognition of how far American race relations had come
since the 1960s. Greenberg hoped that as society became more color-blind,
so would crime fighting. He believed that overt racism was on the decline,
and he chastised African Americans who continued to blame prejudice
for their problems. "If you go off the track," he argued, "don't blame poverty. Don't blame racism. Don't blame lack of opportunity. Blame your-
self." In this, Greenberg was not far from other black conservatives like
Supreme Court Justice Clarence Thomas or writer Shelby Steele. In the
1980s and 90s, Steele argued that African Americans were finally being
judged not by skin color, but by "the content of our character"—just as
Martin Luther King Jr. had once dreamed. Steele, Thomas, Greenberg, and
other black professionals had made it. Why hadn't other African Americans? This question underlay many of the political contests of the era at
the same time that crime continued to dominate policy debates.[38]

Proof that crime had not been completely deracialized by the late 1980s
emerged in the 1988 presidential race. That year, as Greenberg was working on his book, Vice President George H. W. Bush was running against
Massachusetts governor Michael Dukakis. Lee Atwater, a political consultant on the Bush team, came up with a devastating campaign strategy
highlighting the issue of crime. Atwater had grown up not far from
Charleston in Aiken, South Carolina. He recognized early on in his career
that "law and order" and the "southern strategy," parts of the Nixon presidential campaign in 1968, could allow conservatives to dominate both the
South and nation. As Atwater frankly acknowledged to a political scientist in the early 1980s, coded rhetoric about race was a part of this strategy. "You start out in 1954 by saying, 'Nigger, nigger, nigger,'" he explained.
"By 1968, you can't say 'nigger'—that hurts you. Backfires. You say stuff
like forced busing, states' rights, and all of that kind of stuff. . . . [I]f it's
getting that abstract, that coded, then we're doing away with the racial
problem one way or the other, because obviously sitting around saying 'we
want to cut this' is much more abstract than even the busing thing *and* a
hell of a lot more abstract than 'Nigger, nigger.'" In 1988, Atwater linked
race and crime. The young political consultant urged Bush to portray his
liberal opponent as soft on crime. The most effective attack ad of the

election slammed Dukakis for opposing the death penalty and supporting prison furloughs. The ad focused on Willie Horton, a black man who was convicted of a brutal murder and later committed several crimes—including raping a white woman—while on furlough from a Massachusetts prison. The ads never mentioned race, but mug shots of Horton and his connection to rape touched a nerve in the electorate, helping Bush win the election. The power of the Willie Horton ad signified that crime and race remained closely intertwined.[39]

By reducing both crime and complaints of police brutality, Greenberg seemed to be making headway in color-blind law enforcement in Charleston, but then the sleepy southern port city became a front in the war on drugs in the late 1980s. The Lowcountry was not South Florida, but cocaine did begin to influence all levels of Charleston society: from lawyers and suburban businessmen to rural nightclub owners and urban street dealers. Arrests in the late 1980s included a white auction company owner collared for selling 46 percent pure cocaine and a Latino sailor at the Charleston Navy base caught selling 90 percent pure coke. In one of the larger busts, Charleston police confiscated 261 pounds of cocaine being smuggled on a commercial liner at the port. Yet the majority of Charlestonians charged for possession or sale of illegal drugs were street dealers, most of them African American men. Black men were twice as likely as white men to be arrested for dealing in Charleston and three times as likely to go to prison. This disparity resulted in part from differences in policing and prosecuting drug crimes based on the type of cocaine involved—crack or powder. Cheaper than powder, crack cocaine devastated the poor, largely black neighborhoods east and north of downtown Charleston, where it was known as the "Devil's Candy."[40]

Reuben Greenberg came up with a commonsense response to street-level dealing in a town as small as Charleston. He simply stationed officers on the corners and at crack houses where most dealing occurred and at the times it was most likely to happen. Roadblocks and checkpoints caught or dissuaded buyers. These strategies tended to focus on lower income, predominantly black neighborhoods, though they would occasionally snare wealthier white Charlestonians who used drugs. This reflected both the racial and economic segregation in the city and the reality of the drug trade. "There were a lot of wealthy people doing drugs," Officer Herb Whetsell believed, but "they weren't on the corner selling drugs." The Broad Street folks snorted their coke or popped pills behind closed doors. On the East Side, dealing took place in the open. The police went where the dealers were, and they questioned people who seemed out of

Reuben Greenberg, pictured here in 1985, assisting in an arrest, oversaw the Charleston Police Department in an era when the fight against crime and War on Drugs was racialized in American cities. Photograph by Brad Nettles. Courtesy of the Post and Courier.

place. "That's not racial profiling," Whetsell concluded. "That's just good police work."[41]

Greenberg wholeheartedly endorsed this pragmatic approach to policing, even if it sometimes riled civil rights activists and civil libertarians. A test case for this crime-fighting philosophy ultimately ended in the Supreme Court. In 1988, doctors at the Medical University of South Carolina (MUSC) in Charleston saw a disturbing trend in babies being born to mothers using cocaine. Administrators went to the police and city solicitor to determine if they could bring legal pressure on women who were doing drugs while pregnant. Chief Greenberg cochaired a commission to deal with "crack babies," which were seen as both a national tragedy and a potent political issue. The commission recommended that MUSC give doctors the right to screen pregnant women for cocaine use based on lack of prenatal care and other factors. If the tests were positive for cocaine, police could arrest the women. Forty-two women were arrested based on the protocol. All were poor. Only one of them was white.[42]

In *Ferguson v. City of Charleston*, Crystal M. Ferguson and nine other women filed suit against MUSC, the police department, and the city. The women's lawyers argued that the tests for cocaine use by MUSC amounted to warrantless searches that were unconstitutional under the Fourth Amendment. The city argued that no warrant was required because the tests were conducted by doctors, not police, and that the subsequent arrests were justified because this led most of the mothers into drug treatment programs. During the oral arguments before the Supreme Court, the central issues raised by the justices were (1) the role of law enforcement in guiding medical tests and (2) the profiling of women who went to the public hospital. Since tests were done routinely in conjunction with childbirth, the justices quickly got the plaintiffs' lawyer to admit that such tests would have been fine if done for medical reasons. This appeared to presage a victory for the city. Then Justice John Paul Stevens asked, "What about the other hospitals in Charleston? Do they follow the same procedures?" The plaintiffs' attorney saw an opportunity. "No, your Honor," she replied. The Charleston police had "joined with the doctors in the one public hospital to enforce this policy. They did not enforce this policy at the private hospitals, and . . . nobody at another hospital searched their patients in order to use arrest as leverage." Justice Antonin Scalia came to the city's defense, asking whether it made sense for a hospital serving a population with higher instances of drug use to test pregnant women for medical reasons. The plaintiffs' attorney allowed that it might but that these tests were not done primarily for medical reasons. "They set out to target certain people, to test certain people," she argued, "in the context of a police search."[43]

The case was decided 6-3 in favor of Crystal Ferguson and the other plaintiffs. If MUSC wanted to test women for drugs under this policy, they needed a warrant to do so. This case illustrated some significant themes in post–civil rights policing and criminal law. Most of the plaintiffs were African Americans, but the justices and lawyers never mentioned race specifically at the Supreme Court. In that sense, this was a color-blind decision. Yet the MUSC policy and the policing behind it had clear implications for poor residents and particularly low-income African Americans in Charleston. The intent was color-blind, but the effect was not. Class became a proxy for race, and then medical need became a proxy for class, so that by the end of the day, the justices could talk about a case of profiling without explicitly addressing the profile in question. For conservatives like Justice Scalia and Chief Greenberg, it was perfectly justifiable to profile based on the reality of patterns of drug use in Charleston. For liberals, such actions chipped away not only at Fourth Amendment protection against unlawful search and seizure but also potentially at one of the most important civil rights, equal protection of the law.[44]

Charleston lawyer Susan Dunn was one of the liberal activists who argued *Ferguson v. City of Charleston* in the lower courts. A specialist in civil rights and family law, Dunn was a white southerner whose education and upbringing had been shaped by the civil rights movement. Though she was on the opposite side of the political spectrum from Reuben Greenberg, Dunn sympathized with the chief's attempts to address drug abuse in Charleston. She lived in the city. She wanted it to be safe. But she did not conceive of the problem as a "war" on drugs. "It was a situation where there were good intentions," Dunn argued, "but good intentions when you think you're in a war, can lead to Draconian measures." Dunn explicitly acknowledged the issues of race and class in the *Ferguson* case. "I think the drug war added to the ability to profile," she said, "and when you profile . . . it feeds into a kind of racism; it feeds into a kind of classism."[45]

If lawyers, judges, and police officers disagreed about the extent that racism affected criminal justice in the 1980s, they agreed that the real tragedy was the fact that both the perpetrators and victims of urban crime were likely to be African Americans. In the early 1980s, 70 percent of the homicide victims in Chicago and Oakland were black. In Charleston during this same period, 85 percent of violent crimes involved a black assailant and a black victim. After an African American minister was gunned down on the steps of Mount Pisgah Baptist Church on Charleston's East Side, Chief Greenberg spoke out. "No longer do we fear the torch of the Ku Klux Klansmen," the chief told a meeting of 150 black clergy and church officials in 1982. "But now, there's a new fear of our neighbor." City Councilman Robert Ford had organized a local conference about "Black on Black Crime" in 1979. But the problem had only worsened. Ford himself was robbed more than half a dozen times in the years following the conference. Ford and Greenberg had very different strategies to address the problem. Ford believed that economic development of Charleston's poorer neighborhoods was key. Greenberg argued that economics had less to do with crime than people thought, pointing out that three of four Charlestonians arrested for armed robbery had a job. "We can't think that we can stop crime when we have full employment," Greenberg said, before adding provocatively: "There's only been one time that blacks had full employment, and that was the time of slavery."[46]

Unemployment and crime data in Charleston reveal the same complicated picture found in a century of scholarship on this question. There was a relationship between joblessness and crime, but it was not a direct cor-relation, and race only complicated the matter. As Charleston basked in the Sun Belt economic boom in the late 1980s, unemployment dropped to an astonishing 2.6 percent, and crime rates also fell dramatically. As unemployment rose during the recession of the early 1990s, crime rates began to rise as well. Yet crime rates remained high in Charleston even after the recession ended. In 1998, when Lowcountry unemployment had dipped back below 2.5 percent, crime rates in the city were as high as they had been in 1982, when Reuben Greenberg took over as chief of police. Such statistical evidence was small solace to Greenberg. He was right. Em-ployment was not a silver bullet to stop crime; then again, his tough and innovative crime-fighting strategies had not stopped it either.[47]

As Greenberg would be the first to admit, the race against crime is, in one sense, never ending. Some days, the cops win. Some days, the crimi-nals do. Every year, the Federal Bureau of Investigation includes a "crime clock" in its Uniform Crime Report. The clock illustrates the "relative fre-quency" of serious offenses. In 1982, the crime clock showed one major crime every two seconds in the United States. An American was raped every seven minutes and murdered every twenty-five minutes. By 1992, rapes occurred, on average, once every five minutes, and there were nearly three murders every hour. Both the FBI and local officials cautioned against potential misreading of the crime clock, which did not truly re-flect the frequency of crime, just the total number of crimes spread equally across twenty-four hours, 365 days a year. Still, in the words of one Charles-ton officer, "Crime clocks help folks who don't normally deal with crime gain a better awareness of the quantity and seriousness of the crime prob-lem in the community." In Charleston, the numbers were not quite as scary as the national figures, but they still seemed dramatic. Nearly one murder a month and one rape per week occurred in the Lowcountry, ac-cording to the crime clock in the late 1980s. For families of victims, of course, any amount of violent crime was too much, but Charlestonians were three to four times more likely to die in a car crash than in a crimi-nal assault. Reports like the crime clock did more than raise awareness; they contributed to the specter of fear that dominated public discussion. The racial component of that fear was readily apparent in Charleston, even if it remained camouflaged or coded elsewhere.[48]

In this sense, Reuben Greenberg was fighting a very different race against crime. For much of his career, his race shielded him from the kinds of accusations that had hounded white southern lawmen in the past. Greenberg's philosophy of law enforcement did not substantially differ from his white predecessor's, but his department faced far fewer complaints about police brutality or racism, at least in his early years on the job. Even for Greenberg, however, the ideal of color-blind crime fighting proved impossible to achieve. He lived in a society that was far from color-blind with a language that was only superficially race-neutral. In the post–civil rights era, there had been a shift in American political discourse. Discussions about race had revolved around rights in the 1960s and early 1970s, but the rhetoric about rights faded as crime became code for racial problems. Police chiefs like Greenberg knew only too well that crime was a real problem, one that was exacerbated by drugs and other factors. Yet as the wars against crime and drugs eclipsed the war on poverty, the cause of the problem seemed to shift as well. To Greenberg, the problem was no longer racism, and the solution was not more rights; it was more personal responsibility. In the 1980s, most Charlestonians—in fact, most Americans—agreed with the chief. In this race against crime, race lost.

Perhaps it was understandable that the relationship between race and criminal justice remained complicated in the post–civil rights era, but if there was one arena of southern life in which the movement should have settled questions of racial justice it was in public education. The trajectory of Charleston public schools in the wake of several landmark Supreme Court cases in the 1950s and 60s suggests that the question of school segregation remained a vexing one. In some Charleston schools, the decades after the civil rights movement had witnessed dramatic progress in racial integration. In others, however, the stubborn persistence of segregation suggested a more troubling story.

CHAPTER FOUR

Fade to Brown

Keith Major was into computers. Some might have called him a "nerd," others a "brain." To his grandmother and his legal guardian, Ursula Major, Keith was just a really good kid. He had been in gifted and talented programs since elementary school, and he had always done well. Keith was a solid A student. Even though he did not always study as much as he should, he had a bright future. In 1984, Keith Major was about to start high school. Keith and his grandmother lived in a predominantly black, middle-class neighborhood in Charleston. The Majors' home was in Constituent District 20 of the Charleston County Public Schools. This meant that when Keith started high school in the fall, he would be attending Burke.[1]

In 1984, the student body at Burke High School was 100 percent African American. In fact, Burke had been a black school since it was built in 1910 on the site of an old city dump. During the Jim Crow era, Burke received one-third as much funding per student as white Charleston high schools. Charleston's white school superintendent advocated an expansion of vocational programs at Burke in the late 1930s to "supply cooks, maids, and delivery boys" for the local economy. Still the school flourished because it was the only public high school for black students in the Lowcountry. Burke's teachers had degrees from Atlanta University, Fisk, Columbia, Juilliard, and Penn. But in the years since the Supreme Court's 1954 *Brown* decision struck down school segregation laws, Burke had declined. Decades after *Brown*, Burke's student body was still all black, but it had also become overwhelmingly poor.[2]

Ursula Major had grown up in Charleston's black community, and her own children had gone to the city's public schools, including Burke. But she was not about to let her gifted grandson go to a school that had become what she described as a "concentration camp." Major took her grandson to school board meetings and protests. She had grown up in the Jim Crow era. She encouraged her grandson to join the city swim team because she remembered a time when the public pool was segregated. Ursula Major had seen many changes in Charleston and she lived a good life, but she wanted a better life for her grandson. She knew the foundation for that was a good education. After hearing that three white students had been able to transfer out of Burke's district, Major applied for her grandson to transfer to one of the integrated public high schools in the Charleston suburbs. Major's request was denied. "Ms. Major, I'm going to tell you right now," one of the black members of the District 20 school board explained. "I will go against [Keith's transfer], because if we let all the top black students out of this district, what's going to happen to Burke?" After that conversation, Ursula Major agreed to testify in a federal lawsuit to end racial segregation in Charleston.[3]

Any discussion of race, education, and the law must begin with *Brown v. Board of Education*. Writing during and just after the civil rights movement, the first generation of legal scholars, like Richard Kluger, dubbed the 1954 Supreme Court decision "simple justice." The watershed case not only ended legal segregation; it began two decades of liberal *jurisprudence* on the high court. Yet the next generation of scholars rightly pointed out that *Brown* had not actually ended segregation in the short run. Instead, as Michael Klarman argues, it engendered a southern backlash and inspired social movements that brought about real legislative change in the mid-1960s. Fifty years after *Brown*, scholars continued to wrestle with its ambiguous long-term legacies. Provocatively, Derrick Bell argued that the court would have better served black children if it had simply enforced equal funding of black schools. Scholars unwilling to go that far argued that southern whites maintained political power and social segregation by limited, strategic, or constitutional accommodation to the decision. In other words, moderate school reform forestalled real, radical change. As a result, legal historian Anders Walker argued, the ghost of Jim Crow still haunted southern statehouses, cities, and, yes, schools. Education reform in the wake of *Brown* resulted in a desegregation paradox, opening up new opportunities for some black students, while limiting academic support for many others.[4]

Building on this scholarship, I believe that one must look to both the courtroom *and* the schoolroom to determine why segregation still existed in some American schools half a century after the *Brown* decision and, more important, what segregation had come to mean. The definition of segregation has changed over time not just for the courts, but for students, teachers, parents, and administrators. By examining a desegregation case in a small southern city, we can see that in the decades after *Brown*, school segregation became only partly about race. It was actually as much, or more, about class.

In the short run, *Brown* did little to change segregation in Charleston except that black schools finally got more (though not equal) funding in the 1950s. A local challenge in 1963 finally started the process of token integration in the Lowcountry through a "freedom of choice" plan. "If you were the daughter of the NAACP president and wanted to take your life into your hands," a former school district lawyer explained sardonically, freedom of choice meant you could go to an all-white school. Few black students were willing to take that risk. True desegregation began only in the wake of the Supreme Court's 1968 decision in *Green v. School Board of New Kent County*, which ruled that school districts must have racial balance in students, teachers, schools, funding, and even extracurricular activities. In the wake of *Green*, school districts across the South finally began the process of true desegregation.[5]

For black students and administrators, desegregation could be a double-edged sword. Desegregation allowed some black students and teachers to have access to better-funded, formerly all-white educational facilities, but the cost was often a loss of rich traditions and leadership positions as formerly all-black schools were closed. Underfunded as they were, black schools had still been vital community institutions during the Jim Crow era. Charleston's Burke High School had served as an incubator of racial pride and civil rights protest during the 1940s and 50s. "I am proud of being black because of the progress that my people have made in the hundred years since slavery," wrote one Burke student for a 1953 essay contest. Seven years later, Burke students would launch Charleston's first lunch counter sit-in, and one of those student activists, Harvey Gantt, would go on to integrate Clemson University and become the first African American mayor of Charlotte. Looking back on her time at Burke decades later, another student activist recalled with nostalgia: "the fight was instilled in us" there. As oral historian Barbara Shircliffe has argued, black nostalgia in oral history interviews for underfunded, segregated schools recognizes the real cultural value of these community institutions despite their financial and academic drawbacks. More important, such nostalgia should be understood as an indictment of discrimination in the desegregation process, not an endorsement of the racist practices of Jim

Crow education. Desegregation splintered community commitment to Burke, as some African Americans left for formerly all-white institutions. Majority-white schools may have had better facilities, but they were often not as supportive of minority students, faculty, and staff. Historian David Cecelski chronicled the controversy and conflicts that arose in the painful desegregation process in coastal North Carolina, just as Shircliffe found similar stories in Tampa, Florida. As in Charleston, the callousness of some white administrators and teachers in newly desegregated schools across the South made African American students and parents pine for segregated (but somewhat sovereign) black schools.[6]

While Charleston's suburban schools saw the most significant racial desegregation in the 1970s and 80s, black student pioneers in formerly all-white schools found that integration was no silver bullet to end racial discrimination. Living outside of downtown Charleston in a suburb west of the Ashley River, the Riley brothers (no relation to the mayor) left all-black Wallace Consolidated School (grades 1–12) in the early 1970s to become upperclassmen in white-majority suburban schools. The proud sons of a longshoreman, the Rileys had both looked forward to being "big men" on the black campus. At Wallace, Leonard Riley recalled, "We were part of the main fabric of the school, played football, played in the band; . . . [we] had influence, political influence in terms of student government, etc." The facilities and culture were different at formerly all-white St. Andrews. The Wallace shop classroom had been "four times bigger than the science lab," but the lab at St. Andrews seemed state of the art, and many white students had already mastered the slide rule. After he transferred to a majority-white school, Ken Riley quickly gave up his dreams of playing football and focused on simply graduating and escaping from what he saw as a hostile learning environment. "We couldn't get no help from the teachers," Riley remembered, "because they really don't want you [there] to begin with." Leonard Riley experienced this hostility even more directly when he began Algebra III. "You're in the wrong class," a white teacher told him. "This is a college prep class, and you're not college material." Both Riley brothers eventually attended the College of Charleston.[7]

Across the Cooper River from downtown Charleston, Damon Fordham found that desegregated schools in the growing suburbs of Mount Pleasant had similar racial tensions, but mostly in middle school and high school. Fordham's adoptive parents were a teacher and a nurse, and he lived in a fairly integrated middle-class neighborhood. Attending a desegregated elementary school in the mid-1970s, Fordham got along well with his classmates, white and black. Middle school was "a rude awakening."

There, Fordham saw racial violence and racist graffiti on the walls. "Even worse," he said, "was the fact that a number of the white kids who I grew up with . . . sometimes adopted the negative racial attitudes of their peers at Moultrie [Middle School]." Attitudes among black students could be just as troubling. Black students sometimes gave Fordham a hard time because he had white friends and "did not speak so-called Black English." Ironically, he recalled, "many of the same black students who accused me of 'acting white' also gave me grief for having a very dark complexion." Wando High School in Mount Pleasant was only slightly better, in part because of informal and formal segregation within the school. The racial divisions at lunchtime in the cafeteria were the same ones that bothered administrators and social scientists across the country. But few schools outside the South would have had separate buses for the white and black members of the marching band, as Wando did in the late 1970s and early 1980s. Nicknamed "American Bandstand" and "Soul Train," the buses reflected racial divisions at the school and in American popular culture. "Although we were going to the same school," Fordham concluded, "all that was missing were the 'White' and 'Colored' water fountain signs."[8]

Despite the rough transition, Charleston's public schools did begin to adapt to the new reality of desegregated education in the 1970s, incorporating African American history and culture into the curriculum. The district encouraged teachers to highlight contributions of African Americans to local, state, and national history. "In Charleston," a 1972 school district memo explained, "we are trying to make possible a history which will . . . [allow] the community to rise above those conditions of mistrust which divide and destroy the fabric of any society." The district even trained teachers to acknowledge that Gullah (a rural black dialect) was not "bad" English, but a way of speaking with a rich, linguistic tradition.[9]

Not everyone was happy with the changes in public education during the 1970s. John Graham Altman III was an alumnus of St. Andrews High School when it had been an all-white school. His children attended public schools in the same district in the 1970s, but Altman complained to friends that they were not getting the same quality of education he had received. One day, a friend challenged him: "You know so damn much, why don't you run for school board?" He did. He won. He served for twenty years, several of them as school board chairman.[10]

Altman's father had been a New Deal Democrat, and Altman's politics as a young man reflected this political pedigree. The younger Altman was whip smart and pugnacious from an early age. A national champion in debate, he went to law school and then became a press aide to South

Carolina's moderate Democratic governor Fritz Hollings in 1960. Altman's career took a wrong turn in the late 1960s when alcoholism cost him his first marriage. A devotion to the Methodist church and a third marriage finally brought stability to Altman's life in the 1970s, when he won his school board seat. His politics had evolved as well. He became a conservative Republican. Initially, Altman focused on nuts-and-bolts issues like improving discipline and promotion standards in Charleston schools, but he was not cut out to be a behind-the-scenes policy wonk. Newspaper and television reporters quickly learned to rely on Altman for a provocative quip or quote. Over the course of his political career, Altman urged Charleston police to arrest truants, supported the expulsion of students with AIDS, and (jokingly) proposed commemoration of "white history month." To his critics, he was a "buffoon" or, in the words of a local black minister, "one of the craziest white boys I've ever seen." But to his supporters, Altman was a gadfly, a necessary check on bureaucratic inefficiency, liberal school policies, and political correctness run amok.[11]

By the late 1970s when John Graham Altman was first elected to the school board, a system with three types of schools had replaced the old Jim Crow system of segregation in Charleston. There were relatively poor, mostly black, rural and inner-city public schools. There were middle-class integrated suburban public schools, and there were relatively wealthy, mostly white private academies. The school district had no responsibility for the private schools, but white flight to these schools and the suburbs left all-black public schools in the city that stood in stark contrast to the desegregated but often majority-white schools in Charleston's suburbs.

The process of white and middle-class flight to the suburbs took place across the country during the 1960s and 70s, most famously in Detroit, Michigan, and its surrounding suburbs. Moving to the right after nearly two decades of liberal decisions on school desegregation suits, the Supreme Court weighed in on the question of racial segregation between cities and suburbs in its 1974 *Milliken v. Bradley* decision that focused on Detroit. Because "local control of public education in this country is deeply rooted in tradition," the court ruled that even when suburban and city school districts were clearly segregated by race, it was unconstitutional to force desegregation across district lines to achieve racial balance. This decision protected many northern and western metropolitan areas from desegregation suits because they had no history of legal segregation and also because the suburbs tended to be in separate school districts and political jurisdictions from the cities. In the South, the history of legal segregation and unified school districts that covered entire counties meant that southern metropolitan areas were not protected by *Milliken* from federal desegregation mandates. As a result, southern districts tended to be more integrated than northern and western ones by the late 1970s and 80s. For instance, Mecklenburg County (Charlotte) and Wake County (Raleigh) saw initiatives that truly desegregated both cities and suburbs in North Carolina. As historian Matthew Lassiter argued, Charlotte "became a national model for successful school integration" in the 1970s. Charleston had chosen a different path, but that seemed about to change in 1979.[12]

During Jimmy Carter's presidency, the Justice Department began to investigate claims that Charleston County had intentionally drawn school boundaries to keep black students in the countryside and city segregated from mostly white suburban districts. The DOJ threatened to sue to encourage voluntary strategies for integration. John Graham Altman urged the district to fight the feds. "We have never discriminated against black students," he said. "Clearly, some schools are almost all white and some schools are almost all black or all black, but that is not a design by this government. That's a feature of location." In January 1981, in the last days of the Carter administration, the Justice Department sued Charleston County Schools. The NAACP Legal Defense Fund joined the suit. It lasted more than a decade.[13]

Ronald Reagan's inauguration as president and a changing of the guard at the Justice Department slowed the lawsuit but did not halt it. When the case finally went before a federal judge in Charleston in 1987, the DOJ lawyers had their work cut out for them. In the Jim Crow era, Charleston County had not only a parallel school system for black and white students but also a patchwork of more than twenty districts that subdivided the 100-mile-long county. In 1951, the state legislature consolidated twenty-one small districts into eight larger ones. In 1967, the legislature consolidated these districts for tax and funding purposes into a single county-wide district but left student and teacher assignments up to "constituent districts." Members of the local Citizens Councils (a white supremacist group) howled that this was a step toward racial mongrelization. The legislators replied that it was simply a more equitable funding distribution. The Department of Justice argued in the 1980s that the state's real intention was to maintain segregation and that it had in fact succeeded in creating segregated constituent districts, particularly the nearly all-black District 20 in downtown Charleston, which included Burke High School.[14]

A black school in the Jim Crow years, Charleston's Burke High School had never desegregated, but even though *Brown* had not altered the racial composition of Burke's student body, the case and the civil rights movement did have a dramatic impact on the school. Segregation at Burke had become as much economic as racial when black middle-class parents joined the flight from inner-city public schools. Burke teacher Lucille Whipper, who left downtown and Burke in the 1970s, explained it bluntly: "Black people with high incomes started moving to the suburbs." As a black lawyer recalled, "That took the middle-class African Americans away from the Peninsula, and therefore, out of the schools that for history had been well economically mixed, and . . . rendered the District 20 schools pretty much schools for primarily low-income children." Economic segregation underpinned what scholars have called the "resegregation" of the 1970s and 1980s, and yet, discussions of class have been eclipsed by race in the scholarship and case law on segregation. Barring a discussion of economic segregation, lawyers in desegregation cases like the one in Charleston focused primarily on the vestiges of Jim Crow.[15]

Though the Department of Justice brought the initial suit, DOJ lawyers were joined by additional plaintiffs and lawyers from the NAACP Legal Defense Fund. These plaintiffs' stories illustrated the uneven effects of desegregation in Charleston. Richard Ganaway, whose name would ultimately become attached to the suit in *United States of America and Richard Ganaway II et al v. Charleston County School District and State of South Carolina*, seemed at first an unlikely plaintiff. Ganaway had attended segregated black schools in the 1950s, but his kids had always attended desegregated, predominantly white schools. The Ganaways were middle class. Richard Ganaway was a quality assurance inspector for Lockheed, and his wife was a homemaker. The Ganaways had been able to take advantage of the new educational and economic opportunities that emerged after *Brown* and the civil rights movement. But Richard Ganaway was troubled by the fact that not all African Americans in the Lowcountry had those same chances. The district had closed black schools rather than encourage whites to integrate them, he said. The board had made it difficult to transfer from one constituent district to another. When pushed for further examples by the state's attorney, Ganaway grew frustrated. The "only thing I can tell you," he said, is that the law "has served to maintain, not to desegregate, if you will. It certainly has not met the mandate of the 1954 Supreme Court decision."[16]

Unlike the Ganaways, other plaintiffs in the suit did have children in schools and constituent districts that were all-black. Louise Brown, a private nurse in Charleston, had graduated from Burke High School in 1954, and her children went to Burke as well. She complained of rat infestations in District 20 schools, schools that were dilapidated and underfunded.

Talking about one middle school in downtown Charleston, she said: "They don't have money because it's black. . . . [It] is completely deteriorating." Claiming unequal enforcement of discipline and attendance policies, Brown said, "The rules that is set for the black kids is like they are back in slavery time." Edell Simmons, a housekeeper and janitor for the school district, had also gone to Burke. Her son had never gone to school with white children and had never had a white teacher by the time he attended Burke in the 1980s. When asked about the district's "alleged failure to dismantle the dual school system," Simmons simply said, "All I know is that most of the schools that I'm familiar with is totally black."[17]

The defense attorneys for the school district and state of South Carolina did not deny that all-black schools and mostly white schools existed in Charleston, but they did contest the claims that such schools were segregated by law or district policy. They also argued that the district did not discriminate in funding, hiring, or student assignments. When the case began, the school district's attorney was a relatively conservative, well-established Charleston lawyer who had supported John Graham Altman's decision to fight the Department of Justice. Early in the trial, however, several members of the school board decided to change their legal strategy. They hired an ally of Mayor Joe Riley's, a young lawyer who had experienced school desegregation firsthand.[18]

The son of a prominent liberal Charleston attorney, Robert Rosen was a junior in District 20's Rivers High School in 1963 when Millicent Brown became one of the first black students to transfer from Burke to the formerly all-white school. "People have this fantasy about Southern white children playing with black children," Rosen recalled. "That might be true in small towns . . . but in the world I lived in up around Hampton Park, [it] was all white." Rosen had, of course, never gone to school with a black student, but he and his friends, many of them Jewish, tried to welcome their new black classmates. Their support was important to Brown. "For a long time, I ate by myself," she recalled, but "there were some people who began to talk with me and eat lunch with me. . . . They were the Jewish kids. I don't remember any gentile kids befriending me." Segregated within the white community, Jewish students like Robert Rosen sympathized with Brown. Perhaps they had a sense of what she was going through, even though anti-Semitism was much subtler than racism in Charleston during the 1960s.[19]

Dedicated to the same racially progressive ideals that guided his friend Mayor Joe Riley, Rosen attempted to settle the suit with the Department of Justice when the district first hired him. Rosen met with DOJ lawyers in November 1982 and discussed several options to further desegregation, including integrating faculty, enabling inter-district transfers with transportation, redrawing attendance zones, and creating magnet schools. When word of these negotiations leaked to the press, John Graham Altman chastised Rosen: "If you and the Justice Department are . . . negotiating in these directions, we may as well plead 'guilty' to the busing suit." Altman was not alone in his opposition to the remedies proposed by DOJ. Editorializing against magnet schools and other strategies to desegregate city schools, the conservative *News and Courier* wrote, "As everyone knows, District 20 is . . . black to the extent that whites are virtually unseen." But forcing desegregation, the paper argued, was based on the dubious assumption that "black kids can't learn unless they sit alongside white kids." In the face of such opposition, negotiations for a settlement broke down. For the next decade, Rosen dedicated himself to defending the school district.[20]

Opposing Rosen and the attorneys from the state of South Carolina were several attorneys from the Department of Justice, as well as a local lawyer working for the NAACP Legal Defense Fund, Arthur McFarland. The son of a custodian at the Charleston Chamber of Commerce, McFarland had also experienced desegregation when he became one of the first African Americans to attend the formerly all-white Catholic school, Bishop England, in the mid-1960s. When McFarland returned to Charleston in 1974 after graduating from law school and serving as a fellow with the Legal Defense Fund in New York, Charleston schools had not changed as much as he had hoped. "There had been more desegregation in what had been called the suburban schools, but certainly the Peninsula schools were still all-black," he said. "Whites who lived on the Peninsula continued to send their kids to private schools, and the districts that had been predominantly white in the 50s and 60s remained predominantly white." One thing that had changed in Charleston was increased opportunities for black professionals like McFarland, who served for over three decades as a municipal judge in the city. McFarland carved time out of his busy schedule as the chief judge of the municipal court to serve as the Legal Defense Fund attorney for Richard Ganaway in the federal lawsuit against the school district. Though he was on the same side as the lawyers from the Department of Justice, McFarland explained that he was there to make sure that the DOJ did due diligence, not sandbagging the case under pressure from conservative appointees in the Reagan administration.[21]

When the case finally went to trial in the fall of 1987, the DOJ attorneys began by proving what everyone in Charleston already knew—that there were still all-black schools in the Lowcountry more than three decades after *Brown*. The government attorneys asked former school superintendent Dr. Lawrence Derthick to confirm the racial demographics of school after school. Yes, Derthick admitted, there were six elementary schools and two high schools (including Burke) where the study body was 100 percent African American when the lawsuit began. There had been six more elementary schools, two middle schools, and three additional high schools where more than 96 percent of the students were African American. The faculty at all but one of these schools was over 80 percent African American. Many, but not all, of the schools had been founded as black schools in the Jim Crow era, and they were located primarily in three constituent districts, including the city's District 20. But Derthick tried to explain that this was because "the white enrollment was practically nil in District 20, the white parents choosing not to go to public schools." Going school by school, the government attorneys belabored their point until the judge intervened. "Isn't all of this on these charts?" he asked. "No use for him to go over all that."[22]

There were black schools in Charleston, but was this the district's fault? As one way to get at this question, the DOJ investigated the failure of an integrated model school just as the lawsuit was filed. In the mid-1970s, it was clear that the city schools in District 20 were becoming all-black. A group of parents, many of them employees of the College of Charleston, who worked and/or lived in the city, began planning a model school that would be truly integrated. "I honestly believed that the education of children is where the future is, and that it really should be handled within the public school system in integrated schools," testified Helen Clawson, a lawyer and mother of three. "It was very idealistic," she concluded somewhat ruefully. That idealism had driven Clawson to work with others to transform all-black Memminger Elementary School into a model of integration and academic excellence with help from the College of Charleston's school of education. Clawson lived in District 20, but she also recruited parents from other constituent districts to get a critical mass of white families to integrate the school. District 20 was happy to let these families transfer in, but suburban constituent districts were more ambivalent. A large number of interested families lived in District 10, the suburban home of St. Andrews High School. That constituent district school board denied the students' transfer request. An appeal to the county school board was also denied. Discouraged by these rulings, Clawson and other white parents in District 20 remained determined to make the Memminger experiment work. But every year, there were fewer white children in the school. "It was socially isolating," Clawson recalled. "There was only one other little white girl in [my daughter's] class." In the cross-examination, Robert Rosen asked how successful the model school had been in terms of academics. "The goal of integration failed," Clawson said, but she admitted that "the goal of getting a school with quality curriculum and faculty was a tremendous success." Rosen followed, "And the white community hasn't seen fit to take advantage of it?" Clawson, who had moved her own children to private schools, had to admit that was true.[23]

The private schools were the elephant in the courtroom. There were white families in District 20, like the Clawsons, but few of them sent their children to public schools. Mayor Joe Riley sent his kids to a private high school. Robert Rosen sent his kids to private high schools. Most people with means did so. Though private schools played only a small role in courtroom battles over desegregation, they are integral to the larger story of education in the post-*Brown* era, particularly in cities. In the late 1980s, around half of white students in New York, Boston, San Francisco, and Philadelphia attended private schools. About two-thirds of the white students in New Orleans and Washington, D.C., did. White residents in downtown Charleston were not alone.[24]

The private or independent school movement in the South really took off in the 1960s, though there had been private schools in the region since the nineteenth century. Charleston had seventeen private schools in the 1880s, including a Confederate Home School for girls and the Avery Normal Institute for African American youth. The growth of a segregated public school system in South Carolina between 1900 and the 1960s drew students from these private schools. But with court-ordered desegregation beginning in 1963 and accelerating in 1969, private schools became a haven for white students in majority-minority districts. "There can be no doubt that one of the major factors affecting the growth of these schools . . . was the beginning of mass integration of black students into the public schools," concluded one University of South Carolina researcher in the late 1970s. The names of these some of these schools suggested their racial politics. Jefferson Davis Academy (Blackville, S.C.), Robert E. Lee Academy (Bishopville, S.C.), and John C. Calhoun Academy (Walterboro, S.C.) were three of the sixty-nine independent schools founded in South Carolina between 1964 and 1977. If race played a role in the formation of these schools, religion did as well. Supreme Court decisions after World War II, including a 1963 ruling that limited the reading of the Bible in public schools, fueled the rise of independent religious schools in this era. A 1979 school bulletin for Charleston's First Baptist School (founded in the 1940s) emphasized commitment to academics, character, and faith, before taking pains to explain that "this school has no negative, reactionary, or racial motivations." Still, race was a defining factor for many of the area's independent schools. "Whenever we find a private school created in 1964," Robert Rosen explained years after the school suit ended, "it's a segregationist academy, basically."[25]

Though founded long before the desegregation crisis of the 1960s and 70s, Charleston's elite private schools, including Ashley Hall, Porter-Gaud, and Bishop England, saw increased enrollment during this era. Founded in 1909 as a girls' finishing school, Ashley Hall prided itself on educating the best and brightest young ladies not only from the South, but from across the country. Barbara Bush, the wife of one president and mother of another, is the most famous alumna in a list that includes female CEOs, doctors, lawyers, and best-selling authors. Traditionally a boarding school, Ashley Hall gradually shifted its focus to providing an alternative to public education for young white women from upper-class Charleston families. "My sister Anne went to Charleston High, and my younger sister Judy and I switched to Ashley Hall," recalled alumna Gene Burges, "partly because of the coming uproar . . . in the schools with integration." Graduating in 1964, just as Millicent Brown first integrated a public high school in the city, Burges recognized that desegregation was one impetus for her transfer, but it was not the only one. Burges also described a place where academic challenges led to female empowerment. "I loved Ashley Hall," she said. "The teachers really pushed us to do the best we could, and I think that the atmosphere of an all-girls school made those of us who did well feel like we could do anything we wanted to do."[26]

Just as Ashley Hall prepared young women in elite families for college, private military academies and boys' schools served the same function for young men. One of these schools, Porter Military Academy, had been founded just after the Civil War in 1867. A century later, the military academy merged with another boys' school to become Porter-Gaud. Dropping the military curriculum but retaining Episcopal church affiliation, Porter-Gaud served a new function in the era of desegregation. Moving to one of Charleston's inner suburbs in the mid-1960s, the school had also become coed by the 1970s. Comedian Stephen Colbert and artist Shepard Fairey attended the school in the 1980s. Alumni went on to study at Harvard, Northwestern, the Naval Academy, Columbia, Yale, Duke, Stanford, and other elite universities. The tuition of $4,450 per year in the late 1980s kept Porter-Gaud out of reach for many families in Charleston, where the median white household income was about $32,000 a year and the median annual income for black households was about $16,000.[27]

Funding and family wealth were the main differences between private schools like Porter-Gaud and Ashley Hall and their public counterparts, influencing everything from school supplies, facilities, and curriculum to student social life. With academic advantages often came a deeper sense of privilege. "That's all right. That's ok. We'll foreclose your farm some day," fans would chant at sporting events if Porter-Gaud lost to a "lesser" rival. "Since I bounced between both, I can say hands down that private schools are completely cut off physically and socially from the public schools," one Charlestonian remembered of his time as a student in the 1980s and early 1990s. "In public school," he continued, "your identity was shaped by you and your actions, not your last name or your family's notoriety. Private schools were all about status and public schools were all about survival and real life. . . . No one gave a damn who your daddy was or what he did."[28]

Elitism and exclusivity were not unique to prep schools in Charleston, of course, but they were harder to defend in southern private schools during the era of desegregation. Like private academies across the country, Charleston prep schools recognized that both education and reputation might be enhanced by a more diverse student body. Bishop England and Porter-Gaud admitted African American students in 1964 and 1968, respectively. The first African American graduate from Ashley Hall received her diploma in 1974.[29]

As with the students who desegregated the public schools, African Americans who integrated all-white private schools had mixed feelings about their educational experiences. These students were glad to have access to high-quality facilities and college preparatory classes, but they also often faced isolation and prejudice. NAACP lawyer Arthur McFarland recalled that he was not allowed to play basketball for Bishop England his first year there. Finally, in his senior year, he became the first black athlete on a white high school team in the state. Two decades later, Dwayne Green was not sure he wanted to leave St. Andrews Elementary, where black and white students enrolled in about even numbers, to go to private schools like Blessed Sacrament and Porter-Gaud. Born in New York and the son of West Indian immigrants, Green was an outsider in many ways. But it was his race that first set him apart in Charleston's private schools. At Blessed Sacrament, where he was the only African American in his class, Green heard racial epithets and saw black kids from other classes beaten up. By comparison, four African Americans, one Indian, and one Asian American student made his class at Porter-Gaud seem downright diverse. There was no overt racial hostility at Porter-Gaud, but Green did feel socially isolated. Part of it was a limited dating scene, and part was economic. "There were some kids that, their family was very wealthy, had very nice cars, and my parents were very middle class," Green explained. Yet he made friends (including Mayor Riley's son), ran for class president, and had mostly positive memories of his time at Porter-Gaud. Years later, after Green had become the first African American chairman of the board of trustees of his alma mater, his relationship to the school remained complicated. As an aspiring politician, his connections to Porter-Gaud became something of a liability in the black community. "There's a sense that you're not of the black community, because you had the opportunity to go to white schools," he said sadly. "It's damned if you do, damned if you don't." Though his parents had chosen where he would go to school, Green ultimately embraced Porter-Gaud and worked to make it more diverse. "Change in Charleston is so hard to achieve," he said, "because much of the status quo is institutional." Here was an institution Green felt that he could change.[30]

If there remained few African Americans at private schools like Porter-Gaud and Ashley Hall, the numbers of Jewish, Asian American, and Latino students complicated the simple black-white racial divide in Charleston. In the late 1980s, Jewish students still had to answer questions about "whether matzah actually had crushed bone in it or if we really did have animal blood in our wine," one student remembered. "Seinfeld wasn't super-popular," he said, and there was "no Adam Sandler Hanukkah song either." Another student who transferred from Addlestone Hebrew Academy to Porter-Gaud in the mid-1980s remembered the culture shock of going from an Orthodox Jewish school where he spoke Hebrew nearly half of the day to an Episcopal school. For the most part, however, he saw little overt anti-Semitism at the prep school. On the other hand, it was not as if racial and religious differences were invisible. A few weeks after beginning at Porter-Gaud, this student ran into one of his new classmates at the mall. "I just want you to know," the classmate said. "I can't stand niggers, but Jews are just fine with me."[31]

Like Jewish students, Asian American students found that their ethnicity could be a blessing and a curse, helping them when teachers relied on positive "model minority" stereotypes and harming them when they were reminded that they were still not white. Though not as prevalent in Charleston as in bigger southern cities like Houston, Atlanta, or Charlotte, the number of Asian Americans in the Lowcountry had more than doubled between 1970 and 1990, leading to growing visibility if not always acceptance. "As one of the few people of color in a mostly white, middle- and upper-class private school," one Asian American student at Porter-Gaud in the 1980s recalled, "I became increasingly self-conscious over the years of being racially different." Such racial difference was not just a southern phenomenon. The most iconic Asian student of this era was the fictional character Long Duk Dong in John Hughes's 1984 film *Sixteen Candles*. The "Donger" spoke broken English and embodied the stereotypically funny but "foreign" outcast. The racially insensitive treatment of the Donger reflected deeper problems for Asian American students in the 1980s. Perhaps because there had not been a civil rights reckoning for xenophobia and because they were relatively new to southern cities like Charleston, bigotry seemed more overt against Asian Americans. Stereotyped as a "nerd, unsocial, foreign and not cool" and called a "chink," one Asian American alum even wrote a letter to Porter-Gaud administrators warning them of the hostile learning environment. Administrators dismissed these concerns, noting that Asian Americans had done well at the school and that one had even been elected class president.[32]

The federal trial against the school district forced public schools to reckon with racial issues and disparities in ways that the private schools were just beginning to acknowledge. As a result, however, the trial laid bare acrimony just beneath the surface of a small southern city that prized civility and politeness. The federal judge in the case, Sol Blatt Jr., felt this growing racial animosity most keenly. Raised in a small South Carolina hamlet a few hours from Charleston, Blatt was the son of a state legislator who had been a political power broker from the 1930s to the 1960s. Blatt's father had sought ways to maintain segregation in higher education, proposing a separate law school at all-black South Carolina State rather than integrating the University of South Carolina. The younger Blatt had moved beyond defending de jure segregation by the time he became a federal judge, but he was not happy to have such a bitter fight over the legacies of segregation in his courtroom. As the trial dragged on, Judge Blatt pleaded for a settlement from the bench. "I'm particularly concerned about coming up here day after day after day," Blatt said, "because it's just . . . pitting race against race." The judge asked both sides to hire experts to determine if an integration plan that ignored district lines could be the basis of a settlement. Robert Rosen responded skeptically to this request. "I am totally convinced there is no plan we can present to the court that involves geographic rezoning, because we have already desegregated to the maximum extent feasible." "If that's the way you're going to approach the plan," the judge rebuked the defense attorney, "maybe let the state not only pick the expert but draw the plan." Or perhaps, the judge offered facetiously, Rosen wanted simply to follow a plan laid out by the federal government. "Your Honor," Rosen interjected, "we'll go to the expense in good faith and look at the whole zoning [issue]." Though Blatt's local connections and moderately conservative politics made him sympathetic to the school district, the request for a settlement plan looked like he might be favoring the feds and the plaintiffs.[33]

As the experts gathered their research, the court looked into the historical intentions of the state in consolidating the school districts in 1951 and 1967. Many of the men who authored or interpreted these statutes were still alive, and the state asked them point-blank if race was a factor in redrawing the district lines and revising funding or attendance policies. In only one case, the testimony of attorney Robert Figg, was race ever explicitly referenced as a policy rationale by the state's witnesses. Born in 1901, Figg had worked for Charleston and the state of South Carolina in the 1940s and 50s. He had represented a South Carolina school district that ultimately became part of the *Brown v. Board of Education* case. South Carolina schools in the 1950s were "tailored to the people," he said, but "there was resistance to education on the part of the black parents, because they wanted their children in the fields." If some defense witnesses admitted that (questionable) racial assumptions influenced education policies in the 1950s, they denied that race was a factor by the late 1960s. Charles Gibson, who originally authored the 1967 law to consolidate Charleston County schools, went to Porter Military Academy but had grown up in a rural part of the county. "If you lived on one side of [the district line] you got . . . poor educational opportunities," he said. "I realize that money doesn't buy quality education, but I don't know if you can have it without it." So Gibson proposed creating one countywide school district to redistribute tax dollars. Other legislators worried about losing control of neighborhood schools. Robert Figg proposed a compromise — the creation of constituent districts for hiring teachers and assigning students but the consolidation of funding for the larger countywide district. It was not ideal, Gibson thought, but it was better than nothing. "The intent I had [was] not to move kids, but to . . . move the money. . . . Race did not have a whole lot to do with what I had in my mind." A stream of state legislators and school officials testified that the 1967 school consolidation bill was intended to allocate funds more equitably and protect local control of schools, not to maintain segregation. As these witnesses pointed out, segregationists, not civil rights activists, protested school consolidation, going so far as threatening Charles Gibson's life. Without documentary evidence that legislators had redrawn district lines based on race, the court took the word of these men.[34]

If the intent of the law was not to maintain segregation, what about the effect? Clearly, the DOJ and NAACP attorneys argued, Charleston's District 20 black schools were historically underfunded and remained segregated. Leckyler Gaillard, Burke's principal, was a crucial witness for the government's case. Gaillard had begun his career as a math teacher at Burke in 1962 at the end of the Jim Crow era, before rising through the ranks to become principal in 1979. Historically, Burke had always had a strong vocational education center. In the 1980s, it was the best in the county, so good, in fact, that the district bused students in from suburban schools to do some of their classes at Burke. Gaillard was proud of the vocational center, but it came at a cost. The district reduced academic funding based on the number of vocational students. "Consequently," Gaillard explained, "the more vocational programs you have, the more penalized the number of academic teachers you can have." With 300 students in vocational programs and about 1,000 students in academic programs, this presented a problem. Arthur McFarland then asked Gaillard about Burke's facilities. A city street divided the campus. The roof leaked. Classrooms flooded in heavy rains. The cafeteria layout disrupted nearby classes. "I object on the grounds of relevance," Rosen piped up. "Burke has some maintenance problems, along with 59 other schools in the district." The plaintiffs "could have gotten an expert to go look at all the buildings and come in and say that the black schools are inferior to the white schools. . . . They didn't do it, because it isn't true." In fact, district officials had already testified about a $6.5 million renovation of Burke in the early 1980s that made it one of the most modern campuses in the district, with the best performing arts center in the Lowcountry, if not the state. Judge Blatt asked McFarland if he were going to compare facilities of other schools in the district to Burke. McFarland began to explain that he would show that Burke was not the "model" campus that Rosen claimed. The judge interrupted. "I have heard all kinds of testimony about the Burke school," Blatt said. "I know what the problems are at Burke. I have heard them from other witnesses. I know one witness says Burke is a good school and one says it isn't." Frustrated, Blatt allowed McFarland to continue, with a warning: "I'm not going school building by school building, [but] if he wants to talk about Burke and build the record, I am listening." McFarland moved to a different strategy and asked about Burke's white students. At the beginning of the year, Gaillard explained, *one* of Burke's 1,300 students was white, but she had left the school by the time Gaillard testified in the trial. Her foster family said she moved to Georgia. "How would you attract white students to a school like Burke?" McFarland asked. "My interest is attracting the best students on the peninsula to Burke, be [they] black or white," Gaillard responded, "But there are community perceptions that we have been fighting to overcome."[35]

Both sides acknowledged that black schools still existed in Charleston. The debate was whether anything could or should be done about this. Enter the expert testimony. The Justice Department and the NAACP brought in historians to talk about the legacies of Jim Crow, as well as a geographer and an education professor to discuss the influence of school district lines on housing segregation. These experts talked about why after a brief period of integration in the 1970s, the public school population in downtown Charleston had become almost entirely African American. But the city and state attorneys countered with their own experts, a geographer and a sociologist, to show that there was only de facto school segregation in Charleston, as in other cities. The district lines, according to UCLA geographer William Clark, followed boundaries like rivers that divided many parts of the Lowcountry naturally. Judge Blatt asked Dr. Clark directly, "According to your figures, disregarding constituent lines entirely, there is very little you could accomplish in the way of integrating the schools?" Unless the county started "taking them from all over and mixing it up," Clark replied, "if you use adjacent attendance areas across constituent districts," there would be little increase in integration. The final expert for the school district, the last witness to take the stand, agreed with Clark and went a step further. Dr. David Armor contended that even in the few places where redrawing the lines might make a difference, white flight would nullify the intended effect.[36]

Judge Blatt had heard enough. With no settlement in sight and convinced that redrawing the boundaries would have little effect, the judge finally ruled against the Department of Justice and the NAACP Legal Defense Fund in 1990. Yes, the judge acknowledged, black schools still existed in Charleston. But "such schools are predominantly black because the student enrollment in the Constituent Districts in which they are located is predominantly black, and not because of any intent by the Constituent District Board or CCSD." Resting his decision largely on the 1974 Supreme Court case *Milliken v. Bradley* that dealt with majority-black Detroit schools and white suburban districts, Blatt ruled that the school board could not be expected to desegregate an urban (constituent) district where nearly all of the students were African American. In short, racial segregation was the fault not of the school district, but of demographics (white flight), natural boundaries (rivers), and private alternatives. Thus, "this court finds that the defendants have fulfilled their duty to eliminate the dual school system that existed in Charleston County prior to 1954."[37]

After such a contentious trial, public reaction to the decision in Charleston was predictably mixed. "I know from deep in my soul that there's been no discrimination against black students and black employees in this school district," John Graham Altman told a reporter triumphantly. "I knew we were right, and I knew we would win." The suit had cost the district over a million dollars, but Altman and other school board members felt that it was worth it because they feared that a forced integration plan would have cost millions more. As his staff broke out the champagne, the school district's attorney Robert Rosen said simply, "The reason we won is because we've been doing the right thing." Burke teacher Dorothy Wright did not see it that way. "I'm tired of blatant discrimination in the guise of fairness," she said. It is "comical what we do to avoid laws." The plaintiff's attorney, Arthur McFarland, was saddened but not surprised by the judgment. Blatt had ignored the long history of state and district actions to maintain segregation, McFarland argued. He believed that the judge's decision was "highly appealable."[38]

The plaintiffs did appeal to the conservative Fourth Circuit Court of Appeals in Richmond, where Judge Blatt's ruling was affirmed with only a minor qualification by the majority. Yet the dissent was scathing. Despite the fact that the percentages of black and white students were nearly equal in Charleston County, eighteen schools still had 90 percent black enrollment in 1990. "Thirty-eight years after *Brown*," the dissenting judge noted, nearly "half of the school children in Charleston County attend schools that are not integrated." As passionate as this dissent was, it would have little effect on Charleston schools.[39]

The school district had won the legal battle, but the war for the hearts and minds of Charleston students was not over. Even as the lawsuit was drawing to a close, the district began to implement some of the changes that the government's experts in the case had suggested. Before Judge Blatt handed down his decision, the district constructed academic magnet schools to foster integration and provide alternatives to private education. Two of the academic magnet programs were in District 20. A magnet high school was created on the Burke campus in 1988. The magnet school included more advanced placement classes, a mandatory second language, critical thinking pedagogy, connections to local colleges and universities, and a new computer lab. With all of these educational assets, the academic magnet encouraged high-achieving white and black students from throughout Charleston County to transfer to Burke. By 1994, nearly 13 percent of the students at Burke were white.[40]

If the magnet was successful in attracting a more diverse student body to Burke, it did not truly solve the problem of academic segregation, according to Burke alum Jermel President. President's final year at Burke was 1994. A star basketball player, President struggled academically. He did not attend the magnet school, and he recalled a definite divide between magnet and nonmagnet students. Burke students "did not have a good relationship with the [magnet] kids." There was a "virtual separation," he said. "It was like a bunch of smart kids coming into a 'not smart' kids' school." Regular Burke students wanted to know why the magnet students had access to computers and they did not. To President, it all boiled down to funding. Despite the fact that the students shared chorus, band, JROTC, and sports teams, one reporter noted, "There isn't much mingling." This was apparent at lunch, when magnet and non-magnet students ate on opposite sides of the street that divided the Burke campus. In 1996, against the wishes of many in District 20, the magnet school moved from Burke to a new campus on an old Navy base outside the city. One white student who attended the magnet school at its new site found it a "very open and welcoming school for a diverse population," in contrast to the nearly all-white private school she had previously attended. "I had African American friends, Asian friends, homosexual friends, and transsexual friends," this Academic Magnet alum recalled. "I had never felt so welcomed by everyone or exposed to so many different walks of life." With the loss of the relatively diverse Academic Magnet population in 1996, Burke's student body once again became 100 percent African American. Nearly three-quarters of the remaining students were eligible for free or reduced-price lunch. The following year, 97 percent of the students at the Academic Magnet scored above the national average on the Metropolitan Achievement Test. Only 17 percent of Burke students did.[41]

In the wake of the magnet school's departure from Burke, a group of concerned citizens, led by two white businessmen, hired a team of Harvard education researchers to study Charleston schools and propose ways to improve them. The Harvard report praised the academic achievement levels of Charleston magnet schools, where students with the best standardized test scores in the state and region went on to the best universities in the nation. But the report also pointed out that the magnet schools served only about 7 percent of public school students in Charleston. Judge

Sol Blatt had noted this problem during the trial. "I'm sure that magnet schools do bring the school system an integration factor," he said, "but you can't build enough to integrate" the whole district. The Harvard researchers went further, criticizing the racial imbalance at academic magnets in proportion to the student population. Though 60 percent of the public school students in Charleston were African American, 68 percent of the students at the Academic Magnet High School in the late 1990s were white. "This racial preference is indefensible and could lead to litigation," the researchers concluded ominously. Yet in comparison to private schools, which had average nonwhite student populations of less than 10 percent, the magnet schools were fairly integrated. More important, they were free.[42]

The suburban public schools that ringed Charleston were also free, if families could afford to live in these areas. Middle-class whites and African Americans who could leave the city did so. Because of the high proportion of African Americans spread throughout the Lowcountry, Charleston's suburban high schools were actually well integrated, having 26 to 56 percent black enrollments with a countywide population that was about 35 percent African American in the 1990s. Students in these integrated middle-class schools performed as well as or better than the national average on standardized tests.[43]

What about students in District 20? After pouring over census and school data for months, the Harvard researchers came to the unsurprising conclusion that the inner-city schools in Charleston were segregated by race and class. "Thus, we hypothesize," the researchers wrote, "based on this analysis, that a combination of contextual variables—racial isolation plus poverty concentration—are associated with the low achievement scores of students in District 20." Cutting away the education policy jargon, the researchers warned that most students in poor, all-black schools were failing academically. To solve this dilemma, the Harvard research team suggested consolidating Charleston's constituent districts and allowing students to cross the former district lines that isolated the city schools by race and class. This was not to be.[44]

In the decades since the *Brown* decision, family income (class) had become as much a driver of segregation as race. This was as true in Charleston as elsewhere in the South and the nation. Charleston's city schools were still segregated, but they were not segregated the same way schools had been before *Brown v. Board*. When Ursula Major decided where to send her grandson Keith to high school in the mid-1980s, she wanted to send him to an integrated school. But more important, she wanted to send him to a good school. Major dropped out of the federal lawsuit long before Judge Blatt gave his decision. Before the academic magnet came and went from Burke. Before the Harvard researchers wrote their report. Ursula Major sent her grandson Keith to Bishop England, the majority-white, majority middle-class private school that Arthur McFarland had integrated two decades before. Keith Major faced social and academic challenges as one of the "token" minority students at the private Catholic school, but he graduated, went on to college, and later became a Naval Intelligence officer. In the end, the school district had won its case. It had integrated suburban schools. It had built magnet schools that attracted some of the best and brightest students from throughout the Lowcountry, regardless of race. But one way or another, the Charleston County schools had lost many of the kids in District 20, including Ursula Major's grandson Keith.[45]

Not long after Keith Major opted out of a segregated public school in Charleston, another South Carolinian was struggling to get *into* one. In the early 1990s, the Citadel had been racially integrated for a quarter of a century, but the state military college's Corps of Cadets remained all male. One intrepid applicant hoped to change that.

CHAPTER FIVE

Save the Males

Shannon Faulkner was the kind of student who had an opinion about everything. A 3.35 GPA might not have been good enough to be valedictorian of the Wren High School senior class in 1993, but it was an impressive accomplishment for a smart and outspoken student. That student wanted to attend the Citadel. A varsity athlete with Wren's Golden Hurricanes, Faulkner appeared to be the model of a Citadel applicant. Here was a working-class South Carolina kid on an upward trajectory, with grandparents who had made it out of the upstate textile mills through sheer grit and determination. In the winter of 1993, Citadel admissions staff looked over Faulkner's application and liked what they saw. When Citadel staff mailed out thick acceptance envelopes that spring, one went to the address of a certain Wren High School senior. Then, Citadel admissions officers realized that they had made a serious mistake. Shannon Faulkner was female, and the Corps of Cadets was all male. The fat envelope containing her acceptance letter was immediately followed with a slim, tersely worded rejection.[1]

Shannon Faulkner's attempt to gain admission to the Citadel's Corps of Cadets was a logical outgrowth of the civil rights movement in the South Carolina Lowcountry. Faulkner did not call herself a feminist, much less a civil rights activist. She was simply a South Carolinian who wanted to go to one of the state's premier public colleges. Yet, her decision to apply and then fight for admission once rejected based on her sex was emblematic of the expanded struggle for rights in the post–civil rights era. That this struggle focused, in part, on the Citadel was no coincidence. The Citadel had long been a bastion of southern white manhood. In fact, the school prided itself on building southern boys into men. Yet the institution was also an embodiment of national ideals about manhood. As historian and Citadel alumnus Alex Macauley argued, his alma mater "has always been a reflection of not only southern but American values, particularly when it comes to conflating masculinity and citizenship." Insofar as the movements for rights in the twentieth century focused on giving all Americans access to the power that had once been reserved for white men, the Citadel was bound to be a site of those struggles, particularly those related to race, gender, and sexuality. While most scholars have focused on the racial and gender components of changes at the Citadel, I believe that exploring the ways that race, gender, and sexuality shaped the institutional policies and student body of the Citadel better reveals the multiple, sometimes competing, legacies of the civil rights movement. The contests for racial integration in the 1960s, gender integration in the 1990s, and acknowledgment of homosexuality in the Corps of Cadets in the 2000s were very different struggles, but they shared the goals of equal access and equal treatment.[2]

For those who opposed change at the Citadel, this was also a question about rights. It was a question about whether states and public institutions had the right to make their own decisions about admissions requirements. In a deeper sense, however, it was about southerners' rights to defend and define a distinctive, regional construction of manhood. Defense of the Citadel was an attempt to "Save the Males," as the defenders of the all-male Corps of Cadets put it. Southerners had long framed their opposition to civil rights as a defense of the region's "way of life," and this was, in part, an extension of that argument. It was also something unique to the post–civil rights era, an argument about what it meant to be a white southern man when the institutions that had shaped that identity were no longer exclusive. This question was particularly difficult to answer in the case of the Citadel, given the school's history.

Today, the Citadel guards the marshy bank of the Ashley River, one of two rivers that together separate the peninsula of Charleston from the mainland. But when the garrison was first established in the early 1820s, it was more centrally located, just north of downtown, where it was the first line of defense against slave insurrections. Founded in 1822 after Denmark Vesey's aborted rebellion, the municipal guard of armed white men stood at the ready to thwart future uprisings by the region's enslaved African Americans. By 1842, South Carolina officials saw that more than arms were necessary to defend the state and its people. Minds needed to be honed as well. "In this country, where the people are truly and practically the source of all power," the South Carolina governor explained in the 1840s, "they must guard against their own prejudices and passions; . . . in short, they must guard against their own ignorance." With this goal in mind, the state transformed Charleston's small municipal guard into a military school. That school would eventually become the Citadel.[3]

As a state institution, the Citadel's admissions policies were much more egalitarian than those of America's private colleges and universities in the nineteenth century. Half of the cadets at the Citadel paid their way, and the other half came on scholarships from the twenty-nine districts in South Carolina, based on their proportion of the state's population. These "poor but deserving" boys of the state were "maintained and educated at the public expense," according to the law that created the Citadel. Although cadets came from all walks of life, young men from the working class and middle class dominated the ranks throughout the nineteenth and twentieth centuries.[4]

These young men made up the bulk of America's fighting forces in every major military conflict, so it should come as no surprise that Citadel cadets and alumni played crucial roles in American wars. In 1861, cadets fired some of the first shots of the Civil War across the bow of a northern ship, *The Star of the West*, as it sought to resupply the federal garrison at Fort Sumter in Charleston Harbor. During that war, Citadel cadets and alumni rose through the ranks of the Confederate army. Four became generals, and nineteen became colonels. But the school did not fare well at the end of the war, when Union forces conquered Charleston and turned the garrison into their temporary headquarters. The school remained closed from 1865 to 1882, despite the proposal of one Reconstruction-era governor that it become a college for newly freed African Americans. When the school reopened in 1882, it remained all white. School administrators argued that the military curriculum prepared southern boys not only for war but also for peace. "The aim is not to make soldiers," they explained, "so much as to make men, equal at once to the civil and military achievements."[5]

After the Civil War, Citadel cadets and alumni were the guardians of a unique antebellum tradition of southern military manhood. Historians have various explanations for why men from the region tend to gravitate toward the military and military colleges. John Hope Franklin argued that the violence necessary to survive the frontier and subdue slaves reinforced a culture of honor that prized military values and physical aggression. By contrast, Rod Andrew suggested that the support for the military and military education in the South arose from the belief that good soldiers made good citizens. Far from being a conservative force in southern life, Andrew argued, military schools were meritocracies where all white men, at least, were judged on their ability and aptitude, not on wealth or family lineage.[6]

At the beginning of the twentieth century, Citadel freshmen were called "rats." Rats endured three months of hazing and absolute servitude to upperclassmen before they became cadets. One illustration from the Citadel yearbook during this era, captioned "A Scene from Cadet Life," depicted a kneeling freshman about to get paddled by one upperclassman as another looked on with a fearsome switch. In the 1930s, such "ass inspections" left cadets with "literally bleeding posteriors," according to an official history of the school. Physical hazing was only one part of the detail system, which theoretically assigned freshmen to work for upperclassmen in return for mentorship and academic assistance. But stories of abuses led the school's respected president General Charles P. Summerall to discontinue the detail system and crack down on hazing in 1937. In response to Summerall's reforms, seniors at the school rioted in the barracks in what became known as the "Rebellion of '38." The president chastised cadets harshly following the breakdown in discipline. "The efforts that have been made to develop in them qualities of manhood and courage appear to have been wasted," he said. "They have done The Citadel irreparable harm. . . . Their standard of values appears to be too low for them to understand the evil to the college of an outmoded vicious system." Historian Rod Andrew explains that periodic student uprisings reflected a "profound contradiction" in the southern military tradition. "Even as the soldier in southern society stood for discipline, law, and order, he also symbolized defiance and manly resistance to authority," Andrew writes. In part because of this contradiction, Summerall's reforms did not succeed. The official history of the Citadel concludes, "Any serious study of cadet life since 1937 will convince a discerning researcher that complete elimination of hazing at The Citadel remains Utopian."[7]

When General Mark Clark, a veteran of both world wars and the Korean conflict, became president of the Citadel in the 1950s, he defended the arduous rite of passage at the school as the fire that forged an ideal "whole man." The fourth-class system of discipline at the school carried cadets from a hellish freshman year through a vaunted senior year in which they collectively ran the student body. In the 1950s and '60s, this system hardened into a hazing ritual that cadets boasted was tougher than the national military academies. "We will be made men," one cadet from this era proudly claimed of the process. After surviving the fourth-class system, another explained, "You will find that wherever you go, you can say with pride, I AM A CITADEL MAN." This physical adversity was only one aspect of the school's exclusivity.[8]

Since the founding of the Citadel as a defense against slave insurrections, there had been little need to articulate an all-white admissions policy. Then, the civil rights movement of the 1950s and '60s inspired African Americans to challenge the exclusivity of institutions that defined and defended white power. Surviving the physical, psychological, and intellectual challenges at the Citadel and attaining the coveted graduation ring meant that a man had proved himself worthy, and that worthiness opened doors with a network of alumni supporters that included leaders in nearly every field imaginable, from senators to generals, planters to preachers, CEOs to scientists. Without access to the school and this network, African Americans in the South Carolina Lowcountry understood that they would never be truly equal members of Charleston society. Presiding over the school during the first decade of the civil rights movement, General Mark Clark made it clear that he agreed with most cadets and alumni who opposed the racial integration of the school. In a rare, direct reference to his feelings about the civil rights movement, Clark observed: "The American Negro is demanding 'equality' in every phase of life, [but] the blunt fact is that he has been reluctant to accept full responsibility."[9]

In 1966, the year after Clark retired, the first African American cadet walked through the gates of the Citadel. A Charleston native, Charles Foster seemed an unlikely candidate for a civil rights trailblazer. The high school honor student had an easygoing personality when he first joined the Corps of Cadets. He would prove to be an average cadet both academically and militarily. His experience, of course, was anything but average. Hoping to avoid the controversy that attended integration at other southern schools, the Citadel asked the media to downplay Foster's historic significance. In a story that barely ran three paragraphs, the *New York Times* noted that Foster's uneventful entrance went "virtually unnoticed." As a result of soft media coverage, there was little outside pressure on the first black cadet, but internal pressure was a different story.[10]

When Foster arrived on campus, there were no African American professors and very few black administrators at the Citadel. Although African Americans made up nearly half of the school's staff in the mid-1960s, they were relegated to jobs as custodians, cooks, groundskeepers, and laundry workers. The Citadel's unofficial fight song was "Dixie," and fans waved Confederate flags to cheer on the Bulldogs at football games. The atmosphere was not exactly a welcoming one for black cadets.[11]

Racial incidents seriously marred the experiences of Foster and other black pioneers at the Citadel. White cadets screamed racial epithets at Foster from barracks windows throughout his freshman year. One group harassed him wearing white sheets as if they were Klansmen. Foster's original roommate, Dave Hooper, a cadet from New Jersey, also received additional hazing. "I would get the same question every time I went into one individual's room," Hooper remembered. "Did you kill him yet?" Ultimately, Hooper requested a new room assignment. In his sophomore year, Foster was joined on campus by Joseph Shine, a second black cadet from Charleston, but rules against fraternization and perhaps a strategy of self-preservation kept them at a distance from one another. Shine withstood the same racial epithets on campus as Foster. One night, Shine answered a knock at his door to find that someone had drawn a cross with nail polish remover and lit it on fire. The most shocking incident occurred in the early 1970s, when white cadets blindfolded a black cadet named Patrick Gilliard, forced him to stand on a chair, and placed a noose around his neck. When the white cadets kicked the chair out from under him, Gilliard experienced "the longest second of my life" as he fell to the floor. The noose had been looped over a pipe in the ceiling, but not tied down.[12]

The fourth-class system that amplified these horrific incidents of racial hazing also forged interracial bonds between first-year cadets that ironically helped them all survive, according to Alex Macauley, a historian and Citadel alumnus. White cadets understood that although everyone had it rough, black pioneers faced the most intense pressure. "I was a big, hard-nosed football player . . . and [the Citadel] scared me," one white cadet recalled. "How would you like to be a black man coming into the place that fired the first shots of the Civil War?" This awareness deepened the bonds forged by shared adversity. In fact, the ordeals of the fourth-class system of discipline and hazing were intended to forge such bonds, just as military training and boot camp had done for generations. "When people feel that you shared that experience with them and you've come through that experience with them," remembered Joseph Shine, "then they're more inclined to accept you into the brotherhood." For some white cadets, it was the first time they had viewed an African American as an equal, and that epiphany led them to stand with their black classmates. One night in the fall of 1970, the owner of Raben's Tavern, a Charleston bar frequented by many Citadel upperclassmen, refused to serve Joseph Shine in the front room that was reserved for whites only. White Cadets, including Shine's "chief antagonist," walked out of the bar in protest. Echoing many former cadets, Alex Macauley viewed the incident as a turning point in the history of race relations at the school, though it certainly did not end all racial tension.[13]

Few white cadets at the Citadel were influenced as strongly by racial integration as Pat Conroy, the novelist who was a senior when Charles Foster first integrated the school. "This was a tough kid," the white alumnus later said of Foster. "I never heard one kid called nigger more in my entire life." Conroy penned a fictional version of racial integration at the Citadel in his best-selling book *The Lords of Discipline*. The novel's protagonist is Will McLean, a liberal white upperclassman unofficially assigned to see that the black cadet, Tom Pearce, survives his first year and ultimately graduates. "We're a little behind the times," McLean's mentor, a Citadel official, tells him early in the book. "Every other school in South Carolina integrated a good while ago, and God knows we held out as long as we could, but Mr. Pearce is coming through these gates next Monday and he isn't coming to mow the lawn or fry chicken in the mess hall."[14]

As much as *Lords of Discipline* is about race, it is also about masculinity and sexuality. Conroy pits the working-class rebel, Will McLean, against Tradd St. Croix, the effete scion of a wealthy Charleston family. Paternal expectations and a "compulsive need to test the quality of [their] manhood" drive both St. Croix and McLean to attend the Citadel. Mocked as the "honey prince" because of his high-pitched voice and aristocratic upbringing, St. Croix endures homophobic slurs from other cadets. "'Faggot, faggot,' they would scream at him. 'You want to suck me off, faggot?' they would shout, unbuttoning their pants for him." Under this pressure, St. Croix becomes a tragic lesson in gender and sexual insecurity. He leaves his girlfriend when she becomes pregnant. Then he joins a secret society of upperclassmen—the Ten—that brutally hazes "unworthy" first-year cadets. In contrast, Will McLean cares for the woman St. Croix has abandoned and battles the Ten to keep them from torturing and killing the school's first black cadet. *Lords of Discipline* has all of the subtlety of a 1950s melodrama or a steamy romance novel (befitting the airbrushed cover of the paperback), yet it does lay bare the arduous rite of passage faced by Citadel cadets and the connection between this ritual adversity and southern manhood.[15]

Conroy's book and the movie that followed fixed an image of the Citadel as a place where men were made, even if the institution depicted in *The Lords of Discipline* was a flawed one. The fourth-class system continued to harden into a more rigorous and painful process that started with Hell Week for incoming freshmen every summer. Hell Week was always hot and humid. The weather was part of the trial by fire that included racking (yelling), marching, push-ups, shirt-tucks, and haircuts. In the 1960s and '70s, possibly in response to the counterculture fashion of men wearing longer hair, the short haircuts required of first-year cadets grew even shorter. Shaved down to the skin, freshmen at the Citadel became known by the derogatory term "knobs." Throughout their freshmen year, knobs could be quizzed on their knowledge of Citadel traditions by upperclassmen. If they answered incorrectly or committed some other infraction of Citadel regulations, knobs were severely punished. Though such a system may have turned some applicants away, it inspired others. Pat Conroy would later say that the Citadel "taught me the exact kind of man I didn't want to be," but *Lords of Discipline* actually helped recruit a generation of applicants to the school. "This was sort of a notion I got from Pat Conroy's book," remembered Joe Johnson, who went through Hell Week in 1983. "This is a place that will make me a man."[16]

Young men were not the only ones inspired by the challenge of the Citadel. Shannon Faulkner believed that a woman could also withstand the rigors of the fourth-class system. The inspiration for Faulkner to apply was a class discussion about a 1992 *Sports Illustrated* exposé of hazing at the school. That story began with a lurid anecdote about a varsity athlete who was forced to hang naked from his fingertips above a sword placed two inches below his testicles. It was shocking enough that it caught the attention of students at Wren High School in upstate South Carolina. The class discussion quickly moved on from hazing, however. With fifteen females and one male student, the teacher asked the class why women weren't allowed to attend the state school. That question got Faulkner thinking. When she looked into applying, Faulkner found out that Citadel applications did not mention gender, but Wren High School transcripts and advisor recommendations did. Shannon asked the guidance counselor to white out all references to her gender on official forms. Her application went in to the Citadel and to four other schools. The Citadel acceptance was the first to come back. When they later rescinded the offer, Shannon sued the state school. "My parents pay their taxes," Shannon said at an early press conference. "The law just isn't right."[17]

Title IX of the Education Amendments of 1972 complicated but did not necessarily contradict the Citadel's all-male admissions policy. Inspired by the women's movement and more commonly known simply as Title IX, this law prohibited sex discrimination by "any educational program or activity receiving Federal financial assistance." Two exceptions in the law exempted the Citadel. Title IX originally did not affect military schools or schools that had traditionally admitted students of only one sex. Shannon Faulkner and her lawyers believed that the equal protection clause of the Fourteenth Amendment trumped at least the latter of these two exemptions, if not both. There was precedent for their position.[18]

In the early 1980s, a man had challenged the gender-exclusive admissions policies of the Mississippi University for Women (MUW). Founded in 1884, the Mississippi State College for Women had been the first state school in the country to admit only female students. The four-year school offered a range of majors, but it focused on vocational training and nursing. Joe Hogan applied to go to MUW for nursing in 1980 but was turned down because he was a man. "To me, his coming here is diametrically opposed to what for nearly a century, Mississippians have calmly and quietly done well, and that is educate women," Carolyn Vance Smith, the president of the alumni association, told reporters in 1981. "I fear if he is allowed to remain it will damage the uniqueness of this school." Supreme Court Justice Sandra Day O'Connor disagreed. In 1982, the first woman on the high court wrote the majority opinion in the MUW case, ruling that the school's gender-exclusive admissions policy was unconstitutional and that qualified men had a right to attend.[19]

Many of the nation's universities and military colleges had begun changing their admissions policies to reflect the shift in national attitudes that accompanied the women's movement and the passage of federal laws against sex discrimination. Boston College, Harvard, and the University of Virginia all went coed in 1970. West Point, the Naval Academy, and the Air Force Academy admitted women for the first time in 1976. At the service academies, alumni and military brass fought hard against these changes, but ultimately, women's strong academic and military performance quieted critics of gender integration. In the 1990s, dozens of single-sex schools remained. The majority of these schools were private women's colleges. Only two—Virginia Military Institute (VMI) and the Citadel—were public institutions serving men.[20]

By the early 1990s, there had still been no legal rulings on the admissions policies of VMI and the Citadel. The first female attorney general of the United States, Janet Reno, supported challenges to the all-male military schools. Administrators at the Citadel and VMI argued that there should still be a place for public, single-sex military education in the United States. Many cadets and alumni agreed.

Kevin Scott grew up in Georgia and North Carolina, in a family that had a long history of military service. Born in 1967, Kevin was in Junior

ROTC in high school in the mid-1980s when he met several Citadel graduates. Seeing how important the Citadel had been to their lives, Scott applied and enrolled. His family was proud. Even though he had finished Army boot camp the summer before he attended the Citadel, his first week in Charleston was one of the toughest he had ever experienced. "My strongest memory of Hell Week," Scott recalled, "was thinking how odd it was that my 240 pound six-foot-five-inch Army Drill Sergeant from Basic Training was in no way as terrifying as the 140 pound five-foot-five-inch Citadel sophomore cadre corporal that was now shouting at me within inches of my face."[21]

Scott graduated a few years before Faulkner applied to the Citadel, but he retained strong feelings about the gender integration of his school. Raised by a single mom, Scott appreciated strong women, and he felt that discrimination in any form was wrong. Still he believed, like many alumni, that men and women were naturally different and that single-gender education could harness those differences to the educational advantages of students. "I also see The Citadel as a unique place in the world [where] the all-male system could have been maintained," he concluded, "while offering a similar experience to women at other schools in the state of South Carolina."[22]

There were some notable exceptions to the alumni network's opposition to admitting women to the Corps of Cadets. Pat Conroy was an early supporter of women's admission to the Citadel, and Charleston Mayor Joe Riley also made his support for coeducation clear. When Riley had attended the Citadel, it was all male and all white, but the intervening years had taught him the value of diversity. The Citadel could benefit from diversity as well, the mayor argued, displeasing many cadets. Adding his voice to Riley's, Senator Ernest Hollings also supported women's admission to his alma mater. Hollings kept a low profile early on in the controversy, but in May 1993, the senator broke his silence in a letter to the school's president. Although Hollings understood the arguments for an all-male school, he believed that the Citadel could not discriminate based on "race or religion or sex" as a public institution. As one of the lawyers who had defended racial segregation in South Carolina during the 1950s, Hollings learned from the Supreme Court that "single race education" was unconstitutional. He felt that single-gender education was as well. The senator concluded, "Having had a first-hand experience with separate but equal, which is what you plead for in single gender education, I think it should be recorded somewhere that at least one Citadel graduate has learned something about the Constitution."[23]

This was *not* the view of most alumni or administrators in 1993. The Citadel vowed to fight the case in court, and the South Carolina legislature passed a law supporting single-sex education in the state. The school would ultimately pay $5 million (with an additional $3.5 million promised from the state) to create a cadet leadership program for women at Converse College, a private women's school not far from where Shannon Faulkner grew up. The idea behind the "separate but equal" program actually emerged from VMI's fight to remain all male, when the 4th U.S. Circuit Court ruled that single-gender education in Virginia was constitutional if it was available to both sexes. The U.S. Justice Department and the plaintiffs in the cases against the Citadel and VMI refused to accept this line of reasoning, but Citadel alumni took solace in the possibility that separate programs for women and men would save their school.[24]

In addition to Citadel alumni, one of the most vocal groups formed in opposition to Faulkner's lawsuit included mothers and wives of Citadel men. Sallie Baldwin was the president of Women in Support of The Citadel, a group dedicated to grassroots political action against gender integration. Connie Haynie, who helped found the women's group, also founded the Reveille Company ("because America needs one big wake-up call") to sell bumper stickers and T-shirts in support of the Citadel. The motto of the women's group, riffing on an environmentalist slogan to protect endangered whales, was "SAVE THE MALES."[25]

The role of southern women in the campaign against gender integration fit neatly into a tradition of women's conservative activism in the region. From anti-suffrage campaigns to the STOP ERA movement, many southern women fought against women's equality measures, believing that such laws ignored (or even threatened) what they saw as natural differences between the sexes. Differential treatment for women, in this view, was not odious prejudice, but preferential behavior that uplifted southern ladies. There was an undercurrent of liberal women's activism in the South as well, and in the wake of second-wave feminism, some southern women became vocal supporters of gender equality.[26]

One of these women was Patricia Johnson, an officer in the Navy Reserves who attempted to enroll in the Citadel day program for veterans before Shannon Faulkner applied for admission to the Corps of Cadets. Instead of fighting this battle in court, the Citadel closed down the veterans' day program (raising the ire of many male veterans). There was no love lost between Johnson and the women behind the "Save the Males" campaign. Johnson dubbed the more traditional group LAW, or "Ladies against Women." These southern women found themselves on opposite

Connie Haynie (far left) spearheaded the group of Citadel supporters who sought to "Save the Males" by defending single-gender education at the military college when Shannon Faulkner sought admission in the mid-1990s. Photograph by Mic Smith. Courtesy of the Post and Courier.

sides of a long-standing argument about whether gender differences were predominantly biological or cultural.[27]

One of the cultural aspects of this debate revolved around language—how cadets and alumni described their experiences at the Citadel. "My classmates and I endure many hardships that put us in a situation where we must learn to trust and rely on each other," one cadet wrote in the school newspaper, *The Brigadier*, in 1993. "Throughout this process we begin to call each other *classmates* and *brothers* with the most sincere meaning of those two words." William Shakespeare coined the phrase "band of brothers" to describe the bonds forged by military service, and this idea was crucial to the creation of manhood at the Citadel. Incorporating black cadets into this band of brothers had been integral to the success of racial integration at the school. Shannon Faulkner's admission would complicate (or some said destroy) that sense of identity and brotherhood. "Do you think you would be able to share in that brotherhood if you were the first woman at The Citadel?" Dawes Cooke, the school's attorney, asked Shannon Faulkner during her first deposition for the case. "I would hope so," Faulkner replied. "It wouldn't be a brotherhood anymore. It would be a family."[28]

Faulkner took the first step toward joining that family in January 1994, when the court ordered the Citadel to admit her as a day student. As Faulkner strode across campus that first day, she ran into a black cadet named Von Mickle, who stopped to shake her hand and chat briefly in front of the barracks. "I hope you're ready for a challenge," he said. "But I guess I have to commend you. You have a lot of guts, if nothing else, after all that's happened. It's time for women. It's really time." Mickle explained to the press that the Citadel should end what he viewed as a discriminatory policy against women, but he did not believe that Faulkner was necessarily the right woman for the school.[29]

Just as the first African American cadets had faced racial slurs, some opponents of women at the Citadel used sexist and homophobic language to denigrate Faulkner. Vandals spray-painted the words "WHORE," "BITCH," and "LESBO" on her parents' house in Powdersville, South Carolina. People drove through their gardens and changed their voicemail message. Death threats came against Faulkner's parents, and someone put a sign up near their home that read "Die Shannon." Citadel supporters wore T-shirts that referenced the school mascot with the slogan "1,952 bulldogs and one bitch." Faulkner offered to autograph the T-shirts and even wore one herself occasionally, noting that she was at least leading the pack in the shirt's illustration.[30]

In August 1995, the U.S. District Court ruled that the Citadel had to admit Faulkner into the corps. After the Supreme Court once again refused the school's appeal, preparations began in earnest for Faulkner's arrival. The school created a women's bathroom in the barracks and installed video cameras outside a single women's room and panic buttons inside. Accommodations were prepared for the U.S. marshals who would oversee gender integration and make sure that Faulkner was safe.

The temperature hovered in the nineties with the humidity pushing the heat index much higher than that as Faulkner and the other knobs began Hell Week. Citadel administrators grudgingly accepted what many outsiders had seen as inevitable. "As a military person," the school's president said in an opening speech to incoming cadets and their parents, "I salute and move forward." But the president understood that the worst might be yet to come. Harnessing the most fearsome local analogy, he explained, "We are today in a hurricane. And you can put your name on that hurricane. The Citadel finds itself in the eye of the storm. Here, it's calm. It's serene. It's tranquil. . . . Only when you get out of the calm do you enter that hurricane. And then you get beat up." The speech had ominous overtones for Hell Week, but the week itself would prove anticlimactic.[31]

After only a few days, Faulkner checked into the Citadel infirmary with heat exhaustion. She was the seventh cadet to check in. As the week progressed, Faulkner was unable to recover physically or emotionally. On Friday, when she checked out of the infirmary, it was not to rejoin the Corps of Cadets, but to begin "out-processing" from the Citadel. For this combatant in the culture wars of the 1990s, the conflict was over.[32]

Word spread quickly throughout the Citadel and across the country. Cadets cheered. Pundits preached to their choirs. "The feminazis are demanding women in combat," conservative radio host Rush Limbaugh said as he reported Faulkner's withdrawal from the Citadel. "What's happening is that you begin by agitating women and getting them to infiltrate certain male bastions . . . and what it means to be a man is being diluted, being watered down."[33]

What did it mean to be a man if women could survive the traditional rites of passage into manhood? How could there be gender difference if there was also equality? These questions lay at the heart of the controversy over gender integration of the Citadel. For the two journalists who examined this case most closely, Catherine Manegold at the *New York Times* and Susan Faludi at the *New Yorker*, the answers were relatively simple. Manhood, particularly southern manhood, the *New York Times* reporter argued, needed to change to adapt to the changing times. Faludi folded the Citadel story into what she saw as a larger problem with American masculinity. "That [cadets] must defend their inner humanity with outer brutality may say as much about the world outside The Citadel walls as about the world within them," she wrote. "Never mind that their true ideal may not be the vaunted one of martial masculinity, just as their true enemy is not Shannon Faulkner." For Faludi, in other words, this was a case where American culture had not given men a clear, acceptable alternative to the traditional masculinity that the Citadel had long embodied. There was no third way for men, particularly southern men, to address the changes in womanhood that had brought Shannon Faulkner to the Citadel's gates. Sociologist Michael Kimmel tackled the question of gender equality and difference most directly in his work on the Citadel. An expert witness for the Justice Department in the VMI case, Kimmel argued that achieving true gender equality would reveal that the differences between men and women paled in comparison to the vast differences *among* men and women. Using a metaphor popular in military recruiting, Kimmel argued that if the Citadel and VMI forged strong cadets, then they should take a cue from metallurgy. "If you want to make a metal stronger, you do not add more of the same metal. You add a different metal. You make an alloy." For Kimmel, gender integration was "the only way to 'save the males.'"[34]

The "crisis" of masculinity in the 1990s was attributed to many things: the feminist movement, deindustrialization, corporate restructuring, job outsourcing, the end of the Cold War, and the (temporary) downsizing of the American military, to name a few. Faulkner's quest to integrate the Citadel laid bare regional variations on this theme: the struggle over what it meant to be a gentleman in a postfeminist world and the roles of honor, physical adversity, and male camaraderie in shaping southern men. With military bases closing across the country, but particularly in the South in towns like Charleston, the rite of passage into manhood offered by the Citadel may have seemed outdated to some, but to others, it took on even more significance as alternative traditions, institutions, and proving grounds for masculinity disappeared.[35]

The final front of the evolving war for rights and recognition at the Citadel was fought within the school's walls as a group of men who had been part of the brotherhood for decades began to confront the taboo of homosexuality at the institution. When Joe Johnson arrived at Hell Week in 1983, he hoped to prove his manhood like many of the other knobs, but for Johnson the stakes were higher. "I had a lot of self-doubts," he later remembered, "and I had certain inklings that I was gay." Because he had gone through boot camp the previous summer with the National Guard, the Florida native did fine during Hell Week, but that was only the beginning.[36]

Homosexuality may not be the last taboo of southern history, but it is certainly a topic that has, until recently, been little studied. John Howard opened the field with a study of gay culture in Mississippi called *Men Like That*. James Sears continued this investigation with *Rebels, Ruby Fruit, and Rhinestones*, and Patrick Johnson further explored the intersection of race and sexuality through his interviews with black gay southerners in *Sweet Tea*. Contrary to popular notions that there were few if any gay men or lesbians below the Mason-Dixon Line, Howard, Sears, and Johnson found that homosexuality thrived in the South—not just in big cities like Atlanta and New Orleans, but in smaller towns and rural hamlets as well.[37]

Although historians came late to the topic of homosexuality in the South, novelists, playwrights, and other artists have long explored queer life and queer themes in the regional tradition of the "southern gothic." Like many other artists, Charleston writer Harlan Greene was more than a little ambivalent about his hometown. Being a Jewish intellectual was tolerable in Charleston during the 1980s, Greene explained, "but no one in society will want to own up to the burden of homosexuality; for it is too upsetting a truth that unsettles the pleasant fictions of the city." So Greene "corseted" his sexuality in an attempt to gain acceptance by Charleston elites until he "realized that the air in those exclusive places was not rarefied; it was stultifying." Of course, not all gay Charlestonians corseted their sexuality. At midnight, Charleston's famous Battery became the city's "garden of good and evil." Located at the tip of the peninsula with the requisite Confederate monument, the Battery's cannons are permanently trained on the ghosts of Yankee soldiers guarding Fort Sumter in the harbor. The Battery was long a tourist destination by day and a gay cruise park at night. The city only whispered about "men like that" in dark euphemisms, and though they stood night watch over the city's Battery, they were gone by morning. Surely, they never entered the gates of the Citadel.[38]

Long before it became official military policy, the city, the South, and the Citadel practiced their own versions of "Don't Ask, Don't Tell." Citadel administrators were veterans of World War II, Korea, and Vietnam. They were "wise to the ways of the world," Joe Johnson believed, and since it was "an all-male school, they probably [realized] that they had a slightly higher percentage of gay men that gravitated toward that environment for whatever reasons, psychologically, and I think the administration . . . wanted to turn a blind eye to it because they didn't want it to affect enrollment." Though the Department of Defense (DoD) and Reserve Officers' Training Corps (ROTC) had regulations banning openly gay and lesbian military service for decades, the Citadel had no such official policy. The only explicit restriction on cadet homosexual conduct was a centuries-old state statute that outlawed "buggery." In fact, Citadel administrators did "not have record of a cadet being disciplined or dismissed for homosexuality." Instead, the school apparently left policing of homosexuality to the Corps of Cadets itself.[39]

Policing of sexuality was such an integral part of cadet banter at the Citadel in the 1980s and 1990s that it was almost taken for granted. Historian and Citadel alumnus Alex Macauley explored reams of material on the evolving roles of race and gender at the school without turning up much evidence at all about sexuality. In thinking back on his own time at the school, however, Macauley remembered that gay jokes and insults were nearly constant. "If somebody wasn't cutting it, they would be called 'fag,' 'queer.' Band Company was regularly lambasted by rifle companies [with] homophobic slurs," implying that "because they carried instruments[,] they weren't manly." Such sentiment was common in many parts of southern society during this era, but "in terms of the frequency with which the language was used," Macauley believed, "it was peculiar to The Citadel." He continued: "It was used more as a way to denote weakness . . . and there were stories floating around that so-and-so cadet's gay. If the person had effeminate tendencies, then the rumors would dog him around, but to my knowledge, it was never used as a way to run somebody out of the corps." Cadets struggling with their sexuality were not so sure of this.[40]

After Joe Johnson survived Hell Week in 1983, he wondered if his uncertainty about his sexuality was apparent to other cadets. This was an era when hypermasculinity and homophobia coursed through American popular culture and politics. Rambo single-handedly avenged the American defeat in Vietnam, and many Americans believed Reagan's muscular foreign policy cowed the Soviet Union. But as Reagan's tough posture against foreign policy foes dominated the public discourse, he remained largely silent about a burgeoning domestic health crisis, AIDS. Awareness of the AIDS epidemic emerged in the national media, and although there was quite a bit of talk about homosexuality, little of it was positive. Homophobia in the media and the administration reinforced similar sentiments in the military, and homophobic remarks remained a way of policing the boundaries of cadets' masculinity. "I think that when you're in a setting that is 100% guys," Johnson observed, "the differences between guys become more obvious . . . you see gradations in how they're not necessarily conforming to gender stereotypes, for instance." Such awareness could lead to trouble. It did in Johnson's case.[41]

A rumor began to circulate that Johnson was gay. The evidence was circumstantial. He sang in the choir. He majored in French. He liked to draw. In 1984 when Johnson was a sophomore, his company commander called the younger cadet into his room and confronted him with the rumor. Johnson denied it, not just to the older cadet, but to himself. The conversation shocked and scared him. "I'm gonna get a blanket party tonight[,]" he thought, fearing an infamous hazing ritual in which one group of cadets holds down a victim in bed, while another group pummels him. "Some guys are going to come in here and kick my ass." Johnson went through the motions of drill parade over the next few days but couldn't shake the fear. Ultimately, he asked for and received a transfer to a different company. The rumors followed him, but somehow the fear did not. He fell back on his friends, and the life of a cadet was so busy that few people even thought to ask why Johnson did not go on dates with Charleston girls.[42]

For Citadel knobs (the first-year cadets at right), upperclassmen like Joe Johnson (left) were fearsome authority figures and models of manhood. Yet cadets like Johnson who were gay faced even greater fears at the Citadel. Courtesy of Joe Johnson.

For some cadets, the Citadel's informal "Don't Ask, Don't Tell" policy worked. In 1987, the year that Joe Johnson graduated, Kevin Scott became a sophomore. "Being from the South," he said, "I had heard about The Citadel and its long and distinguished military traditions." Meeting several alumni and hearing about how the Citadel helped them in their careers sealed the deal. Scott watched the movie version of *The Lords of Discipline* with his mom the weekend before he arrived on campus and told her that she shouldn't worry; there was no way Hell Week could be that tough. But it was. As a knob, Scott learned to rely on his classmates, and he bonded with them as brothers. When they needed a shirt-tuck, he helped them. If they needed a study partner, he was there. The fact that he had known he was gay from a very young age had little impact on his life as a cadet. He recalled that during one cadet Bible study there was a brief discussion about how "laying with another man" was a sin in the same way that cheating and stealing were, but even this was not spoken with real disdain or hatred. The male bonding that went on among cadets even elicited homoerotic jokes. "If two cadets did everything together (studying, working out, etc.), there was some joking that they were 'married,'" Scott recalled, but he never saw witch hunts or even heard homophobic remarks about particular cadets. Less masculine cadets were judged (sometimes harshly) on academic and military performance, a safe way of policing sexuality without challenging the tacit assumption that all cadets were straight. No one asked Scott if he was gay while he was a cadet, and he certainly felt no need to tell. One thing Scott was outspoken about was the need to keep the Citadel an all-male environment. This was a sentiment shared by most cadets, gay and straight.[43]

As executive editor of the Citadel's student newspaper, *The Brigadier*, in 1994, Chad Youngblood was on the front lines of the battle over gender integration. News agencies from around the world interviewed him, and he oversaw student coverage of the biggest news story in the school's 150-year history. "One of my reasons for wanting to go to The Citadel was because it was all-male," Youngblood recalled years later as an openly gay lawyer in New Orleans. "It's something I get kidded with by my friends when this issue comes up, and it's not because I was gay. At that point, I really thought very little about my sexuality. I wanted to go [to the Citadel] . . . because it was a quality education in a single-sex atmosphere, and I couldn't imagine it working with women there." Youngblood had gone to high school just a few miles away from Shannon Faulkner in upstate South Carolina. A medical condition had almost kept him from attending the Citadel, and he endured Hell Week not once, but twice. He remembers his knob year as "when I formed a bond with some people that I became closer with than I ever had been close to people in my life, outside of my family."[44]

By the time he was a senior, as a result of bad press surrounding Shannon Faulkner's attempt to enroll, Youngblood felt that the strict militaristic system he had endured had become much more "touchy feely" and watered down. Like many cadets who witnessed the battle over gender integration firsthand, Youngblood believed that the enrollment of women weakened the system that had once tested the mettle of the all-male corps. Most Citadel alumni viewed their time at the school through a strange, almost masochistic nostalgia in which today's cadets could never endure the rigors they faced. But the fissure between the "Old Corps" and "New Corps" at the point of gender integration was a chasm. The physical requirements for women cadets had to be different. This was a key argument against admitting Shannon Faulkner or any women to the all-male school.

Much as they might have disagreed with cultural conservatives on other issues, gay Citadel alumni found common cause with pundits who decried the loss of the all-male educational opportunity at the Citadel. Gender politics in this case made for strange bedfellows. Over time, gay alumni mellowed in their opposition to women at the Citadel, but they remained ambivalent. "I am a thirty-four-year-old gay man who lives in the South. I know what it's like to have rights denied to me," Chad Youngblood later explained. But you have to "weigh the right of a handful of females to get an education at one particular school versus the huge change that school has had to undergo to accommodate them." As a college professor, Joe Johnson has thought about the issue quite a bit since women began attending his alma mater. Although he certainly saw homophobia while attending the Citadel, he also believed that the all-male environment allowed for a broader spectrum of masculine identities to emerge. "I still, even now, feel like there should be some place in our society for single-sex institutions of higher education," he said. "There's a real easy slippage from a co-ed setting into an enforced hetero-normativity or an enforced hetero-sexuality that can be subverted when one has a single-gender kind of society." Kevin Scott looked back on the changes at the Citadel more wistfully, "disappointed to see the tradition of the all male environment come to an end . . . the loss of a form of bonding that only comes in an all-male situation." As real as that loss was, the changes at the Citadel may have had benefits that these men could not see when Shannon Faulkner first walked into the school's imposing barracks. Ironically, the admission of women that many feared would undermine the rite of passage and unique bonds of brotherhood at the Citadel forced an acknowledgment that there were multiple rites of passage at the school and different types of men and women who passed them.

Eric Doss grew up in Greenville, South Carolina, not far from Chad Youngblood and Shannon Faulkner, who were seven or eight years his senior. When he told his family he wanted to go to the Citadel, his grandmother was not happy. She tried to dissuade him by giving him Conroy's *Lords of Discipline* for Christmas, sure that he would never want to be a part of "such intolerance and hate and abuse." Doss read the novel in three days and then called his grandmother: "Nanny, that's the greatest book I ever read." He started Hell Week in August 1998.[45]

There were several women in Doss's class. Unlike the female knobs, Doss and the other male cadets had their heads shaved into what his battalion commander called "birth control haircuts." Early on, Doss made the critical mistake of saying the first name of one of the cadre—upperclassmen who train knobs during Hell Week. The cadre exploded. The racking began. Doss wanted to quit. Many of his classmates, including a few of the women, did, but Doss made it. By the time he was a senior, he had become the opinion editor of the *Brigadier* and had been elected vice chairman of the Honor Committee. Although he had initially opposed the presence of women in the Corps of Cadets, by the time he was a senior, Doss had "embraced the reality" of the new corps. In fact, he was encouraged—the same way Will McLean had been encouraged to mentor a black cadet in *Lords of Discipline*—to mentor a female cadet as a prospective member of the Honor Committee: "I just realized that being opposed to women or being hostile toward women as a policy was (a) shortsighted and (b) not consistent with what I'd been elected to do. As much as alumni will tell you that the whole place has gone to hell in a handbasket and it's not as hard as when they were there, the Citadel still serves its mission, which is to create citizen soldiers and to educate young men and now women."[46]

If race and gender relations began to change at the Citadel by the 2000s, the question of sexuality remained a vexing one. "There are certain aspects of military service that . . . are innately homoerotic," Doss explained. "Things as simple as finishing a PT [physical training] run and being sweaty and covered in mud and dirt and half-naked . . . and falling into a pile of your brothers and eighteen guys that just went through the same thing with you. To the outsider, or probably to anyone, that's a little homoerotic." But Doss and most of his classmates did not think about it that way much, because most of them were heterosexual. As a straight Citadel alumnus and former history major, Doss acknowledged that "homosexuals have a long and pretty rich tradition of serving in the military." He knew that gay cadets had graduated from his school, but he thought that acceptance of openly gay cadets might be a long time coming.[47]

In 2003, a year after Eric Doss graduated, Kevin Scott founded the Citadel Gay and Lesbian Alliance (GALA). Unaffiliated with the school or its alumni association, Citadel GALA connected gay or gay-friendly students, faculty, and alumni. It was a support and social network whose members included Joe Johnson, Chad Youngblood, and more than a hundred others. Lindsay Koob, a white gay southern cadet in the mid-1960s, was "mighty pleased and proud" to be a member: "The matter of gays—both at and from The Citadel—remains the final, unspoken civil rights obstacle that continues to separate some of her sons and daughters from the main fold." Chuck Maxwell, a gay African American Citadel alumnus from the mid-1980s, agreed. After seeing a fellow cadet "railroaded out of his battalion because he was gay," Maxwell remembered, "I hid my sexuality and over-excelled." He joined Citadel GALA in 2008. "We have no control over our sexuality," Maxwell said. "I didn't choose to be homosexual any more than being black."[48]

Not everyone in Charleston equated the movements for civil rights, women's rights, and gay rights, but all of these struggles spilled over into the cloistered world of life at the Citadel. How could they not? The Citadel had educated white youth for more than a hundred years before the first African American walked into the barracks. It had been a bastion of southern manhood for a century and a half before the first woman joined the Corps of Cadets. The civil rights and feminist movements aimed to give African Americans and women equal access to institutions like the Citadel precisely because institutional exclusivity had empowered southern white men, just as the policing of homosexuality at places like the Citadel maintained the fiction that only straightness equaled strength. With African Americans, women, and gay alumni wearing the coveted Citadel graduation ring, these movements could claim real victories in Charleston. As Alex Macauley concluded in his book on his alma mater, changes at the Citadel meant that assumptions about race and gender (and perhaps sexuality) would no longer determine "the quality of one's leadership and citizenship."[49]

It is tempting to look at the hard-fought evolution of the Citadel's Corps of Cadets as a microcosm of changes throughout Charleston society and the Lowcountry. A similar argument has been made about the evolution of the U.S. military and the larger changes in American society. Yet the military is not America, just as the Citadel is not Charleston. If the post–civil rights era was defined as much by institutional discrimination as overt personal prejudice or unequal treatment under the law, then an increasingly inclusive admissions policy at the Citadel represented victory in the war for rights. But it was just one battle among many.[50]

A parallel battle was taking place in the political arena. With the repeal of the poll tax and passage of the 1965 Voting Rights Act, African Americans won the right to vote again across the South. In Charleston and countless other places, however, the goal of activists in the post–civil rights era was turning those votes into actual political power.

CHAPTER SIX

Seeing the Elephant

When Civil War soldiers experienced combat for the first time, it was said that they had "seen the elephant."[1] A new elephant, representing the Republican Party, came to dominate South Carolina during the period of Reconstruction. After Reconstruction, however, the Republican Party and its elephant all but disappeared from the South. A century after the Civil War, the southern strategy of national Republican candidates like Barry Goldwater, Richard Nixon, and Ronald Reagan capitalized on reaction to the civil rights movement to convince white southerners to do the unthinkable—vote for the party of Abraham Lincoln. This top-down narrative of the Republican Party's southern strategy reflects a popular understanding of the period, but it is only part of the story. As other scholars have argued, the grassroots story of the Republican renaissance in the South was shaped by religion, education, race relations, suburbanization, and fiscal conservatism in the booming Sun Belt.[2] These factors were all integral to the rebirth of the Republican Party in Charleston and the rest of South Carolina, but Civil War memory and racial redistricting were just as crucial.

Ironically, strong support for Confederate heritage helped the party of Lincoln overcome a century of defeat, turning the Lost Cause into victory at the ballot box, while an unlikely interracial alliance solidified Republican electoral victories. Since the 1980s, Republican candidates in state and local races rallied white working-class and middle-class voters with commemorations and reenactments of the Confederate cause. Membership in Sons of Confederate Veterans and similar historical societies became important for successful Republican candidates. In South Carolina, party leaders fought to keep the Confederate battle flag flying above the statehouse despite a boycott by the NAACP. At the same time, however, white Republicans worked with black Democrats to shake a century of white Democratic rule through the redistricting process. This alliance was even more crucial to the Republican renaissance than the Lost Cause. Redrawing southern electoral districts along racial lines empowered African American candidates, but it also made white Republicans competitive in southern state and local elections. On election days, Republican candidates hoped that white southerners would "see the elephant" once again. In the post–civil rights era, large majorities of them ultimately did.[3]

For much of the twentieth century, there was no viable Republican Party in the Lowcountry. Republican George Washington Murray, a former slave and member of the Colored Farmers Alliance, had represented Charleston in Congress in the mid-1890s, but he was beaten handily in 1896 and literally run out of town a decade later. During the Jim Crow era, the all-white Democratic Party disfranchised black voters, securing nearly all elected positions in Charleston and much of South Carolina. When Peter McGee, a liberal white Democrat, traveled to Columbia to represent Charleston in the state legislature in 1963, he was surprised to meet any Republicans. In fact, the first Republican legislator in the twentieth century had been elected just two years earlier. To a Democrat like McGee, the lack of "active political parties" in the solidly Democratic South was a good thing, allowing different coalitions to form on various issues, instead of simple party-line voting. There may have been a spectrum of political views in the South Carolina legislature of the early 1960s, but the legislators themselves were nearly all male, all white, and all Democrats, as they had been since the end of the nineteenth century.[4]

The civil rights movement changed the Democratic Party, and that, in turn, altered the political landscape in South Carolina and the Lowcountry. Even as Joe Riley was forging an interracial coalition of progressive white and black Democrats in Charleston during the 1970s, a new generation of conservative politicians resuscitated the Republican Party after decades of Rip Van Winkle–like slumber.

Strom Thurmond was one of the first South Carolinians to wake up to this new political reality in 1964. That year, Arizona Senator Barry Goldwater was the Republican Party's nominee for president. As a senator, Goldwater opposed civil rights legislation on constitutional grounds. As a candidate, he believed that the GOP was no longer "going to get the Negro vote as a bloc." Instead, as he explained to southern Republicans, "we ought to go hunting where the ducks are." In other words, seek support among southern white conservatives. Recognizing Goldwater as a kindred spirit, Senator Strom Thurmond threw his weight behind the western renegade's presidential campaign and repudiated his own party in 1964. With the benefit of hindsight, it is tempting to view Thurmond as part of the Republican vanguard among white southerners, but the mass exodus of white southerners from the Democratic Party would not come for decades. Only a few hardy souls followed Thurmond into what must have seemed like the political wilderness in the 1960s.[5]

One of those souls was Arthur Ravenel Jr. The Ravenel family had lived in the Lowcountry for centuries. The blood that ran through their veins was bluer than most, but his side of the family had fallen on hard times. By the time Arthur Ravenel Jr. was born in the 1920s, his father had already failed in the dairy business and was trying his hand at truck farming in St. Andrews Parish west of downtown Charleston. Ravenel signed up for the Marines at the end of World War II, too late to see combat, but long enough to earn access to the GI Bill. He went to the College of Charleston and worked for a time at the local paper mill. Ravenel would eventually launch a successful real estate business, but politics was his true calling. He served as a Democrat in the South Carolina House during the mid-1950s. Forced to join the Pulp and Sulfite Workers of the World when he worked at the paper mill, Ravenel was most proud of passing a right-to-work law during the 1950s that curtailed the power of South Carolina unions. A conservative on most issues, Ravenel was still safely in the mainstream of the southern Democratic Party in the 1950s.[6]

Like Strom Thurmond, Arthur Ravenel's political epiphany came in the 1960s. Inspired by Goldwater's presidential campaign, Ravenel explained: "The Democrat party seemed to be getting more and more liberal, and it looked like the only alternative, the only viable alternative out there, was the Republican Party." Viable was not the way most objective observers would have described the South Carolina Republican Party of the 1960s. When Ravenel switched his party affiliation, there were only a handful of what he called "patronage Republicans" in the Lowcountry. They would get appointments with the post office or other federal agencies when a Republican was in the White House, but they rarely mounted real challenges to Democrats in state and local elections. Ravenel sought to rally a new generation of supporters for the Grand Old Party, but it would take time. Running for a range of state and local positions in the 1960s and 70s, South Carolina Republicans lost far more than they won. In 1968, for example, only five of the 124 legislators in the statehouse were Republicans; by 1970, their number had risen to nine. "The Democrats would have victory parties," Ravenel joked, "and we'd have defeat parties!"[7]

The tide began to turn for Lowcountry Republicans, in part because of the popularity of a rising Republican star from California. Unlike South Carolina Republicans, Ronald Reagan was not accustomed to losing. The popular two-term governor of the Golden State came to Charleston in 1974 to give local Republicans a shot in the arm and lay the groundwork for future presidential campaigns. Lowcountry Republicans praised the Californian for working to cut taxes, government spending, and welfare rolls. Local GOP officials applauded Reagan for reforming "a welfare program that was being abused by unqualified freeloaders," saving California nearly a billion dollars.[8]

With Reagan running for the presidency at the top of the Republican ticket in 1980, GOP candidates in the Lowcountry had high hopes going into the elections. Tommy Hartnett, a former Democratic member of the South Carolina House who switched parties in 1972 before becoming one of three Republicans in the state senate, was the GOP candidate for Charleston's open congressional seat. Internal memos from the Hartnett campaign discussed the pros and cons of a Republican candidacy in Charleston in 1980. The major con was a high percentage of African American voters (34 percent) who were all but guaranteed to pull the lever for the Democrats, but the Hartnett campaign believed that suburban white voters would outweigh the rural and urban black vote. More than half of the district (53.5 percent) was classified as suburban, giving Hartnett what the campaign called a "demographic advantage." Charleston, in fact, had more suburban voters than any other South Carolina district. Like Arthur Ravenel, who was running for state senate in 1980, Hartnett lived in one of those suburbs. Harnett and Ravenel felt sure that most of their suburban neighbors would support their goals of reducing taxes, cutting government social programs, opposing affirmative action, strengthening the military, and getting tough on crime. The Republicans were right. Ravenel and Hartnett may not have won many African American votes in 1980, but they did win their races with strong support from the suburbs and wealthy areas of downtown Charleston. Ravenel joined a much-strengthened Republican delegation from the Lowcountry in Columbia, and Hartnett became the first Republican congressman from Charleston in the twentieth century.[9]

Tommy Hartnett, Arthur Ravenel, and the other Republicans who won Lowcountry races in 1980 clearly belonged to a different party than the one that had sent the Colored Farmers Alliance member George Washington Murray to Congress in the 1890s. Race was not the only difference, but it was the most obvious one. Some of this had come from the top, with Republican strategists like Kevin Phillips arguing in the early 1970s that the GOP did not need "substantial Negro support" to win national elections. Building on Goldwater's Deep South success and following Phillips's recommendations, Nixon pursued a "southern strategy" to woo white votes. Liberals were quick to criticize the racial underpinnings of these strategies. When asked about the Republican Party's ascension in South Carolina, for instance, Charleston Democrat Peter McGee simply answered, "Race. R-A-C-E."[10]

Though it was not always addressed explicitly, race did influence Republican campaigns not only in national elections but also in local elections from the Lowcountry to the Mississippi Delta. Republican opposition to affirmative action was an argument about fairness, but it tapped into a backlash to the civil rights movement. Similarly, Republican campaign rhetoric about cutting welfare may have carried implicit racial messages about reducing government support for minorities. Liberal critics certainly thought it did, and conservative candidates at least understood the power of this rhetoric. In announcing his run for Congress, Hartnett originally planned to say that he was "concerned about the welfare of our state and nation," but in the final text of his announcement, he cut "welfare" and replaced it with concern for the "future." When Hartnett spoke of welfare, he talked about reducing an expensive, inefficient program. Arthur Ravenel shared Hartnett's critical view of public assistance, telling one interviewer that he preferred "workfare" to welfare. Even though Harnett believed that reducing welfare rolls was a good government reform, he later acknowledged that issues like welfare reduction inevitably took on a "racial context" in the political arena.[11]

Race was not simply an implicit part of Republican strategies in the Lowcountry, as a federal lawsuit against Charleston County ultimately revealed. From the 1970s through the 1990s, the federal court found that some white Republican poll watchers sought to intimidate black Democratic voters. Robert Rosen, an attorney for the Democratic Party, recalled that Republicans would "challenge black voters and would be generally obnoxious at the polls and do everything they could do to deter black people from voting, you know, within the law." Such challenges included demanding identification, limiting assistance for illiterate voters, and telling voters with political action committee candidate lists that they could not bring "campaign literature" into polling stations. One of the worst offenders was Sam McConnell, one-time chairman of the Charleston County Republican Party, who would often approach elderly black voters in rural districts and loudly challenge them. Tommy Hartnett acknowledged that passionate "ultra" Republicans like McConnell may have used these tactics but argued that McConnell was the exception, not the rule. Aside from the polls, however, Charleston candidates played the race card in other ways. In the late 1980s and early 1990s, white Republicans *and* Democrats published "shaded" pictures that darkened the faces of their African American opponents. But the boldest and strangest example of race influencing Charleston politics was the brainchild of Republican political consultant Rod Shealy. Shealy's sister sought the Republican nomination for lieutenant governor in 1990. That year, Shealy financed the fake campaign of a black Republican candidate for Congress, complete with campaign literature picturing the "candidate" outside a Kentucky Fried Chicken. A subsequent investigation revealed that the campaign was really a ruse to get out the conservative white vote in the Lowcountry and help Shealy's sister win her race. When Shealy was fined for breaking state election laws, his lawyer unrepentantly explained, "Everyone knows race has been a factor in every political campaign [in Charleston] since the first slave set foot on this shore."[12]

Even though some Lowcountry Republicans used racial issues to win elections, the party actually struggled with the race question, and the very fact that they wrestled with it at all challenges the popular narrative of Republicans' southern renaissance. In the late 1960s and early 1970s, South Carolina Republicans were defensive on race. They argued that state Democrats had no better record than Republicans and that the GOP should not amend its platform to woo minority support. Arthur Ravenel and a few other South Carolina Republicans believed that the GOP should reach out to black voters. They met resistance in the early 1970s. "You speak of attracting Negro voters," the South Carolina Republican Party chairman wrote to one party member in 1970, but how? The Republican Party would not advocate "more give away programs . . . more jobs based on race rather than qualifications." The GOP should not appeal to voters "based on race, creed, or color, but rather on philosophical grounds," the chairman concluded. By the following year, however, the GOP was recruiting an African American for the state executive committee. "The decision to place a black on the committee is both correct and right," explained one internal Republican memorandum in 1971. "Granted that there is perhaps no such thing as an effective black leader among the Party members, [but] we must begin somewhere." Despite their lack of enthusiasm for existing candidates, GOP leaders persevered, hoping to address what they worried was an "image problem" in the black community.[13]

Earl Douglas seemed to be the answer to South Carolina GOP prayers. A conservative black newspaper columnist originally from the state of Washington, Douglas wrote a syndicated column as the "Earl of Charleston." In the 1970s, he lived in the same Charleston suburb as Arthur Ravenel and Tommy Hartnett, and he shared many of their political views. Speaking to the GOP state convention in 1978, Douglas excoriated Democrats for creating the "hell of social welfarism" based on the "philosophy of Marxism." American liberals, Douglas argued, "gave us high unemployment, high taxes, runaway inflation, a declining morality, [and] a high crime rate." In terms of racism, Douglas concluded that the Democrats had it all wrong. He had been a Republican for thirty-three years and a conservative black man for nearly fifty-five, but he did not see himself as a minority. Instead, he was simply an American.[14]

Tragically, Douglas died in 1979, and there were few black Charlestonians waiting to take his place in the leadership ranks of the GOP. To say that Earl Douglas's political views were atypical among black South Carolinians would be an understatement. Republicans nominated a small number of African American candidates from the 1970s through the 1990s. A few even won local elections, most prominently Tim Scott, a black Republican from Charleston, who won a seat on county council in 1995 and, later, a seat in Congress. Yet Scott won with very little black support, and his victories were exceptions to the rule. In the 1980s and 90s, one political scientist noted after studying Lowcountry elections, there was "not a single Republican nominee who was a candidate of choice of the African American voters in the general election" unless the Republican ran unopposed. African Americans made up less than 3 percent of voters in Republican primaries during this era, and their proportion of voters in Democratic primaries climbed to more than 80 percent in presidential election years. As Arthur Ravenel pointed out in 1990, the political trend in the Lowcountry was moving toward a nearly all-white Republican Party and nearly all-black Democratic Party.[15]

If Republicans could not win black votes, some party officials began to realize, perhaps they could find common cause with black Democratic candidates who were also struggling against an electoral system that was heavily rigged in favor of white Democrats. Less than a month after Earl Douglas fired up the GOP state convention in the spring of 1978, Glenn McConnell, the young chairman of the Charleston County Republican Party and brother of "ultra" Republican Sam McConnell, told state leaders that he wanted to reach across the color line. He worked with the state NAACP Political Action Committee to push for more single-member districts in South Carolina. Such a plan, McConnell argued, would benefit both African Americans and Republicans, since each group was a minority in at-large city, county, and state elections. That some of the most liberal black Democrats and conservative white Republicans shared common interests was a lesson that Glenn McConnell and the GOP would not soon forget, particularly when it came time to talk about redistricting.[16]

The redrawing of political district lines, which takes place after each census every ten years, is always a high-stakes, partisan contest. South Carolina Democrats had used redistricting to dilute the power of African Americans and Republicans when the party "redeemed" the state after Reconstruction. The Democrats had gerrymandered the majority-black district that sent George Washington Murray to Congress in the 1890s, for example, so that they could win the rest of South Carolina's congressional races. This strategy—known to political scientists as "packing"—put as many minority voters as possible into one district to dilute their influence in surrounding districts. By the end of the nineteenth century, packing was no longer necessary. Democrats had disfranchised and terrorized black citizens so that they no longer influenced elections anywhere in the state. After the 1965 Voting Rights Act guaranteed black southerners the vote, however, white Democrats in southern states once again used at-large elections and racial gerrymandering to maintain electoral majorities. The federal government fought back.[17]

The Voting Rights Act gave the U.S. Department of Justice the task of reviewing (or "pre-clearing") redistricting plans in states like South Carolina that had a history of disfranchising minorities. When white Democrats in South Carolina redrew district lines in the 1970s and 1980s, they unsurprisingly drew the lines to protect Democratic incumbents. These districts had just enough African Americans to assure a Democratic victory in the general election but not enough to allow an African American candidate to win the Democratic primary. In the early 1970s, the federal government accused the Democrats of intentionally drawing the lines to dilute black voting power. As a result of a federal lawsuit, elections for the South Carolina House of Representatives moved to single-member districts, including more predominantly black districts. The number of black state legislators rose from three to thirteen as a result. Federal legislation and Supreme Court decisions in the 1980s further strengthened the hand of the Justice Department to intervene in the redistricting process. South Carolina's first black state senator in the twentieth century took office in 1983. Although black and white Democrats worked together in the majority, black legislators felt that they were unequal partners in state government. The stage was set for a new political alliance that would remap the landscape of power in South Carolina and the rest of the South.[18]

At the same time that black elected officials were gaining clout in South Carolina, white Republicans were also on the rise. In 1987, Arthur Ravenel Jr. became only the second Republican U.S. congressman from Charleston in the twentieth century. That same year, Carroll Campbell became the second Republican governor of the state since the end of Reconstruction. Campbell had won not only because of his telegenic good looks and Reaganesque conservatism. The rising GOP star also understood the evolving role of race in South Carolina politics as well as anyone in the state. As a candidate, Campbell had recognized the symbolic power of Confederate heritage, particularly the importance of the rebel flag. A Confederate battle flag had flown above the South Carolina Statehouse since the early 1960s, both as a commemoration of the Civil War centennial and as a reflection of white South Carolinians' resistance to federal civil rights initiatives. Black legislators proposed taking it down; Campbell encouraged Republicans to defend the rebel banner. The Confederate flag, he argued in 1986, could be a wedge issue, dividing the "unnatural" and "unstable" coalition of African Americans and working-class whites in the Democratic Party.[19]

If the alliance between black and white working-class Democrats was "unnatural," Campbell and other Republicans were about to forge an even less likely alliance with African Americans through the redistricting process. Campbell easily won reelection as South Carolina governor in 1990, giving the Republicans veto power over the all-important reapportionment fight after the census. Republicans had been looking forward to redistricting, knowing that white South Carolinians were increasingly willing to vote for the GOP. State senator and future congressman Joe Wilson argued in the *Carolina Republican* newsletter that both African Americans and Republicans could benefit from redistricting. In 1991, the South Carolina Republican Party filed suit to have federal judges redraw political boundaries instead of the Democratic-controlled state legislature. The suit alleged that the Democratic plans were racially discriminatory, but as South Carolina journalists understood at the time: "Republican leaders hope that concentrating the heavily Democratic black vote in some areas will create other districts that are Republican."[20]

Thus, black civil rights activists and southern white Republicans became strange political bedfellows, seeking to create majority-minority districts likely to send black officials to southern state houses and the nation's capital. This alliance was the brainchild of Ben Ginsberg, chief counsel for the Republican National Committee in the early 1990s. Republicans recognized that Democrats had used a "pizza pie" approach to slicing up urban areas and other minority regions to give white Democratic candidates access to minority supporters. The GOP argued for "doughnut" districting, which would concentrate minorities into core districts (inside a city, for instance) so that more minority representatives would be elected. For Republicans, the upshot of this strategy was that the districts surrounding the majority-minority district would be whiter and more conservative. Under President George H. W. Bush, the Justice Department began to advocate the creation of more majority-minority districts to fulfill what they saw as the mandate of the Voting Rights Act. "The irony here," explained political scientist Dewey Clayton, was "that the Republican Party, traditionally reluctant to embrace the Voting Rights Act, was now using it as an instrument to advance its own agenda." Still, the Justice Department continued to support majority-minority districts under President Bill Clinton, even though such redistricting greatly weakened the prospects of white Democrats in the South.[21]

This political alliance had a dramatic impact on southern elections throughout the 1990s, most immediately on the congressional level. In 1992, thirteen African Americans were elected in new majority-minority districts. Twelve were from the South. In South Carolina, for instance, the state legislature created the first majority-minority congressional district in the twentieth century. African Americans made up 62 percent of the population in the awkwardly shaped sixth congressional district that covered parts of sixteen counties from Columbia to Charleston. Winning 65 percent of the vote in 1992, Jim Clyburn became the first black congressman from South Carolina in nearly a century. Clyburn was one of thirty-nine African Americans elected to Congress that year, the most in U.S. history. Republicans benefited from these new districts as well. In Georgia, for example, Republican Newt Gingrich easily won reelection in 1992 from a suburban district that had been whitened by creation of a black-majority district in Atlanta. Back in South Carolina, Clyburn's victory all but assured Republican Arthur Ravenel's reelection from the first congressional district, which lost a third of its black voters in reapportionment. Before redistricting, the South Carolina congressional delegation had been split evenly between three Democrats and three Republicans. Afterwards, it tilted toward the GOP, four to two.[22]

Not everyone was happy with the historic congressional elections of 1992. As white Democrats in South Carolina continued to battle Republicans and the Justice Department over redistricting the seats in the state legislature, they received help from an unlikely source, the U.S. Supreme Court. A challenge to the majority-minority districts that shaped the 1992 elections reached the Supreme Court in 1993. The court heard a case dealing with a bizarrely shaped majority-minority district in North Carolina that connected black communities between Durham and Charlotte along a thin strip of the Interstate 85 corridor. Critics joked that if people drove down the interstate with their car doors open, they would take out all of the voters in narrow parts of the district. The district was drawn so strangely, in part, to protect white Democrats in surrounding areas. Newly elected congressman Mel Watt defended his district, arguing that it was North Carolina's only truly "urban" district, allowing black urbanites to elect a representative of their choice. In the majority decision of *Shaw v. Reno*, Justice Sandra Day O'Connor rejected this reasoning and ruled the racially gerrymandered district unconstitutional. Though O'Connor did not believe that "race-conscious decision making is impermissible in all circumstances," she found that the North Carolina district bore "an uncomfortable resemblance to political apartheid." Two years later, in a Georgia case, the court reinforced this decision, ruling that race could not be the "predominant" factor in drawing districts. These rulings limited but did not eliminate majority-minority districts. Justice Department attorneys continued to push for more minority representation in state houses across the South, believing that redistricting still "played a major role in minority voters making dramatic strides toward achieving equal opportunity to elect candidates of their choice."[23]

With mixed messages coming from Washington, white Democrats in South Carolina continued to drag their feet in redistricting the state's house of representatives. In early May 1994, the Justice Department angrily rejected their latest plan. The white Democrats were concerned with "incumbency protection," suggested Justice Department attorney and future Massachusetts governor Deval Patrick. The "disregard for black electoral opportunity" in places like Charleston, Patrick concluded, ran counter to the Voting Rights Act. Despite strong condemnation from the federal government, the impasse in South Carolina continued. On May 10, 1994, black Democrats and white Republicans finally brokered a deal on a redistricting plan that created more majority-minority districts, along with whiter surrounding districts that might favor Republican candidates. Historian Orville Vernon Burton pointed out the irony that the deal was struck on Confederate Memorial Day. It was a "significant political watershed," Burton observed, "the end of white Democratic Party ascendency that had held power in the state since 1876." A historic number of black Democrats were elected to the state house in the fall of 1994, and Republicans took control of the chamber for the first time in the twentieth century.[24]

How much was the Republican renaissance in South Carolina and the rest of the South a product of redistricting? Though Burton saw the interracial redistricting deal in South Carolina as a watershed moment, he ultimately argued that it was simply one step in the gradual process of political realignment for white southerners. Certainly there is truth to this. Republican victories in the 1980s predated the dramatic redistricting fights of the 1990s. In the mid-1980s, the percentage of southern whites who identified as Republicans surpassed Democrats for the first time in American history. Political scientists Earl Black and Merle Black noted that by 1988 45 percent of southern white voters identified as Republicans, compared to only a third who claimed to be Democrats. The number of Democratic officials who left their own party in the 1980s and early 1990s also reinforces the notion that redistricting was not the primary cause of the Democratic demise. Republicans were more than happy to welcome "compassionate conservatives" from the Democratic Party into their ranks.[25]

While the conversion of white voters encouraged elected officials to switch parties, racial redistricting was a key accelerant in this process and to the Republican renaissance more generally. "Many lawmakers with mostly white, middle-class and suburban districts must consider the switch," explained one South Carolina journalist in 1993. There were many more such districts, as rural areas in the Black Belt and black neighborhoods in southern cities were carved into majority-minority districts. By one count, the first few years of the 1990s saw eighty white elected officials in Mississippi leave the Democratic Party for the GOP. Nearly thirty jumped ship in South Carolina in the same period. White Democrats in other southern states followed suit, and in the wake of redistricting, even more made the switch. Some simply opted out. Jimmy Bailey, a white Democrat from Charleston, resigned rather than face a tough reelection fight in 1994, when his district lost more than half of its African American voters to a nearby majority-minority district. John

Graham Altman, a Republican representative from suburban Charleston who won his seat after redistricting, bluntly described the reapportionment process as "political homicide."[26]

The fallout from the redistricting fight created a bitter split between white and black Democrats. As Charleston Democrat Lucille Whipper explained, black legislators were tired of being taken for granted by white Democrats. "It reminds me of the days in slavery," she said. "We wanted to be free, and our benevolent masters said, 'Why do you want your freedom?'" White Democrats did not see it that way. Charleston representative Jimmy Bailey condemned his black colleagues for aligning with Republicans. "The African American leadership sold their souls to gain a few seats and perhaps some plum positions," he later recalled. "There were those of us who said, 'Look, you're cutting off your nose to spite your face.'" In a phone call with Charleston Mayor Joe Riley the night that black legislators joined Republicans on redistricting, Bailey said, "I'm watching the demise of the Democratic Party as we speak." Some observers wondered if the split was so deep that it might lead to a permanent alliance between black Democrats and white Republicans. At least one Charleston Republican knew better. A pragmatic alliance on redistricting was fine, he noted in 1994. But when black leaders said, "Let's talk about the Confederate flag," he warned, "I think you're going to have a problem."[27]

Perhaps no one understood this problem better than Charleston Republican Glenn McConnell. First elected to the state senate with Arthur Ravenel in 1980, the two men liked to joke that Ronald Reagan rode *their* coattails into office. Although Ravenel called himself a "southern patriot," he was not nearly as invested in his Confederate heritage as his friend. Trained as an attorney, Glenn McConnell left the law behind when he and his brother, Sam, became owners of the CSA Galleries in the 1980s. The CSA Galleries sold historically themed artwork and Confederate memorabilia. The store was awash in Confederate battle flags, decorating shot glasses, T-shirts, belt buckles, boxer shorts, and a dizzying array of other goods. Bumper stickers carried messages like "North: 1, South: 0, Halftime." McConnell's interest was personal as well as professional. A member of the Sons of Confederate Veterans, Secession Camp #4, McConnell loved Civil War reenactments.[28]

As a result of his fascination—some said obsession—with the "War between the States," it might have been easy to caricature Glenn McConnell as a southern rube, but people who underestimated the state senator from Charleston did so at their own peril. The former student body president at the College of Charleston was both smart and ambitious. He became

Arthur Ravenel Jr. (third from left) and Glenn McConnell (second from left)
were architects of the Republican renaissance in Lowcountry politics during the
1980s and 90s. Here, they drummed up votes on Election Day in November 1984.
Courtesy of the Post and Courier.

the youngest chairman of the powerful senate Judiciary Committee and then the first Republican since Reconstruction to hold the post of senate pro tempore. Few bills became law without his approval. When he later became lieutenant governor, it was actually something of a demotion. Allies and opponents alike called him one of the most powerful politicians in South Carolina. McConnell was a deeply committed conservative. Unlike his brother and other ultra Republicans, however, McConnell was seen as more of a racial moderate. When Democratic Representative Lucille Whipper went to McConnell's office, she would tease him, "Now, I'm gonna talk to you, but I can't look at all those [rebel] flags." Whipper admired McConnell as a master of senate procedures, and she knew his support was crucial for any bill she proposed. McConnell's conservatism was "not based on a racial thing," Whipper claimed, even if some of the conservative legislation he supported did "impact race adversely."[29]

While Governor Carroll Campbell had been explicit about using the Confederate flag as a wedge issue to divide Democrats along racial lines in the 1980s, McConnell never put his devotion to the flag in those terms. McConnell simply saw it as a symbol of southern sacrifice and patriotism.

Though McConnell himself had come somewhat late to the neo-Confederate cause, he had the devotion of a convert. In the early 1980s, when the remains of a Civil War soldier from South Carolina were found in Virginia, the young state senator fought for the rebel to lie in state beneath the capitol dome. Thus began a lifelong devotion to honoring Confederate memory. By the 1990s, McConnell was the most dedicated and articulate defender of the flag in the South Carolina legislature.[30]

McConnell's initial nemesis on the flag issue was Robert Ford. A veteran of the civil rights movement from New Orleans, Ford first came to Charleston with the Southern Christian Leadership Conference during the hospital strike of 1969. Over the next few decades, Ford worked as a car salesman, newspaper advertising man, and development director for the United Methodist Church, but at heart, he was a community organizer and politician. He liked to boast that he went to jail seventy-three times in the civil rights struggle. His strongest memory of the Confederate flag was seeing it through the bars of a Mississippi prison cell in 1967. To Ford, the flag represented hatred and slavery, not heritage. After nearly two decades on Charleston's city council, Ford won a seat in the state senate in 1993, and he traveled to Columbia with the hope of bringing the Confederate flag off the capitol dome. That path led him through Glenn McConnell.[31]

Although initially opponents on the flag issue, McConnell and Ford later built a friendship and political alliance. Dubbed the "odd couple" by Charleston journalists, the two men could not have been more different. Dressing neatly with a tendency toward the preppy, the Republican state senator was likened to a "Presbyterian minister, studious, and straight-laced." When he debated Ford and others on the Confederate flag, McConnell brought stacks of books and note cards, lecturing in a professorial style. Ford, in contrast, spoke extemporaneously, at length, and with colorful anecdotes from his years as an activist. Ford had a "swaggering style," according to Charleston journalists, that was accentuated by "flashy clothes." Both McConnell and Ford were lifelong bachelors, but while McConnell rarely spoke about his private life, Ford bragged about having numerous girlfriends, describing himself as a "player." Beyond style, the two men represented opposing sides of Lowcountry politics. McConnell's constituents were primarily white, conservative, suburban voters; Ford came from a largely black, liberal, urban district. While McConnell supported limiting the size of government and reducing taxes, Ford sought to expand government programs for the poor and defend civil rights for all minority groups. As different as they were in style and substance, the two men came to know and respect one another in 1993 as they traveled to debate the position of the Confederate flag.[32]

When Democrats initially voted to fly the Confederate battle flag above the South Carolina statehouse in the early 1960s, the measure was so uncontroversial that Peter McGee, who joined the legislature just after it went up, nearly forgot that it was there. In hindsight, he wished that he had pushed to bring it down, but McGee and other white Democrats never mustered the votes to do so, even when they held supermajorities in the legislature during the 1960s and 70s. Although black Democrats lobbied to bring down the flag throughout the 1970s and 80s, they got no traction on the issue with their white colleagues. After Republican Governor Carroll Campbell recognized the symbolic power of the issue for white voters in the 1980s, the Republican Party joined black South Carolinians in keeping the issue alive. Pro-flag advocates, including Glenn McConnell and other Republican leaders, raised funds for television and print ads, arguing that outsiders and radical civil rights groups led opposition to the flag. In their 1994 primary, Republicans asked voters a series of questions about taxes, the Confederate flag, and other issues. Seventy-two percent of Republicans wanted to eliminate property taxes, while seventy-four percent wanted to keep the flag flying above the state house.[33]

Despite the strong support for the Confederate flag among the Republican rank and file, the flag issue proved to be a double-edged sword for the GOP, just as it cut both ways for the Democrats. South Carolina Democrats officially opposed flying the flag, although white conservatives rejected the party line and moderates recognized that the issue could divide the party's interracial coalition. In the GOP, Governor Carroll Campbell toned down his support for the flag, fearing that it would hurt his chances of joining a Republican administration in Washington during the early 1990s. His successor, David Beasley, stumbled dramatically on the flag issue. A former Democrat who switched parties in 1991, Beasley defeated Arthur Ravenel Jr. for the Republican gubernatorial nomination in 1994. Beasley won the general election that year, vowing to defend the Confederate flag. Then in 1996, the Republican governor had a change of heart. Worried about worsening race relations, Beasley said that he prayed about what to do. The governor called for removing the flag from the capitol dome and raising it over a Confederate monument on the statehouse grounds. A tsunami of negative responses swept into Columbia. The governor was a "traitor" and a "scalawag," according to one fax from the "Dixie Defenders." Rank-and-file Republicans wrote angry letters to GOP leaders, withdrawing their financial support for fear that some of their money "might fall into Gov. Beasley's pocket to support his liberal sway." Yet for all of the populist anger that Beasley's proposal stirred, there was also quiet support for a compromise from some GOP backers. The Palmetto Business Forum and the South Carolina Chamber of Commerce—traditional GOP allies—worked behind the scenes to take down the flag, fearing that it was limiting outside investment in the state. With fiscal conservatives pushing for a compromise and cultural conservatives willing to defend the flag to the last, the Republicans seemed just as flummoxed on the flag issues as the Democrats. The split within the GOP helped a Democrat win the governor's mansion in 1998, but it did not bring down the flag. If anything, the battle lines were even more starkly drawn.[34]

At the suggestion of local civil rights activists, the NAACP called for a national boycott of South Carolina, discouraging all business and personal travel to the state until the legislature removed the Confederate banner from the statehouse. With tourism a huge part of the state's economy, particularly in the Lowcountry, the boycott could ultimately cost the state millions of dollars in revenue. Reverend Joe Darby, who drafted the original NAACP sanctions, described the flag as a symbol of a dead country and racism. Growing up in Columbia, the AME minister recalled watching Klansmen display the rebel flag in demonstrations at the capitol on Confederate Memorial Day. By the 1990s, when Darby took a position at Morris Brown AME in Charleston, his opposition to the flag was resolute. "Until South Carolina lays that flag aside," he said, "we're gonna have a problem."[35]

The NAACP boycott brought additional resources and national attention to the fight against the flag, but it also hardened resistance to bringing the banner down. Though he had originally considered a compromise, State Senator Glenn McConnell was offended by the implication of the boycott. The flag was a source of pride to McConnell, not embarrassment. "I'm not going to surrender it now to a reputation of shame," the Republican legislator said in response to the NAACP sanctions. "If there's one thing we learned at Gettysburg," he concluded, "it's to occupy the high ground and don't leave it." Not everyone occupied the high ground in the pro-flag camp, however. Members of the Klan were quite visible at pro-flag rallies at the capitol in 1999 and 2000. McConnell distanced himself from such extremists, but it was harder to disavow enthusiastic GOP leaders and friends like Arthur Ravenel. Returning to the state senate after an unsuccessful run for governor in the mid-1990s, Ravenel spoke to a rally of 6,000 flag supporters in early 2000. "Can you believe that there are those who think the General Assembly of South Carolina is going to . . . roll over and do the bidding of the National Association of Retarded People?" Ravenel said, mixing up the black civil rights organization and an advocacy group for the mentally disabled. Ravenel, the father of a son with Down syndrome, fueled further controversy by apologizing "to the retarded folks of the world for equating them to the national NAACP."[36]

Mayor Joe Riley and other liberal Charlestonians were appalled by Ravenel's comments. After speaking out against flying the Confederate flag over the state house throughout the 1990s, Mayor Riley led a final push to lower the banner in 2000, organizing a protest march from Charleston to Columbia. "The important thing," Riley said, "was to show that South Carolina wasn't a racially polarized state." Still, there were South Carolinians who opposed the famously liberal mayor. "You bring those niggers marching through Calhoun County," one man wrote, "and you will be in the sights of my gun." Charleston Police Chief Reuben Greenberg loaned Riley a bulletproof vest. His wife made him wear it. The fifty-seven-year-old mayor marched twelve hours a day for nearly a week to traverse the 120 miles to Columbia. "Every religious denomination, every business organization, every civil rights organization, college boards of trustees and athletic directors, and average citizens, rank and file, have said: remove the Confederate battle flag," Riley told a few thousand people at the state capitol. "And our legislature . . . hasn't even begun to debate the bill. They are out of step with the people of South Carolina." Meanwhile, 300 flag supporters demonstrated on the north side of the capitol, waving hundreds of battle flags. One flag supporter wore a replica of a Confederate uniform, and another held a sign that read "God Save the South." A third blamed Yankees who had moved down from the North for trying to destroy the southern heritage. As impassioned as both sides were, legislators inside the statehouse held out hope for a compromise. If Republican Senator Glenn McConnell agreed to take the flag down, one Democratic senator noted, "It'll be over."[37]

Once again, the compromise would hinge on an alliance of white Republicans and black Democrats. Senator Glenn McConnell did not relish the idea of taking down the battle flag in the face of the NAACP boycott, but he left a small opening for compromise. "I was rigid that that flag should be preserved, and it should not be removed except with honor," McConnell later recalled. "It could not be settled on the basis of power, because we had the power on our side to keep the flag on the dome." But the Republican senator also came to see the Confederate struggle in a longer history of South Carolinians fighting for rights that stretched back to the

American Revolution and forward to the civil rights movement. Working with Robert Ford and other African American legislators as well as white Democrats, McConnell crafted a compromise to take the battle flag off the statehouse and place it on a monument to Confederate soldiers in front of the capitol. The state would also commission an African American history monument on the capitol grounds, something that black legislators had long sought. Ironically, the Confederate battle flag would actually be *more* visible to capitol visitors in its new location. NAACP activists were not pleased. It was a "sellout," according to Reverend Joe Darby, that only "got the flag halfway down." Despite the continuing opposition of the NAACP, the legislature passed the flag compromise. On a warm Saturday in the summer of 2000, two Citadel cadets in dress uniforms lowered the Confederate battle flag from the capitol dome. A color guard of Civil War reenactors raised a new flag above the monument to Confederate soldiers.[38]

When the dust settled from the flag fight, Glenn McConnell and Robert Ford continued their unlikely political alliance, one that reflected the complicated relationship between white Republicans and black Democrats in the South of the post–civil rights era. The two men worked together on resolutions to establish state holidays for Confederate Memorial Day and for Martin Luther King Day. McConnell supported Ford's efforts to nominate more African American judges, and Ford brought a Confederate flag back into the statehouse to make a point about the importance of celebrating the Civil War's sesquicentennial. Not everyone believed that the partnership between these two Charleston politicians was an equal one. Former state representative Lucille Whipper thought Ford supported McConnell because the Republican was both personable and a political power broker. "He became friendly with Glenn," she recalled of Ford's change of heart about McConnell. "Now, whether that is a mutual friendship or not, I question that." For his part, McConnell was proud to call Ford a friend. Friendship was one thing, however, political power another. In one legislative session after the flag controversy was settled, only two of the sixty-six bills Ford authored passed into law. By contrast, McConnell saw forty-six of the 106 bills he authored become law. Five years after the Confederate flag fight, McConnell led a Republican majority in the Senate. The GOP controlled the governor's mansion, house of representatives, both U.S. Senate seats, and most of the congressional delegation. Black Democrats like Robert Ford continued to win elections in majority-minority districts, but the Republicans won nearly everywhere else. A fierce critic of the alliance between black Democrats and white

Republicans, NAACP activist Joe Darby observed, "In the process of getting a couple more members of the Black Caucus, they actually set the stage for the Republican Party to become pretty much invincible in South Carolina."[39]

All of this had been made possible by the passage and evolution of the Voting Rights Act. A signature accomplishment of the civil rights movement, the act reenfranchised and empowered African Americans throughout the South. Conservative critics continued to challenge the law as unnecessary, unfair, and unconstitutional. This was particularly true, critics argued, of the section of the law that let the Justice Department review changes to state and local voting regulations, including redistricting. One such challenge to the Voting Rights Act reached the Supreme Court in 2009. In oral arguments, Chief Justice John Roberts asked how the Justice Department could support its claim that the preclearance process was still necessary when they rejected only 0.05 percent of changes to state and local voting laws. The government's attorney replied that the threat of rejection kept states from passing discriminatory voting laws. Chief Justice Roberts called this line of reasoning silly, comparing DOJ review to the fabled "elephant whistle." "Well, there are no elephants," he joked, "so it must work." Four years later, the chief justice authored a majority opinion that struck down the section of the Voting Rights Act requiring southern states and other localities with a history of voter discrimination to preclear their electoral changes with the Justice Department.[40]

Chief Justice Roberts may not have seen any elephants, but they were clearly there. The received wisdom on the Republican revolution in the American South holds that the white backlash against civil rights legislation, particularly to Democratic support for laws like the Voting Rights Act, led to the rise of southern Republicans. Certainly, southern whites began to vote for Republican presidential candidates in the late 1960s and continued to do so in increasing numbers through the 2000s. On the grassroots level, however, the civil rights backlash did not lead immediately to a Republican renaissance. In state and local elections in places like Charleston, the Republican revolution was not complete for nearly three decades. Racial redistricting and neo-Confederate politics were central to this transformation.

A true Republican renaissance did not occur in places like the South Carolina Lowcountry until the 1990s, when racial redistricting created an alliance between white Republicans and black Democrats. This interracial bipartisan coalition, with support of the federal government, laid the groundwork for record numbers of black electoral victories in the 1990s in majority-minority districts. Racial redistricting also resulted in white Republican victories in surrounding mostly white districts. White Democrats in the South nearly became extinct, creating a new electoral calculus in the region.

This set the stage for a battle over Confederate memory in South Carolina and other Deep South states. Confederate memory had welded southern whites together with a shared culture, even when they might have been divided on a host of other issues, including geography, religion, and economics. With black politicians pushing to furl the Confederate flag in the wake of the civil rights movement, white Republican candidates could weld together diverse white constituencies by defending the flag and southern heritage. By the 1990s, however, it became clear that the Confederate flag could divide whites as much as it had once united them. Some Republicans, especially business leaders, feared that public celebration of Confederate memory hurt outside investment; other Republicans warned that such investment was not worth selling out southern heritage. Ultimately, a second coalition between white Republicans and black Democrats ended the standoff on the Confederate flag issue in South Carolina, Georgia, and other southern states. Once again, interests converged to maintain the status quo of political empowerment for a black Democratic minority and a white Republican majority.

This uneasy alliance carried southern politics into the twenty-first century, when the divergent economic interests of Lowcountry residents hardened political battle lines. In the early 2000s, the battle would be over union power in a state and region that were famously opposed to unionization. The combination of an increasingly global economy and the continuing effect of race on Charleston's local economy created a combustible situation on the Charleston waterfront. A violent clash between longshoremen and the police in January 2000 inspired the attorney general of South Carolina to charge five longshoremen with rioting. The campaign to free the "Charleston Five" turned the men into symbols of the continuing civil rights struggle, illustrating the ways that politics, labor, and race remained deeply entangled in Charleston.

Shadows in the Sun Belt

The police had been in position for hours. Decked out in full riot gear, they stood ready to defend the nonunion workers at the South Carolina State Ports Authority terminal from what authorities feared would be hundreds of angry longshoremen. A cold rain fell intermittently throughout the evening. What had started as an exciting break from the daily grind of patrols and paperwork had stretched into an interminable night of uneventful guard duty. After more than five hours standing sentry on an empty street, the police were joined by two demonstrators from the International Longshoremen's Association (ILA) Local 1422. The men carried signs that read "Unions promote experience, better economy, better wages." After two more hours of this, news reporters on the scene worried about filing stories no one would read.[1]

Around midnight, a couple of hundred longshoremen marched out of their union hall. They were fired up. Members of ILA Local 1422, nearly all black men, and Local 1771, mostly white men, headed toward the port terminal. The longshoremen were challenging the use of nonunion workers to unload a ship for the second time in the month of January 2000. As the men came down the street, they chanted "I-L-A, I-L-A, I-L-A." New signs appeared that read "The ILA built the port of Charleston." A reporter for the Charleston *Post and Courier* believed that some of the men had been drinking, and he saw a few brandished long sticks. The police line marked the edge of port property, but the longshoremen believed they had a permit to march down the street. "Hold the line," police captains urged as their front ranks girded for conflict.[2]

The melee that followed led to ten injuries and nearly as many arrests. Five longshoremen would eventually be charged by the South Carolina attorney general with the felony crime of rioting. The case of the "Charleston Five" became a minor cause célèbre in labor and civil rights circles, echoing the protests and legal battles of a bygone era. More than three decades after the Charleston civil rights movement climaxed with the hospital workers' strike of 1969, here was another labor struggle that brought to the fore issues of race, class, and gender in the Lowcountry. Yet the longshoremen's struggle was not simply civil rights redux.

The labor struggle that led to the Charleston Five case took place in a very different historical context than the hospital strike. As the journalist Suzan Erem and anthropologist Paul Durrenberger argued in their book, *On the Global Waterfront*, the longshoremen's struggle with Lowcountry authorities was a local skirmish in a war between organized labor and international shipping companies in an increasingly global economy. As labor scholars have observed, unions faced an uphill battle organizing and maintaining power in the face of globalization. This "free-flowing torrent of capital and information," according to labor historian Jeff Cowie, seemed about "to overwhelm workers' grasp on the pace of history." Like many American workers in an increasingly service-oriented economy, most Charleston workers faced globalization alone, with little job security and without the support of a union. By contrast, organized longshoremen were in a relatively strong position to deal with globalization. They could connect to dockworkers around the world, organizing together to defend their jobs and wages. On the state level, the Charleston Five campaign was also a political battle between a union that was increasingly active in progressive, Democratic Party coalitions and a Republican attorney general seeking to defend the South Carolina's right-to-work laws and pro-business economic environment. Locally, the Charleston Five campaign provides an opportunity to assess the economic legacies of the civil rights movement in Charleston, to think about the ways that race still influenced where Charlestonians worked and lived. The movement had helped to make racial discrimination in employment and housing illegal in the 1960s, but three decades later, the job market and social geography of the Lowcountry suggested that there were limits to the economic legacies of the movement.[3] Race and organized labor had been defining features of the Charleston waterfront dating back to the nineteenth century. Just a few years after the Civil War, Lowcountry dockworkers banded together to form the Longshoremen's Protective Union Association

(LPUA). Founded in 1868, the LPUA had become the "most powerful organization of the colored laboring classes in South Carolina" by the mid-1870s, according to the Charleston *News and Courier*. At that time, the union included nearly 1,000 members. Strikes, work slowdowns, and an 1898 brawl between union and nonunion workers on the waterfront maintained the union's power even after Reconstruction. Building on labor activism during the Great Depression, Charleston longshoremen reorganized as Local 1422 of the International Longshoremen's Association in 1936 under the leadership of World War I veteran George German. German ruled the local with an iron fist for three decades, leading the union through the Depression, World War II, the dawn of the Sun Belt boom, and the civil rights movement. A pragmatist more interested in maintaining wages than pushing for civil rights, German encouraged individual union members to join civil rights demonstrations, but Local 1422 remained relatively distant from the movement.[4]

Even if ILA Local 1422 tried to avoid direct intervention into the racial politics of the postwar era, the makeup of the union and the reality of racial segregation on the waterfront meant that race influenced the organization's historical trajectory. A War Department study of the Charleston port conducted in 1940 laid out the racial segregation that defined the waterfront labor market both before and after World War II. "Negro longshoremen and dockhands handle all cargoes between land and water carriers," the report noted, "while white men are generally employed as supervisors, checkers, weighers, etc." The waterfront workforce still reflected this split in the 1950s, when Marion Turner got his first job there. At that time, "a white man in the South wasn't going to do this kind of work," Turner recalled. "It was too hard and dirty." Longshoremen like Turner muscled large quantities of goods—cotton, bananas, cloth, and the like—onto and off ships, largely by hand. The clerks and checkers on the docks were white, as were the executives of stevedoring companies who hired the longshoremen and the men who ran the State Ports Authority (SPA). Yet the racial prejudice that segregated the waterfront also steeled the solidarity of Local 1422, according to Eli Poliakoff, who chronicled the history of the city's longshoremen's unions. Partly because of this racial solidarity, dock work and unions remained segregated even in the post–civil rights era. ILA Local 1422 represented black longshoremen and mechanics; ILA Local 1771 represented white clerks and checkers.[5]

The racial segregation on the docks was emblematic of segregation within Charleston's larger labor force during the civil rights era. Black workers in Charleston hospitals directly challenged employment segregation and discrimination during the 1969 strike, but the entire local economy was divided racially in this era. In 1970, almost 85 percent of black men worked in blue-collar jobs in Charleston; nearly 40 percent of them were classified as laborers. Similarly, around 40 percent of black women were service workers. Only 1 percent of black Charlestonians were classified as professionals, and less than 4 percent were classified as managers in 1970. Given the limited opportunities in the Charleston labor market, longshoremen's relatively good wages attracted ambitious young black men to the docks and the ILA. One of those men was Ken Riley.[6]

Ken Riley grew up west of the Ashley River in the 1950s and 60s when parts of what is now suburban Charleston were still the country. It was "almost a Huckleberry Finn–type childhood," he recalled nostalgically and without irony. "We loved the woods. We swam in ponds. We worked the farms with our dad." But behind this nostalgia lay the reality of a family struggling at times to make ends meet. Ken's father had a number of jobs or "hustles" that made up a modest income. Ken's mother was a cook and dietician for the Charleston County schools. In Riley's early years, he and his older brother, Leonard, traveled with their father as far north as New York doing seasonal farm work. He also remembered going down to the county dump not far from his house to dig for metal to sell to the junkman for extra cash. By the time Ken Riley's father started getting regular shifts as a longshoreman in the mid-1960s, the family's prospects were looking up.[7]

Although Ken and his brother Leonard worked occasionally on the docks during the summer, their mother wanted them to go to college so they could become professionals. In the early 1970s, Leonard went to the College of Charleston to take premed courses, and Ken followed, majoring in business administration. The Riley brothers struggled academically and socially at the college, which had admitted its first African American students only a few years before. Leonard transferred, but Ken stayed. Cofounding the college's first black fraternity and taking upper-division business classes gave him the focus he needed to graduate, but decades later, Ken Riley still described his college years as "the worst days of my life." Much to their mother's chagrin, Ken and Leonard joined their father on the docks, where they could make good money.[8]

"The men on the docks at that time," Riley remembered, "I could get any eleven guys and crush any NFL football line." Even with the connections to the docks through their father, Ken and Leonard were just as green and untested as any other young guys. The older guys had survived decades on the docks. They were rough men, respected and sometimes feared. All of them carried knives, and some carried guns. "For a young bright-eyed guy coming from a college campus," Riley said, "that kind of environment was a little intimidating." The Riley brothers were not afraid of hard work, but this was another level of difficulty and danger. Moving 800-pound bales, lifting 250-pound sacks, and rolling 50-gallon drums, the men had to prove themselves and rely on one another to avoid life-threatening accidents. That trust fed into the solidarity of the ILA. It made the union a brotherhood. Just as Ken and Leonard were learning the ropes and finding a home in the ILA in the 1970s, however, technology was transforming the waterfront in ways that would change the work forever.[9]

The first shipping containers appeared at American ports in the 1960s and 70s, gradually replacing the pallets and loose cargo that longshoremen once manhandled. Cranes now winched twenty- and forty-foot-long metal boxes onto the beds of waiting trucks. No longer would cargo be measured simply by weight but by TEUs (twenty-foot equivalent units). Where it once took nearly forty men four hours to load 200 tons of cargo, it took fewer than fifteen men just minutes to load containers with the same amount of cargo. By the late 1990s, more than a million containers (or TEUs) went through the port of Charleston, making it the fourth busiest port in the United States and the second busiest on the Eastern Seaboard. Shipping company executives and logistics experts called the container "the fundamental building block of international commerce." Unions dubbed it "the longshoremen's coffin." One wrong move by the crane operators, ship captains, or longshoremen could mean disaster and death. When cranes malfunctioned or operators lost focus, tons of cargo in the container came crashing down on the longshoremen. Some also feared that the new technology spelled a slow death for the longshoremen's jobs and union. When Ken Riley joined ILA Local 1422 in the 1970s, about 1,500 longshoremen worked the Charleston docks. Containerization cut that number almost in half. The union made sure that the longshoremen who survived the transition were well paid, but there were fewer good jobs to go around.[10]

Outside the port, the economy and employment landscape had also changed dramatically, as the Lowcountry boomed along with the rest of the Sun Belt South. Since World War II, South Carolina officials had tempted northern and international companies to bring manufacturing jobs to the state. Like other southern states, South Carolina promised low corporate taxes, strong right-to-work laws that kept unionization rates and wages low, and a technical college system that helped workers transition from agricultural to industrial employment. Mocked as "smokestack chasing" by critics, this strategy paid off. From 1950 to 1980, per capita income in South Carolina increased fourfold, going from 60 percent of the national average to nearly 80 percent.[11]

But the magic seemed to wear off in the 1980s, in part because cheap labor in the developing world undercut the competitiveness of a nonunionized workforce in South Carolina and other southern states. For longshoremen, it did not matter if they were unloading imports or loading exports. For the rest of the state, however, the rise of cheap imports destroyed the textile industry and made it difficult to attract new manufacturers. In the 1980s and 90s, tens of thousands of textile jobs bled out of the state. Manufacturing plants for companies like Michelin, BMW, Bosch, and later Boeing offset these losses somewhat, but the boom for workers had ended. Labor organizers blamed this on the state's successful campaign to reduce union representation. By the 2000s, around 4 percent of the workers in South Carolina belonged to unions, the second lowest percentage in the country behind North Carolina. There were also structural reasons for the wage stagnation. South Carolina witnessed a shift in the labor market from industrial jobs to service work, a shift taking place across the United States in the era of globalization. From the 1970s to the 2000s, the share of South Carolinians working in manufacturing dropped from 27 percent to 14 percent, and those working in the service sector rose from 16 percent to 26 percent. In their assessment of this trend, historians Lacy Ford and Philip Stone concluded that workers in the Palmetto State "went from relatively low manufacturing wages to even lower service wages." By 2000, per capita income remained stuck at 80 percent of the national average, leaving South Carolina among the poorest states in the country.[12]

While Charleston certainly reflected these larger economic trends, two factors influenced the Lowcountry economy more than the state or region: a military presence and tourism. For much of the twentieth century, the U.S. Navy, not the port, was the most important employer on the Charleston waterfront. Through World War I, World War II, and the Cold War, military installations provided thousands of jobs to civilians as well as soldiers and sailors in the Lowcountry. The closure of the Charleston Naval Shipyard in 1996 sapped some of those resources, but military-related jobs remained crucial to the local economy. The year after the Navy Yard closed, in fact, the Navy and the Air Force were still two of the top three employers in the Lowcountry. Generally at the higher end of the Lowcountry pay scale, these federal government jobs boosted the local economy and gave good individual benefits.[13]

The other end of the pay scale in the Lowcountry was the service industry, which boomed as Charleston became a tourist mecca. Historic sites, beautiful beaches, golf resorts, arts festivals, and warm weather brought more than 3 million tourists to Charleston each year in the late 1990s. Those visitors pumped about $580 million annually into the local economy. Although Charlestonians complained of increased traffic, few were upset about the economic benefits of tourism. There were some scholars and activists, however, who worried about the types of jobs that tourism and the service economy created. Economists R. Geoffrey Lacher and Chi-Ok Oh argued that more than half of tourism-related jobs in Charleston paid less than $20,000 a year compared to 16 percent of all Lowcountry jobs at that pay level in the 2000s. Lacher and Oh did not address the way race intersected with these job categories, but half of the service workers in the Charleston metropolitan area were African Americans in the 1990s and 2000s. "Black folks, particularly in Charleston, are the cogs in the machine that runs the service economy," NAACP activist Reverend Joe Darby observed. "Those are the motel maids. Those are the porters. Those are the busboys. Those are the folks who do that kind of menial and not always visible work that keeps the service economy going. . . . And I think tourism feeds into that." For Darby and other civil rights activists, battling for better wages was just as important as the fight against legal segregation had been. "It's one thing to be able to go into a restaurant on Broad Street in Charleston," Darby concluded. "It's another thing to be able to get a job that you can afford that."[14]

Three decades after the civil rights movement in Charleston, race remained a hugely influential factor in the Lowcountry labor market. Middle-class and upper-income African Americans had made real gains, but Charleston saw continued economic marginalization of black workers. Between 1970 and 2000, the proportion of African Americans in Lowcountry managerial positions more than tripled from 3.8 percent to 13 percent. Similarly, black participation in professional jobs quadrupled from 2.4 percent to 10.2 percent. These were tangible economic legacies of the civil rights movement. Yet African Americans remained underrepresented in white-collar jobs, considering they made up a third of the Lowcountry workforce. The gender breakdown of these figures suggested that obstacles remained, particularly for black men. Of the 10 percent of Charleston professionals who were African American, for instance, more than 7 percent were black women and less than 3 percent were black men. Interestingly, white women's participation in Lowcountry professional occupations was also higher than white men's—51.7 percent and 34.6 percent, respectively. Black Charlestonians continued to dominate lower paying blue-collar and pink-collar occupations in the year 2000, making up 55.7 percent of Lowcountry laborers and 52.6 percent of service workers. As a result, median black household income in Charleston was $20,000 per year, less than half of the $43,000 median annual income for white households.[15]

The racial income gap in Charleston was greater than in the rest of South Carolina and far greater than in the rest of the country, but it was comparable to other southern cities. This was due in part to the concentration of black poverty in cities, the higher incomes available to urban white residents, and the migration of middle-class residents, many of them white, to the suburbs. The median income gap between black and white households in the United States was about $15,000, according to the 2000 census, but the gaps in the cities of New Orleans ($19,000), Mobile ($20,000), Charlotte ($23,000), and Atlanta ($37,000) were comparable to or worse than Charleston's $23,000 racial income gap. Not all southern cities saw such dramatic racial disparities, but the story was generally a depressing one for urban black workers.[16]

If the gap between southern white and black workers was large, there was an even bigger gap between the average income of blue-collar workers and black longshoremen in the ILA. Relatively high wages made union men symbols of success in the black community and targets for nonunionized competition. As a result of their unique position at the port and decades of negotiations, Charleston longshoremen working full-time made an average of $101,500 in 2000, more than three times the median income in Charleston. In the late 1990s, competitors began to challenge the longshoremen's monopoly on the port. With headquarters in the smaller port of Georgetown, South Carolina, Perry Collins's Winyah Stevedoring, Inc. (WSI) hired nonunion longshoremen to work the Lowcountry docks, dealing primarily with small amounts of "break-bulk" or loose cargo. Compared to ILA longshoremen's six-figure average salaries, WSI paid nonunion longshoremen $25,000 to $30,000 a year. When a small Danish shipping company, Nordana, began looking to save on labor costs in Charleston, they struck a deal with WSI to work their ships at the State Ports Authority docks in 1999.[17]

The ILA Locals 1422 and 1771 saw the Nordana contract with WSI as a threat to the union monopoly on the Charleston waterfront, a wedge that might allow other shipping companies to shift to nonunion labor. With permits to conduct informational pickets, ILA demonstrated against the nonunion workers starting in December 1999. "We are the union, the mighty, mighty union," ILA members chanted at the terminal gates. Local 1422 President Ken Riley promised that the union would protest every Nordana ship that pulled into port until the company reconsidered its use of nonunion workers. Police Chief Reuben Greenberg, who had a good relationship with Ken Riley and the ILA, allowed the longshoremen to protest for a "reasonable amount of time" before asking them to go back to their hall. "We know they are going to move, because they are honorable men," Greenberg told a reporter, and the union protestors did leave the terminal gates when asked. When the next Nordana ship docked in early January 2000, however, the protests were not quite as peaceful. Once again, the union conducted educational pickets at the terminal gates, but a group of ILA members also sneaked into the port and harassed the nonunion workers. One WSI worker claimed that longshoremen threatened him with a knife and pulled him off a small port vehicle, breaking his glasses. Rather than face union longshoremen, the WSI workers fled onto the Nordana ship, raising the gangplank and ramp to keep the ILA members at bay. Eventually, the ship pulled out of port unloaded, leaving about twenty-five containers on the Charleston docks. Police escorted the nonunion workers home to Georgetown. Chief Greenberg explained that no arrests were made because WSI workers could not identify their attackers. Ken Riley did not condone the violence but said, "The guys are angry and frustrated. It's very volatile." Johnny Alvanos, president of Local 1771, the mostly white clerks' and checkers' union, echoed Riley's concerns: "The guys are worried about their jobs. It's definitely explosive. . . . We don't need any more low-wage jobs here."[18]

A showdown looked imminent, but violent escalation was not in anyone at the port's interest. A reputation for efficiency and smooth labor relations had been the basis for the Charleston port's phenomenal growth in the era of containerization, growth that had produced millions of dollars in state revenues, provided hefty profits for stevedoring companies, and protected lucrative longshoremen jobs. Problems on the waterfront would encourage shipping companies to shift to rival ports like Savannah and Norfolk. Local 1422 extended an olive branch to Nordana, offering to work their next ship for free while the longshoremen and the shipping company negotiated a long-term solution. Nordana rejected that offer, saying that it would be too costly to break their WSI contract. With SPA police warning of the potential necessity for "lethal action" when the next Nordana ship docked, escalation seemed inevitable.[19]

Police would be ready for the confrontation. State Ports Authority CEO Bernard Groseclose sent a formal request for "at least 200 officers" to state and local law enforcement agencies when the next Nordana ship arrived in the middle of January 2000. In planning for the protests, Police Chief Greenberg asked Groseclose, "How far do you want to go?" As an officer for the State Law Enforcement Division (SLED) wrote in his notes, the real question was "How far will the state go for the right to work law?" Police informants in the ILA warned that union members planned to sneak into the port. Groseclose wanted to stop that at all costs. Police Chief Greenberg, who would coordinate the operation to protect the port, wanted the SPA to understand the stakes of confronting the ILA. "The union is very strong," Greenberg said. "We can stop this [protest]. However, it will shut the port down." Finally, Greenberg warned "we may have to arrest several hundred people." The plans were set for hundreds of police from every local Charleston jurisdiction, the county sheriff's office, the highway patrol, and SLED to protect the port when the next Nordana ship arrived.[20]

Ken Riley saw buses of law enforcement officers heading to the port on the afternoon of January 19, 2000, and he was worried. As usual, the ILA attorneys had gotten a permit to picket the street in front of the terminal where nonunion workers would handle cargo and containers for the Nordana ship. The police brought armored vehicles, SWAT vans, patrol cars, dogs, snipers, boats, mounted officers, and a helicopter to defend the port. As a Charleston Police Department captain explained in a morning briefing, "We want to have such a show of force to project an image that we can't lose this battle tonight. And it has all the potential of being a battle." Randall Cloud, a volunteer police chaplain, was at the port to minister to the officers and keep everyone calm. When the nonunion workers began to work the Nordana ship that cold, wet evening, they did so under the protection of over 600 law enforcement officers. A handful of officers were on the docks, watching the massive cranes swing containers onto the ship. But most of the police were outside the port terminal on the road in riot gear, waiting.[21]

When the ILA men finally marched out to protest at midnight, the police line stopped the union men in their tracks. Fists flew. Demonstrators pulled one officer's riot stick out of his hands and yanked the man off the line. Because the police had set up a perimeter in front of railroad tracks, there were loose rocks and railroad ties lying around that became ammunition in the hands of the demonstrators. A hail of gravel flew sporadically at police over the next thirty minutes. Many of the rocks were aimed at police lights illuminating the scene. Protestors tipped one light over. "Hey, don't do it," yelled men at the front of the march in ILA jackets. The demonstrators settled down for a few minutes and then started up again. They were a mix of black and white men, most of them in their twenties through their fifties, wearing ILA sweatshirts, flannel shirts, camouflage coveralls, and bulky winter coats. Facing the protestors was a multiethnic force of male and female officers from around the Lowcountry. While most members of the Charleston Police Department had college degrees, the beat cops were literally blue-collar workers. In fact, family ties connected many police and longshoremen. But that night, the division between them was stark. With a helicopter flying low overhead and police dogs barking continuously, a cacophony drowned out much of the demonstration, but a few individual voices cut through the din. "People's jobs on the line!" shouted a black demonstrator. "You're a fuckin' Uncle Tom," one white checker yelled at a black cop. "You want someone to take *your* job?" asked another protestor. Ken Riley rushed out of the union hall once reports of violence started coming in. As he approached the police line, he claimed that he was hit over the head by a policeman's riot baton. Police claimed that he was hit by a protestor's rock. Bleeding from a head wound, Riley left the protest to get stitched up at a local hospital. Union folks told him later that was when the police really fought back.[22]

For the first half of the conflict, the police showed admirable restraint in the face of an incredibly tense standoff. Arrests were made of demonstrators who tried to force their way through the line, but these were handled professionally. Around 12:30, the police announced multiple times over a loudspeaker: "In the name of the people of the state of South Carolina, you are demanded to disburse." Later, the officer added, "There will be no innocent parties." A few minutes later, two police cars and an unmarked white suburban command vehicle drove straight through the protest line, throwing tear gas canisters to clear their way. Tensions rose again. From behind the police line, Chief Greenberg gathered some of his staff together. The chief himself had been hit by a rock just above his eye. "We'll get all of that on film," Greenberg said. "It will justify anything we do after. It will justify anything we do." Years later, Greenberg's memories of the demonstrations still raised his ire. "It was the longshoremen who got out of hand," he recalled. "They came to the demonstration drunk and everything else. They threw bricks—I mean, bricks—and railroad ties.

Police officers were knocked down and beaten." Around 12:40, the ILA leaders succeeded in rounding up the demonstrators and pushing most of them back toward the union hall. When they had retreated about a hundred yards, a phalanx of police marched slowly after them. Although most of the demonstrators had their backs to the police line at this point, South Carolina state troopers fired flares, tear gas, and beanbags. One trooper fired on a protestor at very close range, knocking him to the ground with the force of the shot. Shortly after 1 A.M., most of the protestors were back at the union hall. A few men remained in the street, alternately taunting and talking to the cops. A white demonstrator asked plaintively, "You want poverty? Y'all want poverty?" The police responded with silence. The protest was over. The campaign had just begun.[23]

Although local media coverage of the waterfront protest varied in tone, all of the journalists covering the event called it a riot, and most blamed the union. Union members had certainly not helped their cause by screaming at reporters, shoving photographers, and turning over a television truck near the scene. Natalie Bagwell, a white NBC television reporter, who was forced to hide in the bushes with her cameraman when the protests got violent, delivered the most hyperbolic coverage. The "angry union workers" were "very secretive," Bagwell said. The railroad tracks "were the dividing line and soon, we found ourselves on the wrong side." The railroad tracks did play an important role in the protests, but Bagwell's reporting tied them to a subtle racial metaphor. Back in the studio, the NBC affiliate's African American anchor claimed erroneously that there was "not a big difference between what union and nonunion workers are earning on the docks," suggesting that both groups earned "well above the average pay for most workers in the Lowcountry." In fact, WSI employees made exactly the average pay for African Americans in the Lowcountry, but ILA members could make three to four times that. The ABC affiliate began with a sensational teaser: "It was like a scene from the 1960s— hundreds of angry rioters attacking police and the media." While some reports did ask whether the massive police presence had "baited" union violence (and union president Ken Riley suggested just that), the most charitable reports concluded "it was the union that came off looking bad."[24]

Aside from the public relations disaster, the ILA also had legal problems, with eight union men arrested during the melee and one arrested later. The men arrested the night of the protests were charged initially only with a misdemeanor offense of trespassing on SPA property. Police statements and press photos identified five of the longshoremen breaking through the police line and striking officers with fists or sticks. Four of

The Charleston Five—Elijah Ford, Ricky Simmons, Peter Washington, Jason Edgerton, and Kenneth Jefferson (left to right)—on the Charleston waterfront in the early 2000s when their trial for rioting made them symbols of the continuing struggles of organized labor and civil rights. Courtesy of the Post and Courier.

these five—Kenneth Jefferson, Elijah Ford Jr., Ricky Simmons, and Peter Washington—were African American longshoremen and members of ILA Local 1422. The fifth was Jason Edgerton, a white member of ILA Local 1771. The men were "not saints," as one writer put it. Some had arrest records with minor infractions related to drugs, alcohol, and weapons, but none had serious convictions. After the charges for these longshoremen were upgraded to the felony offense of rioting, they would become known as the Charleston Five.[25]

The high-profile campaign both for and against the Charleston Five would play out in both the media and the courtroom, becoming as much about politics as about the law. South Carolina Attorney General Charlie Condon, a Lowcountry native and rising star in the state Republican Party, saw this case as a litmus test for the state's right-to-work laws. Condon upgraded the charges from trespassing to rioting. "South Carolina is a strong right to work state and a citizen's right not to join a union is absolute," Condon explained in a press release the day after the waterfront protest. "If a person wants to peacefully assemble, that's fine, but attacks against police officers and the news media as well as mob violence will simply not be tolerated." Condon's plan for dealing with the longshoremen involved "jail, jail, and more jail." "There will be no repeat performance by the mob," Condon warned in a second press release, explaining why he sought an injunction against ILA picketing. The injunction ultimately limited the number of ILA pickets to fewer than nineteen demonstrators, but a local magistrate dealt Condon's case against the longshoremen a setback when he dismissed the riot charges, finding that the attorney general presented no evidence against individual longshoremen in their preliminary hearing. Furious, Condon issued another press release, accusing the magistrate of having "usurped the role of the Grand Jury, the Jury, and the Trial Judge." The attorney general quickly called for a grand jury to indict the longshoremen on the riot charges.[26]

A staunch political conservative, Charlie Condon was the perfect foil for the liberal coalition of labor and civil rights groups that sought to "free the Charleston Five." Condon came from an Irish Catholic family in Charleston that had had great success with a local department store that bore the family name. After graduating from Bishop England School, Condon earned a BA from Notre Dame and JD from Duke University. At age twenty-seven, he became the youngest South Carolinian ever elected solicitor in 1980. Condon started out as a Democrat, but like many conservative white South Carolinians, Condon switched his political allegiance to the GOP in 1990. He tacked further to the right politically throughout the 1990s, winning election as the South Carolina attorney general in 1994. A strong proponent of the death penalty, Condon quipped that the state should replace the electric chair with an "electric couch" to increase the efficiency of capital punishment. When Shannon Faulkner won admission to the Citadel, he bemoaned the loss of "single gender heterosexual education." He unsuccessfully sued the NAACP for their tourism boycott of South Carolina over the Confederate battle flag. Condon was in the news so much that one reporter asked rhetorically, "Is he a publicity hound? Or is he an outspoken champion of victim's rights?" The unspoken consensus among Charleston reporters was the former, but that did not stop them from publishing Condon's colorful and quotable remarks. In 1998, Condon easily won reelection as attorney general against a white Democrat who had once been a member of the Ku Klux Klan. A few weeks after he won a grand jury indictment of the Charleston Five in 2000, Condon took to the airwaves, stumping for George W. Bush against John McCain in the state's Republican presidential primary. "The Charleston union riot reminds us why South Carolina is a right to work state," Condon explained in a radio ad for the Bush campaign. "Unfortunately, big labor comes out a big winner in John McCain's campaign finance plan." A vote for McCain,

Condon concluded, "would give union bosses and the liberal media more control over elections." Bush went on to win the crucial primary and the general election. Condon served on his transition team.[27]

As Condon campaigned for Bush throughout South Carolina, the Charleston Five were under house arrest awaiting their trial for rioting. Unable to leave their homes between the hours of 7 P.M. and 6 A.M. except to go to work or union meetings, the men began to feel the weight of the prolonged legal battle. Peter Washington missed his mother-in-law's memorial service and his son's high school soccer and football games. "There's a lot of pressure on him," one family member explained. Newly engaged, Jason Edgerton could not take his fiancée out on dates. Kenneth Jefferson could not help his siblings take care of his aging mother, who struggled with high blood pressure and diabetes. "She lives alone and depends on Kenny," Jefferson's sister told union organizers. "Mom worries about him, and it has made her high blood pressure worse. And the effect on Kenny is that he has withdrawn into a shell." Defense attorneys advised the Charleston Five not to make public statements that might jeopardize their case. As weeks turned into months, house arrest wore on the men and their families.[28]

The fact that the Charleston Five were jailed at home provides a unique opportunity to think about Charleston's evolving racial geography. In the 1960s, these men would have probably been incarcerated in segregated cells or been forced by law and custom to live in segregated homes. By the 2000s, the city's racial landscape was more complex. Scattered throughout the Lowcountry, these five longshoremen's choices about where to live illustrated the ways that suburbanization and gentrification influenced residential segregation in the decades after the civil rights movement.

Traditionally, longshoremen had lived on Charleston's East Side close to the waterfront. One of the Charleston Five, Ricky Simmons, a twenty-year veteran of the ILA, still lived on America Street in the heart of the East Side. For the first half of the twentieth century, East Side residents were an eclectic mix of European immigrants and African Americans, but the postwar decades witnessed a decline in the neighborhood's racial and economic diversity. By 1990, more than 95 percent of East Side residents were African Americans. Median household income was less than $10,000 a year, and only about half of East Side adults had a high school diploma. The *Post and Courier* dubbed America Street Charleston's "most dangerous address." Drug dealing was so open, one resident joked, that the blind musician Ray Charles could see it. Still, some middle-class residents remained loyal to the neighborhood. George Pettigrew taught at Burke High

School and stayed on America Street when many of his colleagues left. Pettigrew was often asked why he lived "in the ghetto." As he told a newspaper reporter, he had grown up there, and his mother and aunt still lived in the neighborhood. "This is home," he said in the mid-1990s. "This is always home."[29]

Between the 1940s and 1990s, working-class and middle-class white Charlestonians left the East Side and much of the rest of the peninsula for new homes in the suburbs, an exodus that contemporary commentators and historians alike called "white flight." There were around 40,000 white peninsula residents in 1940 and fewer than 16,000 in 1990, with the largest drop taking place in the 1960s. Suburbs west of the Ashley River and east of the Cooper River saw sprawling development. Longshoremen, particularly the white clerks and checkers, reflected this shift in Lowcountry living patterns. The only white longshoreman in the Charleston Five, Jason Edgerton, lived across the Cooper River Bridge in Mount Pleasant. That suburban community had boomed since the 1960s, growing from about 6,000 residents in 1970 to over 45,000 residents by 2000. As in the standard narrative of white flight, this population boom was largely an increase in white suburbanites. In 2000, more than 90 percent of Mount Pleasant residents were white.[30]

Yet there are two ways in which the simple white flight model does not completely explain the changing racial landscape of the Lowcountry at the end of the twentieth century, both of which are suggested by the housing choices of longshoremen. First, as suburbs spread outward from Charleston and other southern cities, they incorporated formerly rural areas that included large numbers of African Americans. Kenneth Jefferson, a member of the ILA for seven years when he was placed under house arrest as one of the Charleston Five, lived on the edge of Maryville west of the Ashley River. A historically all-black town, Maryville retained a large African American population after being annexed by Charleston and swept up in suburban development. The union president, Ken Riley, lived just up the road from Maryville and around the corner from the suburban fixture, Citadel Mall, as did his brother Leonard. Their homes looked no different than millions of other ranch houses that dotted suburban landscapes around every American city. Why should they? These longshoremen had upper-middle-class incomes, and their choices of where to live suggest a second fallacy in the white flight model, namely, that the black middle class embraced suburban homes and lifestyles just as the white middle class had. In Kenneth Jefferson's West Ashley neighborhood, for instance, 60 percent of the residents were white and 36 percent were African

American, with relatively little racial difference in income levels. Charles Brave, a black longshoreman originally arrested on the night of the Nordana protests but not charged with the Charleston Five, lived a stone's throw away from white checker Jason Edgerton in a tony, mostly white Mount Pleasant neighborhood.[31]

On the one hand, black suburbanization in the late twentieth century seemed like an expansion of the American Dream and a successful realization of the goals of civil rights activists. Martin Luther King Jr. once hoped to hear freedom ring from the hills of Stone Mountain, Georgia. By the late 1990s, the small town where the second Ku Klux Klan was founded had become a leafy Atlanta suburb with a sizable black population and an African American mayor, despite its mountain-sized monument to the Confederacy. Almost 450,000 African Americans moved to Atlanta suburbs in the 1990s, ultimately making suburban Gwinnett County majority-minority. Similarly, a black middle-class migration out of Washington, D.C., transformed Prince George's County, Maryland, into "a premier African American majority suburb." In fact, nearly half of black residents in southern metropolitan areas were suburbanites by 2000.[32]

If southern suburbs were no longer bastions of segregation, the process of black suburbanization also reflected a less positive trend in the racial geography of cities: gentrification. Sometimes defined as white flight in reverse, gentrification was the return of relatively wealthy residents to cities in the 1990s and the simultaneous displacement of low-income residents who had remained through the "urban crisis" of the postwar era. The racial component of this process in Charleston was impossible to miss, as white gentrifiers shouldered out poorer black residents. This was particularly true on the southern border of the East Side neighborhood, not far from the docks and waterfront.[33]

As in many American cities undergoing gentrification at the end of the twentieth century, several factors facilitated the process in Charleston, including migration from the Rust Belt to the Sun Belt, property speculation, property taxes, baby boomers retiring and returning to cities, and an expansion of urban institutions like colleges and hospitals. Yet two factors seemed particularly crucial in Charleston: historic preservation and tourism. Urban sociologist Regina Bures argued that "the expansion of Charleston's Historic District led to gentrification . . . and increased racial and economic segregation." For Bures, this process started long before the 1980s, when historic preservationists began to push for zoning restrictions that limited property development at the southern tip of the peninsula. Historic preservationists fought successfully to expand the Historic District northward, pushing the dividing line between historical haves and have-nots to Calhoun Street. The proportion of black Charlestonians who lived south of Calhoun dropped from almost 15 percent in 1920 to 2.5 percent in 1990. The northward march of historic preservation stalled in the late 1980s, when East Side residents successfully rebuffed an attempt to incorporate parts of their neighborhood into the Historic District.[34]

But historic preservation was not the only cause of gentrification in the city. Tourism brought visitors who returned as buyers. The *Post and Courier* complained that these "out-of-towners" bought "Southern homes at Northern prices," displacing "many middle class folks—blacks and whites alike." By 2000, fewer than half of the residents of Charleston's Historic District had been born in South Carolina. It was time, Mayor Riley realized, to address the situation. In the summer of 2000, as the Charleston Five remained under house arrest, a mayor's task force began a yearlong study of gentrification.[35]

A political document as much as a policy proposal, the final report of the task force praised the city government for what it had done to preserve diversity and affordable housing in the city, even as it urged more radical government intervention. The task force first defined the problem, noting that median housing prices in the city had risen twice as fast as median family income during the 1990s. The task force recommended reform of zoning regulations that favored single-family homes over denser development on the peninsula and a high-end property transfer tax to finance new affordable housing initiatives. Ten pages of the twenty-two-page report listed the various affordable housing ventures undertaken by the city since 1975 (not coincidentally, the year Mayor Riley was first elected). The list, including deferred loan programs, rental rehabilitation plans, home improvement assistance, public housing, and nonprofit and charitable initiatives like Habitat for Humanity, would have impressed even the most cynical reader. As admirable as these affordable housing programs were, they were offset, some critics argued, by public and private development that actually accelerated gentrification in the city.

Perhaps the most vocal critic of the mayor on this issue was a young African American task force member and city councilman named Kwadjo Campbell. A Desert Storm veteran and College of Charleston graduate, Campbell won a seat on the city council representing the East Side in 1997 by campaigning against gentrification. The post gave Campbell a platform to speak out against the injustices he saw from the door of his America Street apartment. The self-described radical called gentrification "ethnic cleansing," and he laid responsibility for it at the doorstep of city hall, calling Mayor Riley "the chief architect of development in Charleston." For Campbell, the city's condemnation of the East Side's Ansonborough Homes after Hurricane Hugo to make way for an aquarium and ball fields proved that the government was part of the problem. The city's unwillingness to intervene in 2000 when private developers evicted hundreds of low-income and elderly residents from the Shoreview Apartments on the Ashley River to make way for luxury condominiums also angered Campbell. Developers offered fifty affordable units to former Shoreview residents, but most of those evicted found cheaper housing outside the peninsula. As the gentrification battle heated up, the contest between Riley and Campbell, who openly sought to replace the mayor, became bitterly personal, with warring op-eds and open letters in the newspaper. Various legal problems seriously undermined Campbell's campaign, but his commitment to fight gentrification never wavered. Years later, he still saw a role for the city government in supporting affordable housing and linking East Side residents to better paying jobs for military contractors, the Medical University, and the port. If the public and private sectors could not help the East Side, Campbell believed, black residents would be left saying, "Goodbye history, goodbye heritage, goodbye culture, goodbye community cohesion. Goodbye. I've got to go now to North Charleston to find a place I can afford to live."[36]

By the time Campbell and Riley locked horns over gentrification, the process had already dramatically altered the city. Although Riley was concerned about gentrification, the mayor initially downplayed the racial component of this process. "There certainly is no basis for a hypothesis that the African-American population, to any substantial degree, has been replaced by white population," Riley argued in 2001. The numbers suggested otherwise. One in four black Charlestonians living on the peninsula moved out during the 1990s. Many of them moved up the neck of the peninsula toward the city of North Charleston. In 1990, African Americans made up 34 percent of North Charleston's population, but by 2000 they were nearly 50 percent and the largest racial/ethnic group in the city. Some African Americans with means bought homes in Charleston's sister city. After twenty-five years of working as a longshoreman, Elijah Ford Jr., one of the Charleston Five, could afford to live in a beautiful North Charleston home near a picturesque bend in the Ashley River. But many of the former peninsula residents were not so lucky, living in largely segregated, impoverished neighborhoods just above the border between the two cities.[37]

As the process of gentrification played out in Sunday afternoon open houses, Monday morning groundbreaking ceremonies for new condominiums, and Saturday morning moving van rentals, the Charleston Five remained under house arrest, and the ILA struggled to retain its powerful position on the waterfront. The legal and labor issues facing ILA Locals 1422 and 1771 would require the Charleston unions to seek allies across the country and around the world. The quest for allies sent Ken Riley on a journey that would last nearly two years. Along the way, the president of Local 1422 became an international spokesperson for civil rights, organized labor, and the Charleston Five.

Ironically, Riley's quest for allies began with a previously scheduled speech to Lowcountry maritime executives at the Charleston Propeller Club less than one week after the Nordana protests. Riley had addressed the group before and gotten a warm reception, but the waterfront unrest left maritime executives understandably unhappy with the union. This talk would require finesse. As a former business major, Riley was fluent in the language of commerce. He spoke of the ILA's role in fostering "continued productivity, greater flexibility, and cost containment" at the port, boasting that longshoremen in Charleston handled "more tonnage per man hour" than workers in any other port in the nation in 1999. Yet Riley was not afraid to challenge South Carolina's development strategy of promoting "the availability of cheap labor and low union density." Bolder still, Riley criticized South Carolina's poor marks in education, health insurance coverage, infant mortality, illiteracy, and teen pregnancy— human rights issues beyond the purview of the standard Propeller Club speech. That was Ken Riley, always trying to balance a pragmatic view of the relationship between labor and management with an idealistic vision of the union's potential impact beyond the waterfront. The labor leader described recent violence on the waterfront as "a very unfortunate situation and one I do not believe you'll ever see again," but he concluded the speech talking about his pride in the union. "We are socially responsible," he said, and "therefore concerned not only about the welfare of our membership, but the welfare of all working Americans, including you."[38]

Support from Charleston maritime executives was important, but it would not bring Nordana to the negotiating table or pay the legal fees to free the Charleston Five. To tackle those problems, Riley sought help from other longshoremen. Labor leaders in ports around the world understood that the dispute between the Charleston longshoremen and Nordana could undermine union negotiating power not only at the South Carolina Ports Authority but also at all waterfronts connected to the network of global commerce. Help came from across the Atlantic when Spanish longshore-men boarded a Nordana ship in Barcelona in April 2000, warning the captain that European longshoremen would not work Nordana ships loaded by nonunion longshoremen in Charleston. Within a week, Nordana executives had returned to the negotiating table with Ken Riley. It took three days to find a cost-saving and face-saving agreement that both sides could support. Nordana would use union longshoremen in Charleston. They would be smaller crews to reduce labor costs without undermining waterfront wages. Ken Riley later thanked his Spanish union brothers in person at a longshoremen's meeting in the Canary Islands, but first, he had to focus on freeing the Charleston Five.[39]

The Local 1422 president crisscrossed the country raising money for the Charleston Five legal defense and awareness of the stakes for organized labor in South Carolina. In the spring of 2000, Riley addressed a meeting of the International Longshore and Warehouse Union (ILWU), a West Coast union that had a more militant reputation than the ILA. Riley drew the connection between labor and civil rights struggles in the South and explained that it was no coincidence that South Carolina exhibited "an anti-worker, anti-union mentality" and was also the only state without a holiday for Martin Luther King. On a subsequent trip to the Bay Area, Riley was asked about the general climate for black workers in Charleston. "There's discrimination in employment and promotions and unequal pay for the same jobs," he said. "You don't see evidence of open outright hatred, but racism is definitely alive and well." On a trip to Seattle, he talked about the ILA's efforts to protest against South Carolina's flying of the Confederate flag, explaining that the campaign further strengthened the union's connection to the state NAACP and a multiracial progressive alliance in the state. While the connection between labor and civil rights issues helped win some support on the West Coast, Riley constantly brought the issue back to the globalization of the labor movement. "Our industry has become global in nature," Riley told ILWU members. "We know our economy is global in nature, [and] . . . so must our workforce." Members of the ILWU would ultimately donate $267,000 to the Charleston Five legal defense fund, a large portion of the $400,000 raised from unions around the world.[40]

The ILA needed these funds because Attorney General Charlie Condon insisted on bringing the Charleston Five to trial for rioting, and the case dragged on into the fall of 2001. The union and its allies claimed that Condon kept the case alive for nearly two years primarily to gain publicity in advance of a planned run for governor in 2002. In a May 2001 press release, Condon shot back that this was "ridiculous and absurd," saying that the union's "comrades" were simply "trying to divert attention from the very serious criminal charges of riot." A summertime rally for the Charleston Five drew thousands of demonstrators to the state capital, where speakers railed against Condon. In the fall, Riley continued to strategize with union attorneys. He was meeting with them on the morning of September 11, 2001, when he learned of the terrorist attacks on the Pentagon and the World Trade Center. The terrorist attacks and the national security legislation that followed raised the stakes of the case. If the Charleston Five were convicted of felony rioting, new port safety protocols would prohibit them from ever working on the waterfront again. When Charlie Condon was interviewed about the case a few weeks after 9/11, the attorney general drew a strange comparison between the ILA and the terrorists. "I'm not anti-union," Condon said, "but I am against forcing people to join unions in order to get a job. And so, this whole idea of ends justifying means, as we know these terrorists that killed so many people, that's exactly their argument. I think it's important to note that ends do not justify means."[41]

Until the fall of 2001, the case had been fought primarily in the court of public opinion, but after more than a year and a half of house arrest, the Charleston Five finally began to see progress on their case in the court of law. Just one day before Condon gave the interview juxtaposing union and terrorist methods, the Charleston Five defense attorneys filed a motion to disqualify the attorney general from prosecuting the case for "serious professional and prosecutorial misconduct." The defense attorneys argued that Condon's numerous press releases, campaign ad for George W. Bush, and other public statements about the case amounted to misconduct. An addendum to the motion suggested that Condon's comments likening the union men to terrorists were "disgraceful." In response, the attorney general noted that his public comments had to be understood in the context of "a highly publicized case" that had received "vast amounts of media attention" in part because journalists "were on hand for the riot." The union and its allies had launched their own public relations campaign, and his public comments were in no way evidence of "prosecutorial misconduct." Perhaps Condon was right, but the point would soon be moot.[42]

On October 10, 2001, two days before the judge considered the defense motion to disqualify the attorney general, Charlie Condon handed over the reins of the prosecution to Solicitor Walter Bailey. "It is clear," Condon explained, "that we need to keep the focus on the cases themselves rather than being diverted by defense lawyer–created, ILA-sponsored, and politician-instigated sideshows." Mayor Riley, loath to weigh in on the case except to praise the police for a job well done, had asked Condon to give up the prosecution to another attorney. Ned Hethington, a colonel in the Charleston Police Department who had been on the front lines at the protest, told one reporter that the union men "were just caught up in the moment. No good is going to come out of [a trial]. . . . It was a bad night and we need to put it behind us." Charlestonians on both sides of the issue seemed to have had enough. Solicitor Bailey told the Charleston Five attorneys that he was "not a big fan of last minute settlements," but he moved swiftly to work out a plea deal with the defendants. With the trial less than a week away and longshoremen's unions threatening to shut down ports in sympathy for the Charleston Five, the two sides reached a settlement in November 2001. The five longshoremen would plead no contest to a lesser charge, acknowledging their participation in an "affray" instead of a riot. They would serve no more time, and the offense would eventually be expunged from their records. The Charleston Five were free.[43]

In the wake of the legal victory, a relative peace returned to the waterfront. When the construction of a bridge forced the ILA to vacate their old headquarters, the ILA built a new union hall, designed by the architect Harvey Gantt, a local civil rights icon and former mayor of Charlotte, North Carolina. The new headquarters had both a hiring hall and community meeting space, befitting of the ILA local's central role on the East Side. Charlie Condon ran for election as governor and U.S. senator, losing both races in the Republican primaries. When the Republican governor who beat Condon nominated the former attorney general for the board of the State Ports Authority, the outcry was so great that the nomination quickly disappeared. At a 2005 meeting of longshoremen organizers from around the world in Liverpool, England, Ken Riley saw the Spanish union men who had helped bring Nordana to the negotiating table and the ILWU leaders from California who had provided crucial financial support for the Charleston Five campaign. When it was Riley's turn to speak, he was thinking of his father, who had just passed away. "We mourn for the dead and fight like hell for the living," he said, borrowing an apt quote from the militant labor activist Mother Jones. Then he thanked his new friends from around the world. "We come from the American South where labor is oppressed. We continue to win because losing is not an option," he concluded. "You showed us the way."[44]

If the Charleston labor struggle showed that unions could find a way forward in the era of globalization, the lessons for the local economy were more mixed. Yes, the longshoremen had defended their powerful position on the Charleston waterfront. They remained a symbol of upward mobility for blue-collar workers in the Lowcountry. "We've fought for wages high enough so that workers can send their kids to college and afford at least a middle class standard of living," Ken Riley explained. Johnny Alvanos, former president of ILA Local 1771, felt the same way, particularly since he had two kids at the College of Charleston. "That's what the union is all about," Alvanos said, "putting our kids through college." The position on the waterfront was his best option, really his only one. "There is no other job in Charleston. If I didn't have this job, I'd be working in the grocery store."[45]

Most blue-collar and pink-collar workers in the Lowcountry were not represented by a union and did not make middle-class wages. Although this was true of most Charleston workers, it was particularly true of black workers many decades after the civil rights movement. When Martin Luther King Jr. gave his "I Have a Dream" speech, he was speaking to hundreds of thousands of people demonstrating for both jobs and freedom. King knew that without jobs, true freedom would be unattainable. Decades later, middle-class jobs and nice homes were within reach for more black professionals and members of the ILA in the Lowcountry. In this context, the Charleston Five campaign and the continued power of the ILA represented important symbolic victories for economic and racial equality in the post–civil rights era. These victories were also exceptions to the rule in Charleston and in much of the rest of the American South.

CONCLUSION

The civil rights movement was a watershed moment in the history of Charleston, remapping the landscape of power in the Lowcountry and touching nearly all of the area's residents in some way. Whether in education or economics, politics or policing, the post–civil rights era saw incontrovertible evidence of African American empowerment. Yet not all African Americans gained access to power. There were limits to the changes wrought by the movement.

Police Chief Reuben Greenberg and others proved that individual minority success was possible in the post–civil rights era. Greenberg came to believe that race was no longer the governing factor on Lowcountry lives the way it had been before the civil rights movement. We could call this the Booker T. Washington phenomenon, because it had happened before in the wake of Reconstruction. Washington's self-help philosophy and his own example of rising "up from slavery" suggested that the rights revolution following the Civil War had succeeded. An increasingly visible black professional class that included lawyers, doctors, professors, and politicians arose in that era, just as it expanded once again in the post–civil rights era. The main difference between the nineteenth and twentieth centuries was that the later era saw this professional class more integrated into formerly all-white institutions. This integration of the professional class and the success of black officials like Reuben Greenberg were further evidence that the civil rights movement had changed Charleston and other southern cities dramatically and for the better. "I think younger people not in the civil rights generation feel like the sky's the limit," said Dwayne Green, an African American Princeton alum and

Charleston trial lawyer. "You know, you don't feel like there are these barriers. . . . You just feel ambitious, and you feel like 'Hey, I can make a difference.'"[1]

Yet the success of black pioneers and the integration of the black professional class into white professional circles also created divisions within the black community. *Washington Post* columnist Eugene Robinson called this the "disintegration" or "splintering" of black communities in the post–civil rights era. Robinson suggested that African American elites, black middle-class suburbanites, immigrants from the African diaspora, and inner-city African Americans were becoming divided by class and culture in ways that undermined racial unity. Perhaps this was part of the story in Charleston. Did the 7,000 black families making between $50,000 and $100,000 a year in Charleston really have the same interests as the 12,000 families who made less than $15,000 in 2010? What about the nearly 400 black families in town making more than $150,000 per year?[2]

The tumultuous end of Reuben Greenberg's storied career as Charleston's top cop illustrated these new divisions within the black community over the volatile issue of crime. After two decades on the job, Chief Greenberg no longer sugarcoated his feelings about anything, including the relationship between race and crime. African Americans committed more of certain types of crimes than whites, the chief said, and racial profiling was just a pragmatic response to that reality. To Greenberg, it was time for black Charlestonians to take responsibility for the higher crime rates in predominantly African American neighborhoods. When asked about black-on-black crime in 2004, Greenberg said, "I refuse to take responsibility every time one black son of a bitch kills another. I have no control over that. There are social factors much more powerful than anything we can concoct in the Charleston Police Department." The NAACP called for a retraction. Greenberg refused. Although there may have been many reasons for the chief's provocative comments, including personal health problems, the incident revealed divisions in the post–civil rights era between conservative black pioneers like Chief Greenberg and liberal activists like Reverend Joe Darby of the NAACP. After Greenberg retired from one of the most illustrious careers in the history of the Charleston police force, Joe Darby remained troubled by the chief's record and legacy. Darby acknowledged that hiring Greenberg was a "bold move" that "affirmed the need for diversity" in city government, but he felt that as the chief's law enforcement philosophy evolved in a more conservative direction, "he became less of the first black police chief than he did the Negro police chief who happened also to be Jewish."[3]

Although divisions among African Americans based on class and political philosophy may have been magnified by the changes after the civil rights movement, there were many precedents for such divisions in Charleston's long history. When historian Marvin Dulaney came to the Lowcountry to take a position as director of the Avery Institute of Afro-American History and Culture, he saw these divisions and recognized their historical antecedents. In the antebellum era, Charleston's free people of color, many of whom were mixed-race descendants of slaves and masters, occupied and defended a middle ground between blackness and whiteness. These folks and their descendants "thought that they were better than the poor, lower class, dark-skinned blacks or those who had been enslaved," said Dulaney. He believed that may have carried over into the feelings of Charleston's black middle class, even in the post–civil rights era. Unlike other African American communities "where [members of] the middle class are the ones who are advocating for civil rights, trying to change and raise up those from the bottom, and improve education for them," Dulaney felt that "the middle class here [in Charleston] was a bit more distant, almost selfish in a sense." Who could blame them? When opportunities for advancement in careers, housing, and education came in the wake of the movement, middle-class African Americans ran with these opportunities, just as middle-class white southerners had. One example of this seemed to be the case of flight from inner-city educational institutions like Burke High School, which middle-class African Americans and whites had basically abandoned in favor of suburban and private alternatives. As director of Avery Research Center and member of 100 Black Men of Charleston, Dulaney was well aware that there were many middle-class African Americans who took advantage of new opportunities and also remained very concerned about black culture, racism, and poverty. Still, his frank discussion of both historical and contemporary divisions within Charleston's black community suggested the ways that "disintegration" of black communities undercut challenges to racism and inequality in the Lowcountry at the same time that conservative forces in the courts and federal government were turning away from civil rights era remedies.[4]

Just as the civil rights movement had opened up opportunities for individual advancement, the women's movement of the 1960s and 70s faced similar problems. Shannon Faulkner's challenge to the all-male admissions policy of the Citadel clearly owed a debt to early movements for civil rights and women's rights, yet Faulkner disavowed the title of feminist, insisting that hers was an individual quest. As such, it failed. In a different sense, however, Faulkner's challenge was a successful example of how the post–civil rights era witnessed a more expansive definition of rights built on the foundation of struggles for African American equality. Although women's rights activists, gay rights proponents, disability rights advocates, and others used the strategies and language of the black civil rights movement, they were fighting different forms of oppression. They faced discrimination from some of the same institutions, as in the case of the Citadel, but their struggle was different from the black freedom movement that inspired them. To recognize the differences in these movements is not to play to the divisive nature of identity politics. Rather, it is a frank assessment of their unique historical circumstances and contexts. Just as racial integration of the Corps of Cadets did not solve the problems of African Americans in Charleston, women's admission to the Citadel left many questions of gender equality in the South Carolina Lowcountry unresolved. On the one hand, the accomplishments of female cadets since the 1990s and the election of Nikki Haley as the first woman (and Indian American) governor of South Carolina in 2010 were positive indicators of change. On the other hand, South Carolina had fewer women in public office than any other state in the union when Haley won her gubernatorial race. Despite the fact that women made up 56 percent of the state's voters, there were no women in the South Carolina State Senate and no women in the state's congressional delegation that year. Challenging the Citadel's admissions policies had been difficult, but breaking into the good ole boy network in the statehouse seemed a herculean task.[5]

African Americans broke that seemingly insurmountable political barrier long after the end of the mass demonstrations and protests of the civil rights movement. The 1964 Civil Rights Act and 1965 Voting Rights Act made this possible, but civil rights legislation alone did not bring black political empowerment in the Lowcountry or South Carolina more generally. African Americans began to win office in sizable numbers only in the 1990s after working with the federal government and South Carolina Republicans to draw majority-minority districts. This worked, in part, because white Democratic incumbents resisted true black empowerment, leaving the door open for an unlikely bipartisan interracial alliance. White Republicans and black Democrats worked together once again on the Confederate flag compromise. As white Republicans became the new majority, however, it was unclear how much they still needed black political allies.

Debate over a more stringent voter identification law tested this alliance in 2011. To the Republicans who proposed it, the law requiring a state-issued photo identification to vote was a good government reform to eliminate voter fraud. To South Carolina Democrats, however, this was an attempt to disfranchise a certain segment of likely Democratic voters, many of them low-income minorities. The debate broke down along both partisan and racial lines, lines that had become virtually identical two decades after the state's racial reapportionment fight. The Republican representatives and state senators from the Lowcountry all supported the stricter voter identification law. All of them were white. The Democrats were just as unanimous in their dissent. All but two of them were African Americans. One of the two white Lowcountry Democrats actually missed the vote. Signed into law by Republican Governor Nikki Haley, the photo ID requirement could have taken the vote away from over 175,000 South Carolinians. But the Department of Justice rejected the measure under its mandate to preclear changes in southern state election laws. In rejecting the law, the DOJ pointed out that black South Carolinians were 20 percent more likely than their white neighbors to lack state-issued photo identifications, though DOJ attorneys were careful not to suggest that the law was written with a "discriminatory purpose." NAACP President Benjamin Todd Jealous was less circumspect in his criticism of the South Carolina law, calling it "little more than a 21st century poll tax."[6]

The post–civil rights era had seen political empowerment of African Americans in the South Carolina Lowcountry, but it had also seen the rise of parties that were strongly identified with racial groups, to the point where saying that someone was a white Republican or a black Democrat was nearly redundant. There were, of course, exceptions to this rule. The most famous of them was Tim Scott. Scott's trailblazing political career began when he won a seat on Charleston County Council in 1995. In 2008, he moved to the South Carolina House, becoming the first black Republican member of the state legislature in a century. Two years later, Scott ran for an open congressional seat in South Carolina's First District. This was the seat that Arthur Ravenel had held, representing Charleston and much of the rest of the Lowcountry. Scott consistently downplayed his racial identity throughout the campaign. He wanted voters to support him for his conservative political platform. Pitted against an African American Democrat in a majority-white and majority-Republican district, Scott's choice to downplay race was not only a philosophical decision but also a pragmatic one. In the fall of 2010, Charlestonians sent Tim Scott to Congress. He became the first black Republican to represent the Lowcountry since George Washington Murray gave up the seat in 1897. Despite the historic nature of his election, Scott continued to downplay racial concerns once in office, refusing to join the Congressional Black Caucus. "My campaign was never about race," Scott said, before reiterating what he saw as the "race neutral" appeal of his conservative agenda. "My campaign has been about themes that unite Americans—restoring the American Dream by reducing the tax burden, decreasing government interference in the private sector, and restoring fiscal responsibility, and I don't think those ideas are advanced by focusing on one group of people." In other words, Scott believed that his victory was proof that racism no longer limited individual accomplishment and that as a result America's newly color-blind society should stop focusing on race at all. This position made Scott exceptionally popular among the mostly white Republicans in South Carolina. After two years in the House of Representatives, Tim Scott was appointed to fill a vacant seat in the U.S. Senate by Governor Nikki Haley, becoming the first black senator from South Carolina and the first African American member of that chamber from the South since the 1880s.[7]

Viewing his own rise from poverty to power as an affirmation of American individualism, Scott agreed with other South Carolina conservatives who staunchly opposed the collective organizing of labor unions. Early in his first term as a congressman, Scott proposed a bill to deny food stamps to family members of workers on strike. Scott and other South Carolina Republicans argued that the decision by aviation giant Boeing to build a new manufacturing plant in North Charleston in 2011 was a direct result of the low cost of doing business in the Lowcountry. When the National Labor Relations Board (NLRB) investigated a claim that Boeing built the Lowcountry plant to punish labor unions at the company's Seattle factory, South Carolina officials lined up to defend both the company and the state's right-to-work laws. "Every employee has the right to join a union," Governor Nikki Haley said. "What you will find in South Carolina is very few employees want to." Boeing's plant survived the NLRB challenge, opening to great fanfare and hiring thousands of Lowcountry workers. Those workers made far less than their unionized Seattle counterparts. Boeing would find that the benefits they accrued from hiring nonunion workers were complicated by the ways that race continued to influence Lowcountry labor relations. The official Boeing website showed a black employee and white employee working together on the interior of a new plane in South Carolina, but race proved to be an issue at the plant. Within a year of opening the factory, a white employee warned managers that other white workers were using racially offensive language at Boeing, and the Equal Employment Opportunity Commission investigated. A black former employee who spoke to these federal investigators was later fired after a physical altercation with a coworker. His subsequent lawsuit alleged that white workers sang songs about lynching and called African Americans "monkeys." Perhaps these tensions could have arisen anywhere in the country, but the fact that they arose in the Lowcountry so soon after the construction of the new Boeing facility suggested the ways that racism continued to influence the local job market four decades after the hospital strike and ten years after the Charleston Five won their freedom.[8]

Not everyone had a pessimistic view of race in the post–civil rights era. Perhaps no single Charlestonian was more identified with this era than Joe Riley. The mayor remained popular among both black and white Charlestonians from the 1970s through the 2010s. Sworn in for a record tenth term in 2012, Joe Riley had governed Charleston longer than nearly half of the city's residents had been alive. As Riley noted in his inaugural address, Charleston faced many challenges, but it continued to do well in relative terms. Economic recession had hurt the tourist economy as well as the city's small tech sector, but in comparison to the era before the Sun Belt boom, Charleston was still thriving. "A long time ago," Riley observed, "it was said that 'Charleston was too poor to paint and too proud to whitewash.' That has long since passed. A new affluence has graced our city." Rededicating himself to defending affordable housing and diversity, the mayor explained, "There may be on the part of the few the misunderstanding that they live in or have moved to a gated community—affluent and exclusive. But that is not a great city." A great city, Riley concluded, was a diverse one. Maintaining this aspect of Charleston's historic identity and helping those Charlestonians who had not been uplifted by the last fifty years of economic and racial progress were the great challenges that remained for Riley as he began what he said would be his final term in office.[9]

In a sense, Charleston's problem was a reflection of the great paradox that defined the post–civil rights era, the increasing opportunity and even affluence of middle- and upper-income African Americans juxtaposed with the persistent poverty of African Americans in urban and rural areas like Charleston and the South Carolina Lowcountry. White Charlestonians were still far better off than their black neighbors, even with the advances made by the black middle class. The median income for white Charleston households in 2010 was $57,000, more than twice the median figure for black households, which was $24,000. Many Charlestonians—white and black, liberal and conservative, men and women—believed that the civil rights movement changed the city for the better, but they also agreed that the city did not change nearly enough. The civil rights movement "revolutionized life" in Charleston, according to attorney Robert Rosen. "It changed everything in the sense that you now have an integrated society." What the movement did not accomplish, Rosen concluded, was "a real change in the economic reality of a lot of black folks." Judge Arthur McFarland echoed these concerns, noting that despite the advancement of professionals like him, "economically, African Americans have lost in many ways," including a decline of the city's black-owned businesses. Former state representative Lucille Whipper pointed to the displacement of black residents through downtown gentrification, though she herself had voluntarily left the city for the suburbs decades earlier. Whipper's one-time colleague as a Democrat in the statehouse, Jimmy Bailey, had become a Republican, but he still spoke wistfully about how his generation had been inspired by John F. Kennedy and the civil rights movement. The "baby boomers got that message," he said, and "changed the world." "We put laws on the books," Bailey added, "but the effort that followed the laws to make sure we took the next step dissipated." The real estate developer who had lifted himself out of poverty felt an obligation to do the same for others. "Now it's time for us to go back and revisit the one remaining area that still needs to be [addressed]," he concluded, "and that is to get rid of the economic injustice that exists today as it existed back then." Bailey and other Charlestonians were too proud to whitewash this truth. Like most Americans, however, they were unable to make the changes they believed were still necessary. The change did not just involve economics, of course. Together, race and class had long hindered real progress in Charleston and the South. The Jim Crow and civil rights eras had seen race as the dominant form of oppression, but in the post–civil rights era, economic inequality grew more salient, buttressing stubbornly resilient institutional racism to block further change. If that change was going to come, it would not be until a new mass movement for racial *and* economic equality arrived.[10]

Notes

TOO PROUD TO WHITEWASH

1. Southern historians have a vested interest in the arguments about "southern distinctiveness," and recent studies have taken different tacks on the question that concerned W. J. Cash in his 1941 classic, *The Mind of the South*. See, for example, Goldfield, *Still Fighting the Civil War*; Cobb, *Away Down South* and *The South and America since World War II*; Brundage, *The Southern Past*; Burton, "The South as 'Other,' the Southerner as Stranger."

2. Coclanis, *The Shadow of a Dream*, 121, 128; Wood, *Black Majority*, xiv; Stephen Kinzer, "Leading Charleston to Its Past," *New York Times*, Aug. 14, 2001.

3. For a counterargument about Charleston's intentional forgetfulness on issues of race, see Roberts and Kytle, "Looking the Thing in the Face."

4. Dittmer, *Local People*; Payne, *I've Got the Light of Freedom*; Eskew, *But for Birmingham*; Moye, *Let the People Decide*; Self, *American Babylon*; Theoharis and Woodard, *Freedom North*; Theoharis, Woodard, and Payne, eds., *Groundwork*; Lang, *Grassroots at the Gateway*; K'Meyer, *Civil Rights in the Gateway to the South*.

5. Hall, "The Long Civil Rights Movement and the Political Uses of the Past."

6. Gilmore, *The Radical Roots of Civil Rights*; Cha-Jua and Lang, "The 'Long Movement' as Vampire."

7. McGirr, *Suburban Warriors*; Lassiter, *The Silent Majority*; Kruse, *White Flight*; Crespino, *In Search of Another Country*.

8. Evans, *Personal Politics*; Schulman, *The Seventies*; Chauncey, *Why Marriage*; D'Emilio, *Lost Prophet*; Cowie, *Stayin' Alive*.

THE LOWCOUNTRY

1. Fraser, *Charleston! Charleston!* 2–4, 8–9.

2. Ibid., *Charleston! Charleston!* 2–4; Coclanis, *The Shadow of a Dream*, 42–47; Wood, *Black Majority*, 79, 88–91, 152–53. The Native Americans already living in the region did not quietly submit to disease and enslavement. For more on their most effective resistance, see Ramsey, *The Yamasee War*.

3. Fraser, *Charleston! Charleston!* 4–5; Coclanis, *The Shadow of a Dream*, 22; Ball, *Slaves in the Family*; Edgar, *South Carolina*.

4. Morgan, *American Slavery, American Freedom*; John Locke and Lord Ashley Cooper, "The Fundamental Constitutions of Carolina: March 1, 1669," published by the Avalon Project of Yale Law School. See also Edgar, *South Carolina*, 42–46, 82–84; Weir, *Colonial South Carolina*, 54–58, 66–69, 71–73.

5. Coclanis, *The Shadow of a Dream*, 86–87.

6. Wood, "'More Like a Negro Country,'" 131–45.

7. Wood, *Black Majority*, 314–19.

8. Fraser, *Charleston! Charleston!* 151–54; Godbold and Woody, *Christopher Gadsden and the American Revolution*; McDonough, *Christopher Gadsden and Henry Laurens.*

9. Coclanis, *The Shadow of a Dream*, 120, 132–40.

10. Starobin, ed., *Denmark Vesey*; Robertson, *Denmark Vesey*; Pearson, *Designs against Charleston.*

11. Johnson and Roark, *Black Masters*, 107, 170, 205, 212–13, 227; Fraser, *Charleston! Charleston!* 54–55, 199.

12. Starobin, ed., *Denmark Vesey*, 11–12; Robertson, *Denmark Vesey*, 6, 42, 45–46, 88–89, 140. Michael P. Johnson asserted that Vesey was most probably not the ringleader of this rebellion, but, instead, the victim of white political ambitions and paranoia about slave insurrection. While his research calls into question the white account of Vesey's plans, it does not conclusively disprove Vesey's role in an unsuccessful rebellion. Johnson, "Denmark Vesey and His Co-Conspirators"; Gross, ed., "The Making of a Slave Conspiracy, Part 2."

13. Fraser, *Charleston! Charleston!* 244, 252; "The Union Is Dissolved," *Charleston Mercury* (Extra), Dec. 20, 1860. For more on the role of working-class whites in the Lowcountry before the Civil War, see McCurry, *Masters of Small Worlds.*

14. Andrews, *The South since the War*, 1; Fraser, *Charleston! Charleston!* 272, 275.

15. Powers, "Community Evolution and Race Relations in Reconstruction Charleston, South Carolina"; Powers, *Black Charlestonians*; Kantrowitz, *Ben Tillman and the Reconstruction of White Supremacy.*

16. Moore, "The Lowcountry in Economic Transition."

17. Yuhl, *A Golden Haze of Memory*; Severens, "Charleston in the Age of Porgy and Bess"; Sass, *Look Back to Glory*; Heyward, *Porgy*; U.S. Bureau of the Census, *Census of Population: Volume III, Part 2* (Washington, D.C.: GPO, 1932), 788–89; U.S. Bureau of the Census, *Census of Population: Volume II, Part 6* (Washington, D.C.: GPO, 1943), 376, 408.

18. Hamer, "Giving a Sense of Achievement."

CHAPTER 1

1. Rose, *Rehearsal for Reconstruction*; Pollitzer, *The Gullah People and Their African Heritage*; Carawan and Carawan, eds., *Ain't You Got a Right to the Tree of Life?*

2. For more on the term *pater familias*, see Saller, "*Pater Familias, Mater Familias*, and Gendered Semantics of the Roman Household." For more on paternalism and American slavery, see Genovese, *Roll Jordan Roll*. The best early studies of the Charleston Movement are O'Neill, "From the Shadow of Slavery"; Fink and Greenburg, *Upheaval in the Quiet Zone*. See also Chafe, *Civilities and Civil Rights*, 8.

3. Clark and Brown, *Ready from Within*, 104.

4. Clark and Brown, *Ready from Within*, 23, 27; Fields, *Lemon Swamp and Other Places*, 138; Charron, *Freedom's Teacher*, 50–80.

5. Carawan and Carawan, *Ain't You Got a Right to the Tree of Life*, 140–43.

6. For more on the early civil rights movement on the Sea Islands and around Charleston, see Carawan and Carawan, *Ain't You Got a Right to the Tree of Life*, 140–69; O'Neill, "From the Shadow of Slavery," 180–97; Charron, *Freedom's Teacher*, 223–24.

7. Clark, *Ready from Within*, 42–53; O'Neill, "From the Shadow of Slavery," 177, 190–91; Charron, *Freedom's Teacher*, 218–35, 244–63.

8. O'Neill, "From the Shadow of Slavery," 98–100.

9. O'Neill, "From the Shadow of Slavery," 91–97, 101–7; "South Carolina: The Man They Love to Hate," *Time*, Aug. 23, 1948; Thomas R. Waring memorandum, March 4, 1988, *Post and Courier* Archives. J. Waties Waring, "Dissenting Opinion from Harry Briggs, Jr., et al v. R. W. Elliot, Chariman, et al," June 23, 1951, 6, 19–20. Atlanta Branch of NARA (Identifier: 279306), http://www.archives.gov/southeast/education/resources-by-state/briggs-v-elliot.html, Dec. 23, 2011.

10. McGee interview with author (2008). Though it did not inspire a mass movement or national media attention, Burke High School students launched the first Charleston sit-in on April 1, 1960. For more on this, see Hale, "'The Fight Was Instilled in Us.'"

11. Bernard Fielding interview by Felice Knight, SC Civil Rights Anthology Project (2004), in author's possession; O'Neill, "From the Shadow of Slavery," 223–38.

12. Gaillard, *Boards to Boardrooms*, 261–63; Fraser, *Charleston! Charleston!* 412–17.

13. Bill Saunders interviewed by Felice Knight, South Carolina Civil Rights Anthology (2004, Interview 1), transcript in the Bill Saunders Papers, Avery Research Center (hereafter ARC).

14. Ibid.

15. Mary Moultrie and Isaiah Bennett interviews with author (1995). It was regular practice for the RN to give nurses' aides and LPNs reports on the patients, yet many white RNs did not feel that black nurses' assistants needed to know this information.

16. Moultrie interview and *Charleston News and Courier*, April 17, 1994.

17. Racist language used regarding workers covered in Mary Moultrie and Jesse Jefferson interviews with author (1995). The wage differentials were outlined in an HEW report, summarized in the *News and Courier*, June 18, 1969. The union requested recognition in a telegram from Isaiah Bennett to John E. Wise, vice president of the Medical College, Hospital Strike Collection, ARC.

18. Elsa F. McDowell, "Medical College Former President Recalls Upheaval," *Post and Courier*, March 19, 1989; Lynne Langley, "MUSC's McCord Dies," *Post and Courier*, Jan. 6, 1996. Dr. McCord refused my request for an interview in 1995.

19. Moultrie stated the union position in a telegram to hospital administrators March 17, 1969, Hospital Strike Collection, ARC.

20. Moultrie, Bennett, and Naomi White interviews with author (1995); O'Neill, "From the Shadow of Slavery," 272.

21. Picketers at the Old Slave Market, described in the *News and Courier*, March 23, 1969; quote about and by McCord in O'Neill, "From the Shadow of Slavery," 281.

22. Abernathy, *And the Walls Came Tumbling Down*, 516–39. For more on the SCLC, see Peake, *Keeping the Dream Alive*; Fairclough, *To Redeem the Soul of America*.

23. For more on South Carolina labor laws and history, see Fink, "Union Power, Soul Power"; Fink and Greenberg, *Upheaval in the Quiet Zone*. See also Korstad, *Civil Rights Unionism*.

24. *News and Courier*, March 23 and 24, 1969.

25. Moultrie interview with author (1995) and with Steve O'Neill (1989). For more on women in the civil rights movement, see Crawford, Rouse, and Woods, eds., *Women in the Civil Rights Movement*; Payne, *I've Got the Light of Freedom*; Robnett, *How Long? How Long*; Collier-Thomas and Franklin, eds., *Sisters in the Struggle*.

26. Mary Moultrie interview with Jean-Claude Bouffard (1982), ARC; Mary Moultrie, Bill Saunders, and Rosetta Simmons interview with Kerry Taylor (2009), Citadel Oral History Program, the Citadel (hereafter COHP); Saunders interview with Felice Knight (2004), Bill Saunders Papers, Avery Research Center; Jerry Butler, "Only the Strong Survive," *The Iceman Cometh* (Mercury Records, 1968).

27. *News and Courier*, April 5, 1969, April 17, 1994. Some of the workers who did not go on strike said they could not because they were single mothers bringing in the only income for their families, but many of the strikers were single mothers themselves. O'Neill interviews with Jefferson and Moultrie.

28. *I Am Somebody*, Icarus Films (American Federation for Non-Violence); *News and Courier*, April 1, 1969.

29. *News and Courier*, April 3 and 10, 1969. Anonymous interviews with two former faculty members and the author (1995).

30. *News and Courier*, April 5 and 11, 1969; Abernathy, *And the Walls Came Tumbling Down*, 555; Moultrie, Simmons, and Saunders interview with Taylor (2009).

31. *News and Courier*, May 2 and 14, 1969; Abernathy, *And the Walls Came Tumbling Down*, 555. For a disavowal of violence by strikers, see White, Jefferson, and Moultrie interviews with author (1995). For Saunders's take on violence during the strike, see his interviews with Felice Knight (2003) and Kerry Taylor (2009), ARC, as well as Fink, "Union Power, Soul Power," 15.

32. *News and Courier*, April 25 and May 5, 1969; *I Am Somebody*, Icarus Films.

33. *News and Courier*, May 2, 7, and 14, 1969.

34. *News and Courier*, May 12, 1969; Abernathy, *And the Walls Came Tumbling Down*, 553; Fink, *Upheaval in the Quiet Zone*, 143.

35. *News and Courier*, May 16, June 10–18, 1969.

36. O'Neill, "From the Shadow of Slavery," 88.

37. Moultrie, Bennett, Jefferson, and White interview with author (1995). Simmons quoted in the *News and Courier*, July 18, 1969.

38. Moultrie and Bennett interviews with the author (1995). For the political legacies of the strike, see Fink, "Union Power, Soul Power," 19; O'Neill, "From the Shadow of Slavery," especially chapter 6.

CHAPTER 2

1. Joseph H. "Peter" McGee interview with author (2008); Joe Darby interview with author (2008); Robert Ford interview with author (2008); Joseph P. Riley interview

with author (2008); Joseph P. Riley Jr. interview with Felice Knight for the South Carolina Civil Rights Anthology (2004), in author's possession.

2. Kruse, *White Flight*, 6; Lassiter, *Silent Majority*, 3.

3. McGee interview with author (2008); Hamer, "Giving a Sense of Achievement." Though the city population declined slightly over the course of the 1940s (probably a result of early suburban growth), the population of Charleston County exploded in the decade, adding 43,751 people (a 36 percent increase and more than the previous half century combined). U.S. Bureau of the Census, *Census of Population: Volume I, Number of Inhabitants, South Carolina* (Washington, D.C.: GPO, 1952): 40–48, 40–67.

4. Tony Bartelme, "Civic Leader Joseph Riley Dies at 80," *Post and Courier*, Aug. 9, 1992; "Joseph P. Riley Sr.: Life of Service," *Post and Courier*, Aug. 11, 1992.

5. Dottie Ashley and Colette Baxley, "Mayor Riley's Mother Dies at 81," *Post and Courier*, Sept. 15, 1996; "Helen Schachte Riley," *Post and Courier*, Sept. 18, 1990; Susanne Emge interview by author (2008).

6. Dottie Ashley and Colette Baxley, "Mayor Riley's Mother Dies at 81," *Post and Courier*, Sept. 15, 1996; David W. MacDougall, "Joseph Patrick Riley, Jr." *Post and Courier*, March 17, 1990.

7. David W. MacDougall, "Joseph Patrick Riley, Jr." *Post and Courier*, March 17, 1990; "Joseph P. Riley, Sr.: A Life of Service," *Post and Courier*, Aug. 11, 1992; Emge interview with author, Oct. 28, 2008; Joseph P. Riley Jr. interview with author (2008).

8. Pat Brennan interview with author (2008); Emge interview with author (2008); Riley Jr. interview with author (2008).

9. Riley Jr. interview with author (2008); Emge interview with author (2008).

10. Joseph P. Riley Jr. interview with Felice Knight for the South Carolina Civil Rights Anthology (2004), in author's possession; Riley Jr. interview with author (2008).

11. Emge interview with author (2008).

12. Moore, *Carnival of Blood*, 211–12; Riley interview with Felice Knight, South Carolina Civil Rights Anthology (2004), in author's possession. See also Ritterhouse, *Growing Up Jim Crow*.

13. Emge interview with author (2008).

14. Riley Jr. interview with author (2008); Brennan interview with author (2008).

15. Brennan interview with author (2008); Riley Jr. interview with author (2008); Baker, *Cadets in Gray*; Andrew, *Long Gray Lines*; Conroy, *The Lords of Discipline*; Manegold, *In Glory's Shadow*.

16. Marsha White, "Charlestonians Honor Memory of J. F. Kennedy," *Post and Courier*, Nov. 23, 1983; Riley Jr. interview with author (2008).

17. Mendel Rivers, "Communist Threat" speech; Mendel Rivers Papers, South Carolina Historical Society (hereafter SCHS) Box 29 (File 1962–3), 3.

18. Rivers, "What the Military Means to the Low Country in Dollars and Cents," Rivers Papers, SCHS, Box 29 (File N.D.-6), 1–2; Schulman, *The Seventies*, 112.

19. Johnson, *The Sorrows of Empire*, 39.

20. Letter from W. F. "Red" Raborn to Mr. Joe Riley, May 1968; letter from Harvey P. Jolly to Mendel Rivers, Aug. 31, 1968; letter from Mendel Rivers to Joseph P Riley, Feb. 9, 1968; Rivers Papers, SCHS, Box 26 (File Correspondence February–March, April–May, August–September, 1968).

21. Rivers, "What the Military Means to the Low Country in Dollars and Cents," Rivers Papers, SCHS, Box 29 (File N.D.-6), 1–2.

22. Rivers, "Integration" (partial speech); Rivers Papers, SCHS, Box 29 (File 1962–8), 18.

23. Riley Jr. interview with Knight. SC Civil Rights Anthology (2004), in author's possession.

24. Riley Jr. interview with Marvin Lare. SC Civil Rights Anthology (2005), in author's possession. In the Jim Crow era, most southern teachers hewed closely to the "Dunning School" interpretation of Reconstruction, which I outlined here and which had become popular nationally in the early 1900s, based on the work of Columbia University scholar William A. Dunning and several of his students. Historians across the country revised this interpretation in the 1950s, so that by 1963–1964, even the "New South" class at the Citadel rejected the Dunning interpretation. For more on the Dunning School, see Muller, "Look Back without Anger," 334.

25. Fraser, *Charleston! Charleston!* 276; Powers, "Community Evolution and Race Relations in Reconstruction Charleston, South Carolina," 217.

26. Fraser, *Charleston! Charleston!* 408–12.

27. Ibid., 412; Gaillard, *Boards to Boardrooms*, 261–63, 305; Fraser, *Charleston! Charleston!* 412–17.

28. MacDougall, "Joseph Patrick Riley, Jr.," *Post and Courier*, March 17, 1990; Macauley, "An Oasis of Order."

29. MacDougall, "Joseph Patrick Riley, Jr.," *Post and Courier*, March 17, 1990.

30. Dottie Ashley, "Charlotte Riley," *Post and Courier*, May 24, 1997.

31. McGee interview with author (2008).

32. "J. P. Riley Jr. Seeks Seat in S.C. House," *Evening Post*, March 8, 1968; "Rep. Riley to head U.F. Division," *News and Courier*, Aug. 12, 1972; Nancy Hawk interview with author (2008); Evans, *The Provincials*, 272.

33. "J. P. Riley Seeks Seat in S.C. House," *Evening Post*, March 8, 1968, "Riley Announces Bid for Re-Election," *James Island Journal*, March 19, 1970; MacDougall, Joseph Patrick Riley," *Post and Courier*, March 17, 1990; Nicole Achs, "1991 Municipal Leader of the Year," *American City and County*, Dec. 1991; Riley interview with Knight, SC Civil Rights Anthology (2004), in author's possession.

34. Fraser, *Charleston! Charleston!* 418.

35. Gaillard, *From Boards to Boardrooms*, 318–19.

36. Saunders interviewed by Knight, SC Civil Rights Anthology (2004, Interview 4), in author's possession, Fraser, *Charleston! Charleston!* 424.

37. McGee interview with author (2008); Riley interview with Knight, SC Civil Rights Anthology (2004); Riley interview with Lare, S.C. Civil Rights Anthology (2005) in author's possession. The letter itself appears to have been lost. Riley no longer has a copy, and attempts to locate a copy in Gaillard's papers were unsuccessful. These quotes are from interviews with McGee and Riley based on their memories of the letter.

38. Riley interview with Knight, SC Civil Rights Anthology (2004), in author's possession; Gaillard, *From Boards to Boardrooms*, 351–54.

39. Riley interview with Knight, SC Civil Rights Anthology (2004), in author's possession; Fraser, *Charleston! Charleston!* 428.

40. Nancy Hawk interview with author (2008); "Nancy D. Hawk," *Post and Courier*, Oct. 19, 2008; Barbara S. Williams, "Reflections on a Life Well Lived," *Post and Courier*, Oct. 26, 2008.

41. Hawk interview with author (2008).

42. For background on the historic preservation movement in Charleston, see Weyeneth, *Historic Preservation for a Living City*; Yuhl, *A Golden Haze of Memory*, 24–49; Brundage, *The Southern Past*, 183–213.

43. Weyeneth, *Historic Preservation for a Living City*, 60–63, 70–71.

44. Ibid., 58–59; Yuhl, *Golden Haze of Memory*, 46–47.

45. McGee interview with author (2008); Hawk interview with author (2008).

46. Hawk interview with author (2008); Henry O. Counts, "Riley Promises Unification for City," *News and Courier*, Dec. 16, 1975.

47. Hawk interview with author (2008). Riley won the election with 51 percent of the vote, including 75 percent of African American votes cast. Fraser, *Charleston! Charleston!* 428. See also Barbara S. Williams, "New City Administration to Be Closely Watched," *News and Courier*, Dec. 14, 1975. While Riley welcomed a racially balanced city council, the switch from at-large voting to single-member districts was really responsible for the changing makeup of the council in the mid-1970s.

48. Barbara S. Williams, "Inaugural Departs from Old Customs," *News and Courier*, Dec. 16, 1975.

49. Henry O. Counts, "Riley Promises Unification for City," *News and Courier*, Dec. 16, 1975.

50. Teaford, *The Metropolitan Revolution*; Counts, "Riley Promises Unification for City," *News and Courier*, Dec. 16, 1975.

51. Keller, "The Impact of Black Mayors on Urban Policy"; Biles, "Black Mayors"; Swain Jr., "Black Mayors, Urban Decline and the Underclass"; David Slade, "Riley Visits James Island to Push Annexation," *Post and Courier*, June 21, 2005; Joe Riley Jr. interview with author (2008); John E. Bourne Jr. interview with author (2008); Ken Riley interview with author (2008); Robert Ford interview with author (2008).

52. Elsa McDowell, "Riley Voted Most Powerful," *News and Courier*, Nov. 29, 1987; Kerri Morgan, "The Riley Years: Shaping Charleston since 1976," *Post and Courier*, May 10, 1992; Peter McGee interview with author (2008); Nancy Hawk interview with author (2008); Jimmy Bailey interview with author (2008).

53. For more on the politics of publicly memorializing slavery (and Denmark Vesey) in Charleston, see Roberts and Kytle, "Looking the Thing in the Face."

54. Lofton, *Denmark Vesey's Slave Revolt*, vii–viii.

55. Ibid., viii–ix.

56. Bailey interview with author (2008); McGee interview with author (2008); Greenberg interview with author (2006); Riley interview with Knight, SC Civil Rights Anthology (2004); Riley interview with Lare, SC Civil Rights Anthology (2005), in author's possession.

57. Riley interview with Knight (2004), in author's possession.

58. Riley interview with Knight (2004), in author's possession; Edward C. Fennell, "Senator Praises Riley for Achievements," *News and Courier*, Nov. 7, 1981.

59. U.S. Bureau of the Census, *Census of Population: Volume I, Number of Inhabitants, South Carolina* (Washington, D.C.: GPO, 1952), 40–48, 40–67; U.S. Bureau of the Census, *Census of Population, South Carolina* (Washington, D.C.: GPO, 1972), tables 24. 34; McCullough and Moore, "Exercising Dominion over Metropolitan Growth," 4; Fraser, *Charleston! Charleston!* 426; Kyle Stock, "20 Years Charleston Place," *Post and Courier*, Aug. 28, 2006.

60. Kruse, *White Flight*; Lassiter, *The Silent Majority*. For a fictional critique of development in Atlanta, see Wolfe, *A Man in Full*.

61. John Graham Altman interview with author (2008); Kerri Morgan, "Mayor's Efforts a Costly Labor of Love," *Post and Courier*, May 10, 1992.

62. Dottie Ashley, "Charlotte Riley: Dancer-at-Heart Delights in City's Cultural Awakening," *Post and Courier*, May 24, 1997; Jack Kroll, "Spoleto Comes to Charleston" and "Spoleto West," *Newsweek*, June 6, 1977; Paul Hume, "Menotti Discovers a New World—In Charleston," *Washington Post*, May 22, 1977. The *New York Times* published more than a dozen articles on the festival in its inaugural year.

63. Weyeneth, *Historic Preservation for a Living City*, 94–95, 97–98; Huth, "Should Charleston Go New South?"

64. Huth, "Should Charleston Go New South?" 34–37; Hawk interview with author (2008).

65. Weyeneth, *Historic Preservation for a Living City*, 100–2; McGee interview with author (2008); Huth, "Should Charleston Go New South?" 37.

66. Weyeneth, *Historic Preservation for a Living City*, 99–100; Hawk interview with author (2008); Herb Frazier, "Charleston Place off the Hook on Loan, for Now," *Post and Courier*, July 19, 1989; Charles de V. Williams, "Charleston Place Cornerstone of Downtown Growth," *Post and Courier*, Feb. 28, 1999; Kyle Stock, "Twenty Years Charleston Place," *Post and Courier*, Aug. 28, 2006.

CHAPTER 3

1. Testimonials to Greenberg's leadership during the storm flooded into the *Post and Courier* after Hurricane Katrina devastated New Orleans, and Charlestonians realized that they had been lucky in more ways than one. "Riley, Greenberg's Hugo Leadership," in letters to the editor, *Post and Courier*, Sept. 13, 2005.

2. Greenberg interview with author (2006); Ned Hethington interview with author (2008); Herb Whetsell interview with author (2008); Ligure "Duke" Ellington interview with author (2008).

3. Ibid.

4. Fraser, *Lowcountry Hurricanes*, 240–47.

5. Ellington interview with author (2008); Hethington interview with author (2008); Greenberg interview with author (2006).

6. Greenberg interview with author (2006); Hethington interview with author (2008).

7. Dulaney, *Black Police in America*, 81–103, 109–14; Bolton and Feagin, *Black in Blue*, ix–x. See also Michael S. Serrill, Thomas McCarroll, and B. J. Phillips, "The New Black Police Chiefs," *Time*, Feb. 18, 1985; Agyepong, "In the Belly of the Beast."

8. Greenberg, *Let's Take Back Our Streets!* 138–40; Greenberg interview with author (2006).

9. Ibid.

10. Greenberg, *Let's Take Back Our Streets!* 142–58; Sara Horne-Greenberg interview with author (2008).

11. Greenberg interview with author (2006).

12. Ibid.

13. Fox Butterfield, "Police Chief's Success in Charleston, S.C., Is What's Raising Eyebrows Now," *New York Times*, April 28, 1996; Horne-Greenberg interview with author (2008).

14. Shirley Greene, "New Chief Sees Safer Charleston," *News and Courier*, April 4, 1982. Reuben Greenberg interview with author, Dec. 9, 2006.

15. Dulaney, *Black Police in America*, 2–4, 13, 16, 116; Jordan, "Police and Politics"; Oldfield, "On the Beat." Four black officers remained on the Charleston force in the early 1900s, and the department hired the son of one of these men for a few months in 1920. But for all intents and purposes, Charleston had a white police force during the first half of the twentieth century.

16. Dulaney, *Black Police in America*, 32, 44; "Our Negro Policemen" *News and Courier*, Oct. 18, 1953; Coyte W. White, "Five Years on City Force, Negro Police Prove Worth," *News and Courier*, April 30, 1956. See also Cambridge Jenkins Papers, ARC. Jenkins was one of the first African Americans hired by the department in 1950.

17. "Police Moving to New Station," *Charleston Evening Post*, Jan. 22, 1974; Ellington interview with author (2008); Hethington interview with author (2008).

18. Karen Amrhine, "City Policewomen Complete Classes," *Charleston Evening Post*, Oct. 14, 1972. There had been women employed by the force as crossing guards and dispatchers before 1972, but this was the first class of women who would become beat cops and officers. Ellington interview with author (2008).

19. Ellington interview with author (2008); Edward C. Fennell, "New Police Leaving Cars to Join Community," *Charleston News and Courier*, Aug. 1, 1977; Gardner Miller, "East Side Police Work Unique Beat," *Charleston News and Courier*, Dec. 26, 1977.

20. Bobby Isaac, "Police Filing Records of Non-Criminal Interrogation," *Charleston News and Courier*, Sept. 16, 1973; Shirley Greene, "Change Tactics, Police Are Told," *Charleston Evening Post*, Oct. 23, 1980; "Blacks Say Police Power Abused, Ill-Used," *Chronicle*, Nov. 21, 1981.

21. "Police Brutality? You Decide," *Chronicle*, Nov. 15, 1975.

22. "Charleston Police Chief Dead; Praised in '69 Hospital Strike," *New York Times*, Nov. 1, 1981. Author interviews with Hethington (2008), Whetsell (2008), and Ellington (2008).

23. Eleanor Flagler, "Riley Accents Positive in State of City Address," *News and Courier*, Jan. 25, 1978; Mary Glass, "Riley Promises Safer, Stronger City," *News and*

Courier, Jan. 14, 1981. Federal Bureau of Investigation, *Uniform Crime Report for 1980*, 41, 64, 128. The Charleston metropolitan area included Berkeley, Charleston, and Dorchester Counties. Per 100,000 inhabitants, the violent crime rates for the metropolitan areas were as follows: Charleston (799.8), Cleveland (794.1), Charlotte (706.9), and Chicago (585.0). Such comparisons are difficult because of the differences between the way metropolitan boundaries are drawn and the way crime was reported in each locale, but even within South Carolina, Charleston had a relatively high crime rate.

24. Ed Magnuson, "The Curse of Violent Crime," *Time*, March 23, 1981; Aric Press, "The Plague of Violent Crime," *Newsweek*, March 23, 1981 (the *Newsweek* cover was titled "Epidemic of Violent Crime," though the article referred to a "Plague"); James A. Martin, "Crime: It Can Strike Anyone, Anytime," *News and Courier*, Sept. 19, 1982.

25. Ibid.

26. Ronald Reagan, "Radio Address to the Nation on Crime and Criminal Justice Reform, September 11, 1982," Public Papers of President Ronald Reagan, Ronald Reagan Presidential Library, http://www.reagan.utexas.edu/archives/speeches/1982/91182a.htm, viewed on December 9, 2014; Edward C. Fennell, "Riley Urges Longer Jail Terms in 'State of the City' Address," *News and Courier*, Jan. 13, 1982.

27. Shirley Greene, "New Chief Sees Safer Charleston," *News and Courier*, April 4, 1982; Whetsell interview with author (2008); Hethington interview with author (2008).

28. Hethington interview with author (2008); Ellington interview (2008); Whetsell interview with author (2008).

29. Horne-Greenberg interview with author (2008); Anne Legare, "Police Chief's Wife Juggles Busy Lifestyle," *Charleston Evening Post*, Jan. 25, 1984.

30. "Greenberg Named Chief of Police of Charleston," *State*, March 18, 1982; Thomas Waring, "Charleston Police Chief Weathers Storms," *News and Courier*, Jan. 3, 1983; Charles Francis, "Blacks Back City Police, Coalition Says," *News and Courier*, Jan. 5, 1991.

31. Federal Bureau of Investigation, *Uniform Crime Reports* 1982 (p. 102); 1983 (p. 357); 1984 (p. 347); 1985 (p. 340); 1986 (p. 340); 1987 (p. 323); 1988 (p. 329); 1989 (p. 335); Greenberg, *Let's Take Back Our Streets!* 124. Murder cases cited were reported by Greenberg in his autobiography and do not match exactly the number in the Uniform Crime Reports.

32. Barry Siegel, "Black Police Chief Skates Past Skeptics," *Los Angeles Times*, Oct. 3, 1983; "Reuben Greenberg," *Time*, Feb. 18, 1985; Jane Shealy, "Celebrity," *News and Courier*, Feb. 9, 1986; Marshall Ingwerson, "Talking Fast and Moving Faster in Charleston," *Christian Science Monitor*, March 4, 1987; "Chief of Police Stands Apart in South Carolina," *New York Times*, June 14, 1987; Vern E. Smith, "A Frontal Assault on Drugs," *Newsweek*, April 30, 1990; Drew Jubera, "The Reuben Greenberg Show," *Atlanta Journal Constitution*, May 20, 1990; Reuben Greenberg, "Let's Take Back Our Streets," *Ebony*, April 1991.

33. Greenberg interview with author (2006); "Religion: Jewish Negro," *Time*, Feb. 1, 1960; Lester, *Lovesong*; Carson, "Black-Jewish Universalism in the Era of Identity Politics."

34. Rosengarten and Rosengarten, eds., *A Portion of the People*; Millicent Brown interview by Kirk Heidenreich (1998), Millicent Brown Papers, ARC; Evans, *The Provincials*, 271–72.

35. Greenberg, *Let's Take Back Our Streets!* 188–91; Brian Bain, Susan Levitas, and Time Watson, *Shalom Y'all* (Satchel Entertainment, 2002); clipping from the *Forward* (March 1993) in Box 1, Folder 1, Greenberg Collection, ARC.

36. Greenberg, *Let's Take Back Our Streets!* 6, 39, 63–64, 93, 116, 120; Vito, Maahs, and Holmes, *Criminology*, 21–22; Banfield, *The Unheavenly City*; Wilson, *Thinking about Crime*; Wilson and Herrnstein, *Crime and Human Nature*.

37. Greenberg, *Let's Take Back Our Streets!* 6–7, 50–51, 79–81, 213–14; Joseph Burger, "Goetz Case: Commentary on Nature of Urban Life," *New York Times*, June 18, 1987.

38. Greenberg, *Let's Take Back Our Streets!* 29–30, 125–26, 130, 134–36; Steele, *The Content of Our Character*.

39. Lamis, *The Two-Party South*, 26, 306, 310–31, and Lamis, ed., *Southern Politics in the 1990s*, 7–8; Susan Estrich, "The Politics of Race," *Washington Post Magazine*, April 23, 1989. The official Bush campaign ad did not include photos of Willie Horton, but campaign supporters aired a version of the ad that did picture the convicted murder.

40. Prentiss Findlay, "Expert Says 'Crack' Is Easy to Get," *News and Courier*, Nov. 6, 1986; Richard Green Jr., "Busted," *News and Courier*, Dec. 4, 1988; Richard Green and Steve Mullins, "Court Survey Reveals Disparity in Outcome of Narcotics Cases," *News and Courier*, Dec. 4, 1988; Skip Johnson, "Officials Say Drug Crack Making Inroads Locally," *Evening Post*, June 28, 1988. See also Federal Bureau of Investigation, "Drugs in America: 1980–1995," *Uniform Crime Report* (1996), 280–84; Stephanie Barna, "A Local War on Drugs," *Charleston City Paper*, Feb. 18, 1998; Nelson, "He Made a Way out of No Way," 21.

41. Hethington interview with author (2008); Greenberg, *Let's Take Back Our Streets!* 20–31; Greenberg, "Less Bang-Bang for the Buck"; Whetsell interview with author (2008).

42. Gagan, "*Ferguson v. City of Charleston, South Carolina*"; *Ferguson v. City of Charleston*, 532 U.S. 67 (2001). For local coverage of the issue of mothers addicted to cocaine, see Elsa F. McDowell, "Cocaine Capturing More Women as Victims," "Rachel's Baby," and "Cocaine's a Killer for Children Born to Users," *News and Courier*, Aug. 23, 1989.

43. Ibid.

44. *Ferguson v. City of Charleston*, 532 U.S. 67 (2001); Susan Dunn interview with author (2008); Ellen B. Meacham, "Women Say They Feel Vindicated by 6-3 Ruling in Drug Test Case," *Post and Courier*, March 23, 2001.

45. Dunn interview with author (2008); Stephanie Harvin, "Susan Dunn: An MUSC Drug-Testing Lawsuit Has Turned into an Eight Year Challenge for a Charleston Lawyer," *Post and Courier*, March 3, 2001.

46. Aric Press, "The Plague of Violent Crime," *Newsweek*, March 23, 1981; "Our Worst Enemy: Black on Black Crime," *Charleston Chronicle*, Nov. 7, 1981; Bill Kovarik, "Greenberg Denounces Black Crime Wave," *News and Courier*, Nov. 21, 1982; Charles

Francis, "Black-on-Black Crime Worries Black Leaders," *News and Courier*, Sept. 25, 1985.

47. Cantor and Land, "Unemployment and Crime Rates in the Post–World War II United States"; Smith and Devine, "Crime and Unemployment"; Fraser, *Charleston! Charleston!* 436; "Local Area Unemployment Statistics: Charleston–North Charleston–Summerville, SC," U.S. Department of Labor, Bureau of Labor Statistics (1990–2009); Federal Bureau of Investigation, *Uniform Crime Reports* (1982–1998).

48. Federal Bureau of Investigation, "Crime Clock," *Uniform Crime Reports* (1982, 1992), 4–5; Bill Steiger, "Crime Time," *News and Courier*, Oct. 25, 1987; Chris Sosnowski and Richard Green Jr., "Basic Details Key to Safe S.C. Roads," *Post and Courier*, Aug. 19, 1997.

CHAPTER 4

1. Deposition of Ursula Major, *United States of America and Richard Ganaway, et al., v. Charleston County School District and the State of South Carolina* (Sept. 9, 1987). Deposition included in the Robert Rosen Papers, Series III, Box 6, File 22, ARC; Keith Major correspondence with author (2012).

2. Baker, *Paradoxes of Desegregation*, 20, 24, 40–41.

3. Keith Major correspondence with author (2012); Ursula Major deposition, *Ganaway, et al., v. Charleston County School District* (Sept. 9, 1987), Rosen Papers, Series III, Box 6, File 22, ARC; Sandra Bennett, "Denial of Student's Request to Transfer Called 'Unfair,'" *News and Courier*, April 17, 1984.

4. Kluger, *Simple Justice*; Wilkinson, *From Brown to Bakke*; Patterson, *Brown v. Board of Education*; Bell, *Silent Covenants*; Klarman, *From Jim Crow to Civil Rights*; Walker, *The Ghost of Jim Crow*; Baker, *Paradoxes of Desegregation*.

5. *United States of America and Richard Ganaway II et al v. Charleston County School District and State of South Carolina*, 738 F. Supp. 1513; 1990 U.S. Dist. Lexis 7020 (June 5, 1990), 8–9; Robert Rosen interview with author (2009), 4; *Green v. County School Board*, 391 U.S. 430 (1968).

6. Hale, "'The Fight Was Instilled in Us,'" 19, 27–28; Shircliffe, "We Got the Best of That World," 59–62; Cecelski, *Along Freedom Road*.

7. Leonard Riley interview with the author (2009); Ken Riley interview with author (2008).

8. Damon Fordham correspondence with author (2010).

9. "A Syllabus for United States History for the High Schools of Charleston County: A Document to Provide Supplementary Information with Emphasis on Ethnic Contributions Especially that of the Afro-American to America's Story" (Charleston County School District, 1972), vii; "Progress with Pride" (Charleston County School District, 1969–1970), 12. Documents are from the South Carolina Room of the Charleston County Public Library (hereafter CCPL).

10. John Graham Altman III interview with author (2008).

11. Altman interview with author (2008); "J. G. Altman Jr. Dies in Hospital," *Charleston Evening Post*, March 18, 1974; "J. G. Altman III Is Press Aide to Governor,"

Charleston News and Courier, June 17, 1960; Kerri Morgan, "Chas. County School Board OKs AIDS Policy," *Charleston News and Courier*, Jan. 14, 1986; Dawn Brazell, "John Graham Altman," *Charleston Post and Courier*, June 18, 1994; Lucille Whipper interview with author (2009); Joe Darby interview with author (2008).

12. *Milliken v. Bradley*, 418 U.S. 717 (1974); Orfield, Eaton, et al., *Dismantling Desegregation*; Berger and Orfield, eds., *School Resegregation*. For more on desegregation in Charlotte, see Lassiter, *The Silent Majority*, 123.

13. "Charleston Schools May Face Busing," *Charleston Evening Post*, Dec. 1, 1980. "Charleston School Officials Cry Foul over Segregation Charge, *State*, Dec. 21, 1980; "Charleston Officials Discuss Suit," *News and Courier*, Jan. 13, 1981; Altman interview with author (2008).

14. Robert Rosen, "Case Summary: *United States of America and Richard Ganaway, II e al v. Charleston County School District and State of South Carolina*" (2006) in the Robert Rosen Papers, ARC; Baker, *Paradoxes of Desegregation*, 171–72.

15. Baker, *Paradoxes of Desegregation*, 172–74; Whipper interview with author (2009); Arthur McFarland interview with author (2010); Orfield, Eaton, et al., *Dismantling Desegregation*; Berger and Orfield, eds., *School Resegregation*.

16. Richard Ganaway deposition in Rosen Papers (Series III, Box 6, File 10), 11–13, 22.

17. Louise Brown deposition in Rosen Papers (Series III, Box 6, File 8), 14–16; Edell Simmons deposition in Rosen Papers (Series III, Box 6, File 7), 14.

18. Robert Rosen, "Case Summary: *United States of America and Richard Ganaway, II et al v. Charleston County School District and State of South Carolina*" (2006) in the Robert Rosen Papers, ARC; Florence Barone, "Charleston School Board Lumbering toward Compromise on Desegregation," *State*, Aug. 15, 1982.

19. Robert Rosen interview with author (2009); Millicent Brown interview with Kirk Heidenreich (1998), in the Millicent Brown Papers, ARC. See also Brodkin, *How Jews Became White Folks & What That Says about Race in America*, 40–44, 171–74.

20. "Resistance to Magnet School," *News and Courier*, May 5, 1981; Florence Barone, "Charleston School Board Lumbering toward Compromise on Desegregation," *State*, Aug. 15, 1982; Steve Mullins, "Justice, Rosen Talk Voluntary Busing," *Charleston Evening Post*, Dec. 28, 1982.

21. McFarland interview with author (2010).

22. Dr. Lawrence Derthick testimony (Day 1), 2, 20, 83–88, from Rosen Papers (Series V, Box 9, File 2), ARC.

23. Helen Clawson testimony (Day 3), 189–92, 195, 199, 204–5, Rosen Papers (Series V, Box 9, File 4), ARC; Anna Cox testimony (Day 3), 150–51, 156–57, 182–83, Rosen Papers (Series V, Box 9, File 4), ARC.

24. Reardon and Yun, "Private School Racial Enrollments and Segregation," 6–7. Joe Riley's kids graduated from Porter-Gaud School in Charleston. Two of Robert Rosen's three kids went to a public magnet school (Buist) in downtown Charleston for elementary and middle school, but then they transferred to Andover and Porter-Gaud for high school. Robert Rosen correspondence with author (2011).

25. Steeley, "A History of Independent Education in South Carolina," 62, 71, 90–97. For listing of private schools in the state, see South Carolina School Directory, 1970–1971 (S.C. Department of Education, 1970), 139–45; South Carolina School Directory, 1978–1979 (S.C. Department of Education, 1978), 142–51; South Carolina School Directory, 1984–1985 (S.C. Department of Education, 1984), 126–35; Directory of South Carolina Schools, 1992–1993 (S.C. Department of Education, 1992). Directories in CCPL. Supreme Court cases limiting the role of religion in public schools include *Engel v. Vitale*, 370 U.S. 421 (1962) and *Abington School District v. Schempp*, 374 U.S. 203 (1963). Robert Rosen interview with author (2009).

26. www.ashleyhall.org, December 9, 2014; Gene Burges interview with author (2009).

27. www.portergaud.edu, December 9, 2014; Greene, *Porter-Gaud School*; Porter-Gaud tuition figures for the 1980s from a correspondence from Margie S. Stanbrook and Jabari Spruill to the author (2011); median household incomes for Charleston County are from the U.S. Census Bureau 1990, Social and Economic Characteristics of South Carolina (tables 9, 13)

28. Alexander Krings correspondence with author (2011); Jonathan Brilliant correspondence with author (2011).

29. McFarland interview with author (2010); Jabari Spruill interview with author (2011).

30. McFarland interview with author (2010); Dwayne Green interview with author (2009). When Keith Major went to Bishop England in the 1980s, he recalled being one of the "token" black students, who saw bigotry by teachers and counselors. As just one example, the guidance counselor did not have information about historically black colleges and universities because she thought so poorly of them. Keith ultimately attended an HBCU, despite this counselor's opposition. "That lady is generally perceived to have been a bigot by my fellow alumni," Keith said. Major correspondence with author (2012).

31. Jonathan Brilliant correspondence with author (2011); Anonymous interview with author (2011).

32. U.S. Census Bureau 1970, South Carolina, General Population Characteristics (table 34); U.S. Census Bureau 1990, South Carolina, Social and Economic Characteristics (tables 6, 167). Charleston County had 932 people of Asian or Pacific Island descent in 1970 and 2,509 in 1990. Anonymous 1 correspondence with author (Sept. 13, 2010), 1–2. For more on the "model minority" stereotype and Asian American integration into white culture during this era, see Wu, *Yellow*, 1, 39–77; Alison Macadam, "Long Duk Dong: The Last of the Hollywood Stereotypes," National Public Radio, March 24, 2008.

33. Sol Blatt Jr. interview with author (2009); Baker, *Paradoxes of Desegregation*, 32; Judge Blatt pleaded for a settlement several times during the trial. The quotes come from Day Five (p. 5) and Day Seven (pp. 67, 88–90). See also Day Ten (p. 12) transcript (Series V, Box 9, Files 5-6, and 9), Rosen Papers, ARC.

34. Robert Figg testimony (Day 22), 4–20, 40–44 (Series V, File 2, Box 10), Rosen Papers, ARC. Deposition of Charles Gibson (Series III, Box 6, File 4), 9, 24, 30, 35,

56, 63, 76, 102. See also testimony from Joseph McGee, Robert Scarborough, and Thomas Hartnett (Day 23) and Charles Gibson (Day 24) (Series V, Box 10, Files 3–4).

35. Leckyler Gaillard testimony (Day 8), 101–2, 108–11, 115, 120–23, 137, 140–41 (Series V, Box 9, File 7), Rosen Papers, ARC.

36. Kerri Morgan, "Expert Testifies Chas. Schools Are Segregated," *Charleston Post and Courier*, March 15, 1988; Edmund L. Drago testimony (Day 12) and Joe T. Darden testimony (Day 18), 4–6, 51–54 (Day 18), a–5, 37–45 (Series V, Box 9, Files 11, 18–19); William Clark testimony (Day 26), 116–17; David Armor testimony (Day 32), 97–98 (Series V, Box 10, Files 6, 12), Rosen Papers, ARC. See also *United States of America and Richard Ganaway II et al v. Charleston County School District and State of South Carolina*, 738 F. Supp. 1513; 1990 U.S. Dist. Lexis 7020 (June 5, 1990), 12.

37. *United States of America and Richard Ganaway II et al v. Charleston County School District and State of South Carolina*, 738 F. Supp. 1513; 1990 U.S. Dist. Lexis 7020 (June 5, 1990), 25.

38. Eric Frazier, "Desegregation Suit Thrown Out," *Charleston Evening Post*, June 6, 1990; Altman interview with author (2008); Rosen interview with author (2009); McFarland interview with author (2010).

39. 960 F2d 1227, *United States II v. Charleston County School District and State of South Carolina* (Nos. 90-1812, 90-1816), United States Court of Appeals, Fourth Circuit, March 12, 1992.

40. Robert Burke testimony (Day 20), 72–73 (Series V, Box 9, File 20), Rosen Papers, ARC; John Vernelson, "Burke Picked for New Magnet School," *Charleston News and Courier*, Feb. 9, 1988; David P. Sklarz, "Academic Magnet Program at Burke High School" (unpublished report in ERIC Database, 1988); "Ledger Sheet of Membership and Attendance by School and District," Charleston County School Board, April 22, 1994. Vertical File—Schools, CCPL.

41. Jermel President interviewed by author (2010); John Vernelson, "Burke Picked for New Magnet School," *Charleston News and Courier*, Feb. 9, 1988; Angela Rucker, "Burke Parents, Staff Speak Out on Magnet Move," *Charleston Post and Courier* (Jan. 19, 1996); Robert Behre and Susan Hill Smith, "About Face on School; Riley to Lobby for Magnet at Burke," *Charleston Post and Courier*, May 30, 1996; Susan Hill Smith, "Bidding Burke Farewell: Magnet School Moving to Former Base," *Charleston Post and Courier*, Dec. 21, 1996; Sandy Krings correspondence with author (2011); "Demographic Characteristics of Charleston County Schools" in the *Annual Report of the Metropolitan Achievement Tests* (Spring 1997), 39, CCPL; Charles Willie et al., "Equity and Excellence: A Plan for Educational Improvement of the Charleston County Public Schools" (April 1998), 19, 105, CCPL.

42. Christina Nifong, "Unexpected Allies on Racial Inequality," *Christian Science Monitor*, July 14, 1997; Motions (Day 10), 4, 13 (Series V, Box 9, File 9), Rosen Papers, ARC; Willie et al., "Equity and Excellence," 76–77, Jabari Spruill, "African American Graduates at Porter-Gaud (1970–2010)" (unpublished report in author's possession, 2011); "Polygon," Porter-Gaud School Yearbook (1990); "Ashley Hall Fact Sheet" (2010), www.ashleyhallorg, July 23, 2010.

43. Willie et al., "Equity and Excellence," 48, 105.

44. Willie et al., "Equity and Excellence," 125.

45. Deposition of Ursula Major (Series III, Box 6, File 22) in the Robert Rosen Papers, ARC; Keith Major correspondence with author (2012).

CHAPTER 5

1. Manegold, *In Glory's Shadow*, 109–16.

2. Maccauley, *Marching in Step*, 2.

3. Thomas, *The History of the South Carolina Military Academy*, 3–4, 12–18; Bond, *The Story of the Citadel*, 4–15.

4. Bond, *The Story of the Citadel*, 16; Baker, *Cadets in Gray*, 2.

5. Baker, *Cadets in Gray*, 5–30, 187; Bond, *The Story of the Citadel*, 81, 87; Thomas, *The History of the South Carolina Military Academy*, 343.

6. Franklin, *The Militant South, 1800–1861*; Andrew, *Long Gray Lines*. See also Wyatt-Brown, *Honor and Violence in the Old South*.

7. Manegold, *In Glory's Shadow*, 45; Nicholson, *A History of the Citadel*, 133, 140–41; Andrew, *Long Gray Lines*, 72–77.

8. Macaulay, *Marching in Step*, 32–33.

9. Ibid., 54.

10. Megget, "Citadel of Trauma;" "Citadel Enrolls First Negro," *New York Times*, Sept. 7, 1966.

11. Macaulay, *Marching in Step*, 65, 73.

12. Megget, "Citadel of Trauma"; Macaulay, *Marching in Step*, 68, 71, 78.

13. Macaulay, *Marching in Step*, 69, 71–72, 74.

14. Meggett, "Citadel of Trauma;" Conroy, *The Lords of Discipline*, 32, 177.

15. Conroy, *The Lords of Discipline*, 156, 177, 229, 489–90.

16. Joe Johnson interview with author (2008); Allen "Kevin" Scott correspondence with author (2007); Joel Lake correspondence with author (2007); Eric Doss interview (2007); Manegold, *In Glory's Shadow*, 121; Susan Faludi, "The Naked Citadel," *New Yorker*, Sept. 5, 1994, 69.

17. R. Reilly, "What Is the Citadel?" *Sports Illustrated*, Sept. 14, 1992, 70–74, 76–78, 81; Andrea Gross, "Shannon's Quest," *Ladies Home Journal*, Feb. 1995, 96–100; Manegold, *In Glory's Shadow*, 157–61.

18. Title IX of the Education Amendments of 1972. 20 U.S.C. §§ 1681–1688.

19. Reginald Stuart, "Mississippi College Enrolls First Man," *New York Times*, Aug. 30, 1981; "School Officials Say Ruling Won't Alter Goal to Aid Women," *New York Times*, July 2, 1982.

20. "Data: Coeds," *New York Times*, Jan. 7, 2007; Baumer, *West Point: Molder of Men*; Lovell, *Neither Athens nor Sparta*; Lipsky, *Absolutely American*. By 1993, there were still over a hundred single-sex schools, the majority of them for women, but only two of them—the Citadel and VMI—were public schools.

21. Correspondence with Allen "Kevin" Scott (2007).

22. Ibid.

23. Christopher Brown, "Citadel Celebrates Its 150th Anniversary," *Post and Courier*, March 19, 1993; Hollings to Lt. Gen. Claudius Watts, III, May 13, 1993 and Hol-

lings to David S. Boyd, June 24, 1993, in "The Citadel" File, Box 436, Ernest F. Hollings Papers, South Carolina Political Collections, University of South Carolina (hereafter SCPC).

24. Manegold, *In Glory's Shadow*, 200; Ron Eyester, "Citadel Back in Court after VMI Ruling," *Brigadier*, Feb. 10, 1995.

25. "Women in Support of the Citadel Takes Action" *Brigadier*, May 13, 1994; Manegold, *In Glory's Shadow*, 206.

26. Wolfe, *Daughters of Canaan*, 142–43, 197–99; De Hart, "Second Wave Feminism(s) and the South."

27. Manegold, *In Glory's Shadow*, 140–43, 206.

28. Zachariah Pratt letter to the editor, *Brigadier*, Jan. 28, 1993; "Faulkner's Bold Whim Ends in Defeat," *Post and Courier*, Aug. 20, 1995.

29. Frank Wooten, "Media Mob Follows Faulkner's Every Move," *Post and Courier*, Jan. 13, 1994; Tony Bartelme, "Cadets' Day Was Emotional See-Saw," *Post and Courier*, Jan. 13, 1994.

30. Andrea Gross, "Shannon's Quest," *Ladies' Home Journal*, Feb. 1995, 96, 98.

31. Manegold, *In Glory's Shadow*, 214.

32. "Faulkner's Bold Whim Ends in Weary Defeat," *Post and Courier*, Aug. 20, 1995.

33. Manegold, *In Glory's Shadow*, 268–69.

34. Manegold, *In Glory's Shadow*, 312; Faludi, "The Naked Citadel," 80; Kimmel, "Saving the Males," 513–14.

35. See Faludi, *Stiffed*; Ehrenreich, *The Hearts of Men*.

36. Johnson interview with author (2008).

37. Howard, *Men Like That*; Sears, *Rebels, Ruby Fruit, and Rhinestones*; Johnson, *Sweet Tea*.

38. Greene, "Charleston, South Carolina," 60, 64.

39. South Carolina Code of Laws 2008, §16-15-120, *http://www.scstatehouse.gov/code/t16c015.htm*, Sept. 24, 2009. The U.S. Supreme Court's decision in *Lawrence v. Texas* (2003) ruled this and other state bans on sodomy unconstitutional; correspondence from Dr. L. Jeffrey Perez, vice president of external affairs at the Citadel, to the author (2009).

40. Macauley, *Marching in Step*; Macauley interview with author (2008).

41. Johnson interview with author (2008). For a classic explanation of the politics of AIDS, see Shilts, *And the Band Played On*.

42. Johnson interview with author (2008). Most of the alumni that I interviewed were not out to themselves when they were at the Citadel, and they probably would have seen homosexual activity as breaking the school's code of conduct. But they did not talk explicitly about this, and none discussed sexual activity while at the school. One straight alumnus reported rumors of gay sex on campus, but they remained rumors.

43. Correspondence with Allen "Kevin" Scott (2007).

44. Interview with Chad Youngblood (2007).

45. Eric Doss interview with author (2007).

46. Ibid.

47. Ibid.

48. Lindsay Koob, "My Time at El Cid"; Nick Smith, "The Citadel Gay and Lesbian Alliance Welcomes Former and Current Cadets," *Charleston City Paper*, Oct. 13, 2008, 36–37.

49. Alex Macauley, *Marching in Step*, 210–11, 215.

50. On the evolution of military policy regarding race and the larger civil rights movement, see Moye, *Freedom Flyers*.

CHAPTER 6

1. The phrase "seeing the elephant" was first used decades before the Civil War to mean any number of adventures or fools' errands. It was especially popular among 49ers during the California Gold Rush. For more on the phrase, see Holliday, *The World Rushed In*, 116; Horwitz, *Confederates in the Attic*, 165.

2. Lassiter, *The Silent Majority*; Kruse, *White Flight*; Crespino, *In Search of Another Country*; Lassiter and Crespino, eds., *The Myth of Southern Exceptionalism*.

3. For more on Confederate memory and southern politics, see Poole, *Never Surrender*, 197, 203–7; Goldfield, *Still Fighting the Civil War*, 40, 302–4, 312–14.

4. Gaboury, "George Washington Murray and the Fight for Political Democracy in South Carolina"; McGee interview with author (2008); C. Bruce Littlejohn, "The Re-Arising of the Republican Party in South Carolina," Address to the University of South Caroliniana Society (1999), in Modern Political Collections, University of South Carolina (herafter MPC).

5. Carter, *The Politics of Rage*, 218; Black and Black, *The Rise of Southern Republicans*, 139–41; Crespino, *Strom Thurmond's America*, 165–84. Crespino suggests that Thurmond became a Republican, in part, because he might have faced a strong challenge in his next Democratic primary race two years later.

6. Ravenel interview with author (2011).

7. Ibid. Bass and Poole, *The Palmetto State*, 134.

8. Press release and notes (January 1974), "Ronald Reagan Visit" Folder, Box 1, Republican Party of South Carolina (RPSC) Papers, SCPC; Barbara Williams, "Reagan Optimistic for GOP Chances," *New and Courier*, Jan. 24, 1974.

9. "Observations on the Political Situation in the First Congressional District of South Carolina" (1980) and Hartnett Campaign Announcement Draft (1980) in Hartnett Files, Box 22, RPSC Papers, SCPC. League of Women Voters interview with Tommy Hartnett (1981) and Arthur Ravenel Jr. (1987) in Congressional Delegation Interview Files, Box 20, League of Women Voters Papers, SCPC. Ravenel actually supported some affirmative action programs, while Hartnett opposed them.

10. Phillips, *The Emerging Republican Majority*, 468; McGee interview with author (2008).

11. For a critique of racial messaging on welfare and other issues, see Mendelberg, *The Race Card*, 6, 10–11. Hartnett Campaign Announcement Draft (1980) in Hartnett Files, Box 22, RPSC Papers, SCPC. League of Women Voters interview with Tommy Hartnett (1981) and Arthur Ravenel Jr. (1987) in Congressional Delegation Interview Files, Box 20, League of Women Voters Papers, SCPC; Hartnett interviewed

by Dan Carter, included in Carter's expert testimony, *U.S. v. Charleston County Council*, Civil Action No. 2-01 0155 11 (2001), 37.

12. Dan Carter expert testimony, *U.S. v. Charleston County Council*, Civil Action No. 2-01 0155 11 (2001), 21–22, 26–28; *U.S. v. Charleston County*, 316 F.Supp.2d 268 (D.S.C. 203), 287–89, 295–96.

13. Ray Harris letter to John N. Hardee, December 3, 1970, Elections 1970 File, Box 16, RPSC Papers, SCPC; Memo from Jim Duffy to Ken Powell, March 5, 1971, Powell File, Box 5, RPSC Papers, SCPC; Executive Committee Meeting Minutes, January 28, 1978, Republican Party Committees File, Box 9, RPSC Papers, SCPC.

14. "Remarks by Earl Douglas," April 8, 1978, 1978 State Convention File, Box 12, RPSC Papers, SCPC.

15. Theodore Arrington expert testimony, *U.S. v. Charleston County* (2003), 16, 26–27, 60; Dan Carter expert testimony, *U.S. v. Charleston County* (2003), 29; Ravenel interview with author (2011).

16. Executive Committee Meeting Minutes, April 29, 1978, Republican Party Committees 1978 File, Box 9, RPSC Papers, SCPC.

17. Clayton, *African Americans and the Politics of Congressional Redistricting*, 16–17, 38. With a Democratic majority, Charleston County Council moved to at-large elections in 1967, two years after the passage of the Voting Rights Act. Dan Carter expert testimony, *U.S. v. Charleston County Council* (Civil Action No. 2-01 0155 11, August 31, 2001), 26.

18. "Carter Sees Two Options in Reapportionment Issue," *Greenville News*, Feb. 23, 1974; "Justice Department Gives Primary Green Light" *Columbia Record*, June 22, 1974; Burton, "Legislative and Congressional Districting in South Carolina," 298.

19. "Campbell: Flag Support not Political," *Greenville News*, March 31, 1994; Goldfield, *Still Fighting the Civil War*, 313–14. For more on Civil War's influence on South Carolina politics, see Poole, *Never Surrender*.

20. Joe Wilson, "Reapportionment: A Sleeping Giant," *Carolina Republican* [n.d.]; Tim Flach, "Redistricting Impasse Sparks State GOP Suit," *Greenville News*, Oct. 5, 1991.

21. Clayton, *African Americans and the Politics of Redistricting*, 41–42; Grofman, ed., *Race and Redistricting in the 1990s*, 2–3; Burke, *Racial Gerrymandering, Redistricting, and the Supreme Court*, 71–78.

22. Clayton, *African Americans and the Politics of Redistricting*, xi, 114; Arthur Ravenel Jr., "Clyburn Helped by Gerrymandering," letter to *Post and Courier*, Aug. 24, 1993; Steve Piacente, "Is District Better Off with Clyburn?" *Post and Courier*, June 11, 1995.

23. Burke, *Racial Gerrymandering, Redistricting and the Supreme Court*, 8–9, 97; Clayton, *African Americans and the Politics of Redistricting*, 66, 104–6, 126, 130; *Shaw v. Reno*, 509 U.S. 630 (1993); *Miller v. Johnson*, 515 U.S. 900 (1995).

24. Patrick letter to Robert J. Sheheen, speaker of the South Carolina House, May 2, 1994, Issues: Redistricting File, Box 25, RPSC Papers, SCPC; Burton, "Legislative and Congressional Districting in South Carolina," 309–11.

25. Burton, "Legislative and Congressional Districting in South Carolina," 311–13; Black and Black, *The Rise of Southern Republicans*, 26–27; "Elected Officials Who

Have Switched to the Republican Party," *Carolina Republican*, May 1990, *Carolina Republican* File, Box 7 RPSC Papers, SCPC; Dale Perry, "Aiken County Representative Becomes Second to Switch to GOP within Week," *Greenville News*, Aug. 18, 1993.

26. Robert Tanner, "State's Political Evolution Shaped by Race and Money," *State*, Aug. 22, 1993; Cindi Ross Scoppe, "28 Democrats Have Joined GOP Ranks," *State*, Sept. 15, 1991; Nina Brook, "GOP to Rule S.C. House," *State* Nov. 15, 1994; "Senator Hayes Latest Democrat to Convert," *Greenwood Index-Journal*, Dec. 1, 1994; Warren Wise, "Census Results to Alter Districts, GOP Power," *Post and Courier*, Dec. 11, 2000.

27. Burton, "Legislative and Congressional Districting in South Carolina," 309–10; Whipper interview with author (2009); Bailey interview with author (2008).

28. Ravenel interview with author (2011); McConnell interview with author (2008).

29. McConnell interview with author (2008); Whipper interview with author (2009); Ford interview with author (2008); Ken Riley interview with author (2008).

30. McConnell interview with author (2008); Nina Brook, "Two Senators Lead Pro-Flag Ad Charge," *State*, Nov. 12, 1993; Yvonne Wenger, "The Odd Couple," *Post and Courier*, Jan. 14, 2009.

31. Ford interview with author (2008); John Heilprin, "Charleston Activist, Columbia Statesman," *Post and Courier*, Sept. 7, 1997.

32. McConnell interview with author (2008); Ford interview with author (2008); Yvonne Wenger, "The Odd Couple," *Post and Courier*, Jan. 14, 2009; John Heilprin, "Charleston Activist, Columbia Statesman," *Post and Courier*, Sept. 7, 1997.

33. Nina Brook, "2 Senators Lead Pro-Flag Ad Charge," *State*, Nov. 12, 1993; "Who Is behind the Plot to Remove Our Heroic Flag" (advertisement), *Spartanburg Herald-Journal*, Aug. 8, 1994; Betsy Peoples, "Republicans Support Keeping Battle Flag," *Spartanburg Herald-Journal*, Aug. 10, 1994.

34. "Democrats Want Flag Removed," *Post and Courier*, May 8, 1994; Tim Flach, "Campbell: Flag Support Not Political," *Greenville News*, March 31, 1994; "Flag Debate Brings Words of Hate," *Post and Courier*, Feb. 24, 1997; Cindi Ross Scoppe and Lee Brandy, "Beasley's Lost Cause," *State*, July 13, 1997; Daniel Wells and Holmes "Brad" Epting letters to Henry McMaster, SC GOP Chairman, June 1997, in McMaster 1997 File, Box 5, RPSC Papers, SCPC.

35. Joe Darby interview with author (2008).

36. Rachel Graves, "McConnell Defends Capitol's Confederate Flag," *Post and Courier*, Aug. 29, 2009; Schuyler Kropf, "Senator Apologizes to Mentally Disabled, Not NAACP," Jan. 11, 2000; Ravenel interview with author (2011).

37. Rachel Graves, "Riley, Coble Offer Flag Compromise," *Post and Courier*, Sept. 4, 1999; Riley Jr. interview with author (2008); Marlon Manuel, "SC Flag March Ends in War of Words," *Atlanta Journal-Constitution*, April 7, 2000; David Firestone, "Long March Ends in South Carolina," *New York Times*, April 7, 2000. For more on the politics of Confederate memory and the flag, see Goldfield, *Still Fighting the Civil War*, 302–4, 312–14.

38. McConnell interview with author (2008); Ford interview with author (2008); Joe Darby interview with author (2008); Warren Wheat, "Cadets Will Lower Confederate Flag," *State*, June 28, 2000; "Finality on the Flag," *Post and Courier*, July 2, 2000. McConnell was quick to say that there was no quid pro quo agreement to build an

African American history monument in exchange for putting the flag in front of the capitol.

39. McConnell interview with author (2008); Ford interview with author (2008); Whipper interview with author (2009); Darby interview with author (2008); Yvonne Wenger, "The Odd Couple," *Post and Courier*, Jan. 14, 2009; Wenger, "Senator Ford to Celebrate Civil War Anniversary," *Post and Courier*, April 7, 2011.

40. *Northwest Austin Municipal Utility District Number One v. Eric Holder, et al.* (No. 08-322) Oral Arguments, April 29, 2009; *Northwest Austin Municipal Utility District v. Holder*, 573 F. Supp., 2d 221; Adam Liptak, "Supreme Court Invalidates Key Part of Voting Rights Act," *New York Times*, June 25, 2013.

CHAPTER 7

1. Charleston Police Department video, January 19–20, 2000, in the Charleston Five Collection, ARC. For a news reporter's perspective, see Suzan Erem interview with Tony Bartelme (2005), Charleston Five Collection, ARC; Tony Bartelme, "Water Front Riot," *Post and Courier*, Jan. 20, 2000.

2. Ibid.

3. Erem and Durrenberger, *On the Global Waterfront*; Cowie, *Capital Moves*, 2; Cowie, *Stayin' Alive*.

4. Poliakoff, "Charleston's Longshoremen." For more on the connection between labor and civil rights, see Korstad, *Civil Rights Unionism*; Honey, *Going Down Jericho Road*.

5. United States War Department, "The Port of Charleston, S.C." (U.S. Army and U.S. Maritime Commission, 1940), 101–5, Charleston Five Collection, ARC; Poliakoff, "Charleston's Longshoremen," 260–61. For more on racial segregation of the unions, see Suzan Erem interview with Larry Young (2005), Charleston Five Collection, ARC.

6. U.S. Equal Opportunity Commission, "Equal Employment Opportunity Report: Job Patterns for Minorities and Women in Private Industry, Volume 2" (1970), 109–11.

7. Ken Riley interview with author (2008).

8. Ken Riley interview with author (2008); Leonard Riley interview with author (2009).

9. Ibid.

10. Tony Bartelme, "Thinking inside the Box; Trailers Changed Industry," *Post and Courier*, May 21, 2000; "East Coast Ports," *Journal of Commerce*, Aug. 30, 2004; "U.S. Waterborne Foreign Container Trade by U.S. Customs Ports," Charleston Five Collection, ARC; Chris Sosnowski, "Death at the Port; 22-Ton Container Falls on Truck Driver," *Post and Courier*, Aug. 14, 1997; Ken Riley interview with author (2008).

11. Ford and Stone, "Economic Development and Globalization in South Carolina."

12. Cobb, *The South and America since World War II*, 209–10; Ford and Stone, "Economic Development and Globalization in South Carolina"; Erem and Durrenberger, *On the Global Waterfront*, 94–95. The German corporation Bosch was the biggest private manufacturing interest in the Lowcountry in the 1990s, according to the "Manufacturers Directory: Charleston Region, South Carolina" (Charleston Chamber of Commerce, 1996), 10.

13. "The Charleston Region: Major Employers Directory" (Charleston Chamber of Commerce, 1997), 5. The loss of the Navy shipyard was offset somewhat by the relocation of the Space and Naval Warfare Systems Center (SPAWAR) Atlantic Head Quarters to Charleston in the 2000s. "SPAWAR Reorganizes with Division HQ in Charleston," *Charleston Regional Business Journal*, Sept. 29, 2008.

14. Linda L. Meggett, "Perks of Coastal Living Add Up to Tourist Dollars," *Post and Courier*, Feb. 28, 1999; Denesha Graham, "Tourists Signal Unofficial Summer," *Post and Courier*, June 1, 1999; Lacher and Oh, "Is Tourism a Low-Income Industry?" Black participation rates in the Charleston service sector were 51.9 percent (1990), 52.8 percent (2000), and 49.79 percent (2010). The decline in the 2000s was partly a result of the growing number of Latino workers in this industry (3.4 percent in 2010). "Job Patterns for Minorities and Women in Private Industry" (Equal Employment Opportunity Commission, 1990), 460; "Job Patterns for Minorities and Women in Private Industry: 2000 EEO-1 Aggregate Report, Charleston–North Charleston, SC MSA" (Equal Employment Opportunity Commission, 2000); "Job Patterns for Minorities and Women in Private Industry: 2010 EEO-1 Aggregate Report Charleston–North Charleston, SC" (Equal Employment Opportunity Commission, 2010); Darby interview with author (2008).

15. "Job Patterns for Minorities and Women in Private Industry: Volume 2" (Equal Opportunity Commission, 1970), 111; "Job Patterns for Minorities and Women in Private Industry: 2000 EEO-1 Aggregate Report, Charleston–North Charleston, SC MSA" (Equal Employment Opportunity Commission, 2000); "South Carolina Community Profiles: Family Income in Charleston County" and "South Carolina Community Profiles: Poverty Status by Race in Charleston County" (South Carolina Budget and Control Board, 2002). Poverty rates among African Americans in Charleston County in 1999 were more than three times higher than white rates, with 29.9 percent of the black population below the poverty line compared to 8.7 percent of white Charlestonians. This did reflect a decline of African American poverty rates from 34.2 percent in 1989. The growing number of African Americans in white-collar jobs was a phenomenon replicated across the cities of the South, but not so much in the rural areas. By 1990, 37 percent of black urban workers had white-collar positions, a 25 percent increase in the 1980s alone. Cobb, *The South and America since World War II*, 189–90.

16. "Atlanta in Focus: A Profile from the 2000 Census" (Washington, D.C.: Brookings Institution, 2003), 58. Income data from the 2000 Census of Population and Housing, searchable by city as "Historical Median Income by Races Data," http://www.usa.com/charleston-sc-income-and-careers—historical-median-household-income-by-races-data.htm, July 10, 2013. Savannah and Richmond had smaller racial gaps ($14,000 and $15,000, respectively).

17. Tony Bartelme, "Thinking inside the Box; Trailers Changed Industry," *Post and Courier*, May 21, 2000; Erem and Durrenberger, *On the Global Waterfront*, 33–37, 42–47, 65.

18. Tony Bartelme and Herb Frazier, "Dockworkers Protest," *Post and Courier*, Dec. 2, 1999; Ken Riley interview with author (2008); "Memorandum from SPA Police Chief Captain Lindy Rinaldi to Anne Moise of SPA," Jan. 5, 2000, SPA Police Report by Sgt. Cishek (undated), Affidavits of Malcolm Barnwell and Don Elliot, WSI em-

ployees, Jan. 11, 2000, Charleston Five Collection, ARC; Tony Bartelme, "Workers Storm SPA Terminal," *Post and Courier*, Jan. 4, 2000.

19. "Memorandum from Captain Rinaldi to Mrs. Moise," Jan. 5, 2000, Charleston Five Collection, ARC; Erem and Durrenberger, *On the Global Waterfront*, 41, 46–47; Tony Bartelme, "Waterfront Riot," *Post and Courier*, Jan. 20, 2000.

20. Bernard Groseclose letter to Captain Reginald Gosnell, Jan. 10, 2000, SLED Notes, January 3, 2000, "Operations Plan—South Carolina Department of Public Safety" (no date), "Statement of Facts," Charleston Police Department, Jan. 19, 2000, Charleston Five Collection, ARC.

21. Erem and Durrenberger, *On the Global Waterfront*, 16; Charleston Police Department video (Jan. 19–20, 2000), Charleston Five Collection, ARC.

22. Charleston Police Department video (Jan. 19–20, 2000), Charleston Five Collection, ARC. This video is six hours long, with several different angles shot by multiple police and news media cameras over the course of the day and night of January 19–20, 2000. See also Erem and Durrenberger, *On the Global Waterfront*, 28–31; Tony Bartelme, "Waterfront Riot," *Post and Courier*, Jan. 20, 2000.

23. Charleston Police Department video (Jan. 19–20, 2000), Charleston Five Collection, ARC; Erem and Durrenberger, *On the Global Waterfront*, 28–31; Tony Bartelme, "Waterfront Riot," *Post and Courier*, Jan. 20, 2000; Reuben Greenberg interview with author, Dec. 9, 2006; "Ltc. Edward L. Hethington Statement," Jan. 27, 2000, Charleston Five Collection, ARC.

24. Charleston Police Department video (Jan. 19–20, 2000), Charleston Five Collection, ARC; Tony Bartelme, "Waterfront Riot," *Post and Courier*, Jan. 20, 2000.

25. Charleston Police Department Jail Log (January); R. A. Vance, "Charleston Police Department Supplementary Report (OCA #0001396)," Jan. 20, 2000; Michael S. Niblock, "CPD Witness Statement," Jan. 27, 2000; Cpl. Christine Middleton, "CPD Witness Statement," Jan. 27, 2000; S. M. Dutton, "CPD Witness Statement," Jan. 27, 2000; Det. Jeff Osburn, "Arrest Warrant for Kenneth Jefferson," Feb. 1, 2000, all in the Charleston Five Collection, ARC. "Not saints" quote from Erem and Durrenberger, *On the Global Waterfront*, 162. CPD booking reports listed known prior offenses for those arrested on January 20. Kenneth Jefferson was arrested weeks after the demonstrations based primarily on a photo published in the *Post and Courier* on January 21, 2000, and a corroborating statement by a CPD officer.

26. "Condon Says Union Rioters Who Attack Police Will Be Put 'Under the Jail,'" Office of the Attorney General, Jan. 20, 2000; "Condon Announces Charges Upgraded for ILA Rioters," Office of the Attorney General, Jan. 21, 2000; "Statement of Attorney General Condon on Magistrate's Decision to Dismiss Dock Riot Charges," Office of the Attorney General, Feb. 1, 2000, in the Charleston Five Collection, ARC.

27. Richard Green, "No Confusing the AG Candidates," *Post and Courier*, Sept. 20, 1998; Schuyler Kropf, "Charged Words May Color Condon Campaign," *Post and Courier*, Feb. 11, 2001; Schuyler Kropf, "Condon Drops Lawsuit against the NAACP," *Post and Courier*, Sept. 5, 2002; Suzan Erem interview with Tony Bartelme, Feb. 9, 2005; "South Carolina Attorney General Charlie Condon Radio Advertisement Transcript," Charleston Five Collection, ARC; Erem and Durrenberger, *On the Global Waterfront*, 98–99, 126. Charlie Condon did not respond to interview requests from this author.

28. Lee Sustar, "Why You Should Defend the Charleston Five" (Chicago: Center for Economic Research and Social Change, 2001), 10–11.

29. Eric Frazier, "Residents Say Their Street Has a Future," *Post and Courier*, Sept. 18, 1995; Glenn Smith, "Revival of America Street," *Post and Courier*, Sept. 11, 2011. The 1990 Census of Population and Housing statistics for racial demographics come from census tracts 9 and 13.

30. Kruse, *White Flight*. For numbers on suburbanization, see "Gentrification Task Force Report" (City of Charleston Department of Planning and Neighborhoods, July 2001), 5; Mount Pleasant demographics from the 2000 Census of Population and Housing; "Regional Indicators, 1992–1993: Population, Income, Employment, Construction" (North Charleston, S.C.: Berkeley, Charleston, Dorchester Council of Governments, 1993). Suburbanization spread to Berkeley and Dorchester Counties by the 1970s and 1980s. The population of Goose Creek (Berkeley County) rose from 3,656 in 1970 to 24,692 in 1990. Similarly, the population of Summerville (Dorchester County) rose from 3,839 to 22,519.

31. "Census Tract 26.05 Profile," South Carolina Community Profiles, SC Budget and Control Board (data from the 2000 Census of Population and Housing); Jason A. Zwiker, "Neighborhood Watch: The Historic Village of Maryville-Ashleyville Fights to Keep Its Identity," *Charleston City Paper*, Nov. 3, 2004; Barney Blakeney, "Another View, Segregation, Integration, Gentrification," *Charleston City Paper*, May 23, 2007; Suzan Erem interview with Peter Wilbourne and Armand Derfner (2005), Charleston Five Collection, ARC.

32. Kevin Sack, "Birthplace of Klan Chooses a Black Mayor," *New York Times*, Nov. 22, 1997; Ehrenhalt, *The Great Inversion and the Future of the American City*, 91–92, 97; "Atlanta in Focus: A Profile from the 2000 Census" (Washington, D.C.: Brookings Institution, 2003), 18; Johnson, *Black Power in the Suburbs*, 1, 4–5; Wiese, "African American Suburbanization and Regionalism in the Modern South."

33. Ehrenhalt, *The Great Inversion*, 3–4; Sugrue, *The Origins of the Urban Crisis*; "Gentrification Task Force Report" (City of Charleston Department of Planning and Neighborhoods, July 2001), 3–5.

34. "Gentrification Task Force Report" (City of Charleston Department of Planning and Neighborhoods, July 2001), 6–7; Bures, "Historic Preservation, Gentrification, and Tourism," 196, 204–7.

35. Brian Hicks, "Task Force Tries to Slow—Not Stop—Gentrification," *Post and Courier*, Aug. 7, 2000; Regina M. Bures and Colleen Cain, "Dimensions of Gentrification in a Tourist City," paper proposal for the 2008 meeting of the Population Association of America, 6.

36. Joseph P. Riley Jr., "Text of Letter to Campbell," *Post and Courier*, Aug. 2, 2000; Clay Barbour, "The Forces That Define Kwadjo Campbell," *Post and Courier*, Sept. 17, 2000; Kwadjo Campbell, "Commentary: Councilman Says His Complaints 'Far from Unfounded,'" *Post and Courier*, April 1, 2001; Kwadjo Campbell interview with author (2013).

37. Jason Hardin, "Defining Downtown's 'Black Exodus,'" *Post and Courier*, April 15, 2001; "North Charleston Comprehensive Plan Update" (Atlanta: Robert and Company, 2008), 12–13.

38. Ken Riley, "Propeller Club Speech" (January 2000), Charleston Five Collection, ARC.

39. Erem and Durrenberger, *On the Global Waterfront*, 84–86; Tony Bartelme, "Shipper, ILA End Standoff," *Post and Courier*, April 19, 2000.

40. "Remarks by ILA Local 1422 President Kenneth Riley to the ILWU Longshore Caucus," March 1, 2000; David Bacon, "Charleston—The Front Line for Labor Rights" an interview with Ken Riley and Bill Fletcher, July 15, 2001; Michael Honey, "An Interview with Ken Riley," July 19, 2001, in the Charleston Five Collection, ARC; Tony Bartelme, "Remaining 'Charleston 5' Make Plea Bargain," *Post and Courier*, Nov. 9, 2001; Tony Bartelme, "World's Dockworkers Gather in Charleston," *Post and Courier*, March 6, 2002.

41. "Condon Responds to Charges by S.C. Progressive Network Concerning the Five Defendants Indicted for Riot in Charleston," press release by the Office of the Attorney General, May 31, 2001; transcript excerpt of "Live Five Talk Back with Charlie Condon," October 3, 2001, Charleston Five Collection, ARC; Tony Bartelme, "Rally for Longshoremen," *Post and Courier*, June 10, 2001; Andy Savage interview with author (2011); Armand Derfner interview with author (2013).

42. Letter from Andrew Savage to Armand Derfner and Lionel Lofton, July 16, 2001; "Defendant's Motion to Quash the Indictment or to Disqualify the Attorney General," *State of South Carolina versus Kenneth Jefferson and Jason Newman Edgerton*, Oct. 2, 2001; "State's Memorandum in Opposition to Defendant's Motion to Quash the Indictment or to Disqualify the Attorney General and Supplement," *State of South Carolina versus Kenneth Jefferson and Jason Newman Edgerton*, Oct. 11, 2001; Tony Bartelme, "Condon Gives Up Charleston Five Case," *Post and Courier*, Oct. 11, 2001.

43. Bartelme, "Condon Gives Up Charleston Five Case," Oct. 11, 2001; Erem and Durrenberger, *On the Global Waterfront*, 147–65; Solicitor Walter Bailey letters to Andrew Savage and Lionel Lofton, Oct. 25, 2001 and Nov. 1, 2001, and Andrew Savage letter to Bailey, Nov. 6, 2001, in the Charleston Five Collection, ARC.

44. Robert Behre, "New Longshoreman's Hall Impressive," *Post and Courier*, Sept. 2, 2002; Schuyler Kropf and Brian Hicks, "Gubernatorial Hopefuls to Meet on June 25," *Post and Courier*, June 12, 2002; Schuyler Kropf, "Demint's Rivals Likely to End Run in Politics," *Post and Courier*, June 24, 2004; Robert Behre, "Condon SPA Slot Opposed," *Post and Courier*, May 3, 2007; Erem and Durrenberger, *On the Global Waterfront*, 165, 177–79, 186–89.

45. David Bacon, "Charleston—The Front Line for Labor," July 15, 2001; Erem interview with Johnny Alvanos (2005), in the Charleston Five Collection, ARC.

CONCLUSION

1. Greenberg interview with author (2006); Green interview with author (2009).

2. Robinson, *Disintegration*; "Household Income in the Past 12 Months (Black or African American Alone Householder)," American Community Survey, U.S. Census Bureau, 2010.

3. Phillip Caston, "Local NAACP Seeks Greenberg Apology," *Post and Courier*, Jan. 10, 2004; Darby interview with author (2008).

4. For more on free people of color in the antebellum period, including slave owners, see Johnson and Roark, *Black Masters* and *No Chariot Let Down*. Dulaney interview with author (2008).

5. "South Carolina Commission on Women," http://www.oepp.sc.gov/sccw/index. html, Aug. 15, 2012.

6. Yvonne Wenger, "Debate Rages over South Carolina's Voter ID Law," *Post and Courier*, May 19, 2011; Michael Winter, "Justice Dept. Rejects South Carolina Voter ID Law," *USA Today*, Dec. 23, 2011; Thomas E. Perez, assistant attorney general of the United States, letter to C Havarid Jones Jr., assistant deputy attorney general of South Carolina, Dec. 23, 2011, archived at the Brennan Center for Justice, New York University, http://brennan.3cdn.net/594b9cf4396be7ebc8_0pm6i2fx6.pdf, Aug. 20, 2012. Five members of the Lowcountry delegation missed the vote on this law. One white Republican and one black Democrat who were not there noted that they would have voted for and against it, respectively. Ultimately, the Supreme Court struck down the section of the Voting Rights Act that required DOJ preclearance of voting law changes in places like South Carolina that had a history of voter discrimination. Adam Liptak, "Supreme Court Invalidates Key Part of Voting Rights Act," *New York Times*, June 25, 2013.

7. Katherine Q. Seelye, "South Carolina Candidate Shrugs off History's Lure," *New York Times*, June 25, 2010; "South Carolina Elects Black GOP Congressman," *Washington Post*, Nov. 2, 2010; Schuyler Kropf, "Scott Won't Be Part of Caucus," *Post and Courier*, Dec. 2, 2010; Stephen Largen and Schuyler Kropf, "Haley Picks Scott to Replace DeMint," *Post and Courier*, Dec. 18, 2012.

8. Largen and Kropf, "Haley Picks Scott to Replace DeMint," *Post and Courier*, Dec. 18, 2012; Frank Wooten, "Scott Accentuates the Positive," *Post and Courier*, Jan. 5, 2013; Katy Stetch and David Slade, "Boeing's Whopping Incentives," *Post and Courier*, Jan. 17, 2010; Warren Wise and Bo Peterson, "Solomon, Boeing Retaliated," *Post and Courier*, June 18, 2011; Brendan Kearny, "Ex-Boeing Worker Claims Racism and Retaliation," *Post and Courier*, Feb. 12, 2012; http://www.boeing.com/boeing /commercial/charleston/index.page, July 16, 2013.

9. Brian Hicks, "Riley's City Already a Great One," *Post and Courier*, Jan. 11, 2012; "Inaugural Address Mayor Joseph P. Riley, Jr.," Jan. 9, 2012, 11; Jeanne Cummings, "Freshmen Learn to Use Bills the DC Way," *Politico*, April 21, 2011.

10. "Median Income in the Past 12 Months" (Charleston County), American Community Survey, U.S. Census Bureau, 2010; Rosen interview with author (2009); McFarland interview with author (2010); Whipper interview with author (2009); Bailey interview with author (2008).

Bibliography

AUTHOR INTERVIEWS

Alan Ali

John Graham Altman

Anonymous (4)

Jimmy Bailey

Casey Behrendt

Isaiah Bennett

Sol Blatt Jr.

John Bourne Jr.

Pat Brennan

Jonathan Brilliant

Gene Burges

Kwadjo Campbell

Al Cannon

Joseph Darby

Armand Derfner

Eric Doss

Marvin Dulaney

Susan Dunn

Ligure "Duke" Ellington

Susan R. Emge

Robert Ford

Damon Fordham

Dorothy Tincken Green

Dwayne Green

Reuben Greenberg

Nancy Hawk

Ned Hethington

Sara Horne-
   Greenberg

Jesse Jefferson

Joe Johnson

Sandy Krings

Joel Lake

Alex Macauley

Keith Major

Glenn McConnell

Arthur C. McFarland

Joseph "Peter" McGee

Mohamed Melhem

Mary Moultrie

Jermel President

Arthur Ravenel Jr.

Joe Riley

Ken Riley

Leonard Riley

Robert Rosen

Andy Savage

Kevin Scott

Jabari Spruill

Tim Street

Herb Whetsell

Lucille Whipper

Naomi White

Chad Youngblood

ARCHIVES

ARC   Avery Research Center for African American History and Culture,
       College of Charleston

CCPL   South Carolina Room, Charleston County Public Library

COHP   Citadel Oral History Program, The Citadel

NARA   National Archives and Records Administration

SCHS   South Carolina Historical Society

SCPC   South Carolina Political Collections, University of South Carolina

NEWSPAPERS AND PERIODICALS

Atlanta Journal-
   Constitution

Brigadier (Citadel)

Charleston Chronicle

Charleston City Paper

Charleston Mercury

Charleston Post and
   Courier

Charlotte Observer

Christian Science
   Monitor

Columbia Record

Ebony
Greenville News
Newsweek
New York Times

New Yorker
Spartanburg Herald-
    Journal
State (Columbia, S.C.)

Time
Washington Post

BOOKS

Abernathy, Ralph. *And the Walls Came Tumbling Down*. New York: Harper & Row, 1989.

Andrew, Rod. *Long Gray Lines: The Southern Military School Tradition, 1839–1915*. Chapel Hill: University of North Carolina Press, 2001.

Andrews, Sidney. *The South since the War*. Boston: Ticknor and Fields, 1866.

Baker, Gary. *Cadets in Gray: The Story of the Cadets of the South Carolina Military Academy and the Cadet Rangers in the Civil War*. Columbia, S.C.: Palmetto Bookworks, 1989.

Baker, R. Scott. *Paradoxes of Desegregation: African American Struggles for Educational Equality in Charleston, South Carolina, 1926–1972*. Columbia: University of South Carolina, 2006.

Ball, Edward. *Slaves in the Family*. New York: Ballantine, 1998.

Banfield, Edward C. *The Unheavenly City: The Nature and Future of Our Urban Crisis*. Boston: Little Brown, 1970.

Bass, Jack, and Scott Poole. *The Palmetto State: The Making of Modern South Carolina*. Columbia: University of South Carolina Press, 2009.

Baumer, William H., Jr. *West Point: Molder of Men*. New York: D. Appleton-Century, 1942.

Bell, Derrick. *Silent Covenants: Brown v. Board of Education and the Unfulfilled Hopes for Racial Reform*. New York: Oxford University Press, 2005.

Berger, John Charles, and Gary Orfield, eds. *School Resegregation: Must the South Turn Back*. Chapel Hill: University of North Carolina Press, 2005.

Black, Earl, and Merle Black. *The Rise of Southern Republicans*. Cambridge: Harvard University Press, 2002.

Bolton, Kenneth, and Joe Feagin. *Black in Blue: African American Police Officers and Racism*. London: Routledge, 2004.

Bond, O. J. *The Story of The Citadel*. Richmond: Garrett and Massie, 1932.

Brodkin, Karen. *How Jews Became White Folks & What That Says about Race in America*. New Brunswick, N.J.: Rutgers University Press, 1998.

Brundage, W. Fitzhugh. *The Southern Past: A Clash of Race and Memory*. New York: Belknap Press, 2005.

Burke, Christopher M. *Racial Gerrymandering, Redistricting, and the Supreme Court*. Westport, Conn.: Greenwood Press, 1999.

Carawan, Guy, and Candie Carawan, eds. *Ain't You Got a Right to the Tree of Life?* Athens: University of Georgia Press, 1989.

Carter, Dan T. *The Politics of Rage: George Wallace, the Origins of the New Conservatism, and the Transformation of American Politics*. New York: Simon & Schuster, 1995.

Cash, W. J. *The Mind of The South*. New York: Vintage, 1941, 1991.

Cecelski, David. *Along Freedom Road: Hyde County, North Carolina, and the Fate of Black Schools in the South*. Chapel Hill: University of North Carolina Press, 1994.

Chafe, William H. *Civilities and Civil Rights: Greensboro, North Carolina and the Black Struggle for Freedom*. Oxford: Oxford University Press, 1980.

Charron, Katherine Mellon. *Freedom's Teacher: The Life of Septima Clark*. Chapel Hill: University of North Carolina Press, 2009.

Chauncey, George. *Why Marriage: The History Shaping Today's Debate over Gay Marriage*. New York: Basic Books, 2004.

Clark, Septima, and Cynthia Stokes Brown. *Ready from Within: A First Person Narrative, Septima Clark and the Civil Rights Movement*. Trenton, N.J.: Africa World Press, 1990.

Clayton, Dewey M. *African Americans and the Politics of Congressional Redistricting*. New York: Garland, 2000.

Cobb, James. *Away Down South: A History of Southern Identity*. Oxford: Oxford University Press, 2005.

———. *The South and America since World War II*. Oxford: Oxford University Press, 2011.

Coclanis, Peter. *The Shadow of a Dream: Economic Life and Death in the South Carolina Low Country, 1670–1920*. Oxford: Oxford University Press, 1989.

Collier-Thomas, Bettye, and V. P. Franklin, eds. *Sisters in the Struggle: African American Women in the Civil Rights–Black Power Movement*. New York: New York University Press, 2001.

Conroy, Pat. *The Lords of Discipline*. Boston: Houghton Mifflin, 1980.

Cowie, Jefferson. *Capital Moves: RCA's Seventy-Year Quest for Cheap Labor*. New York: New Press, 2001.

———. *Stayin' Alive: The 1970s and the Last Days of the Working Class*. New York: New Press, 2010.

Crawford, Vicki L., Jacqueline Rouse, and Barbara Woods, eds. *Women in the Civil Rights Movement: Trailblazers and Torchbearers, 1941–1965*. Brooklyn, N.Y.: Carlson, 1990.

Crespino, Joseph. *In Search of Another Country: Mississippi and the Conservative Counterrevolution*. Princeton, N.J.: Princeton University Press, 2007.

———. *Strom Thurmond's America*. New York: Hill and Wang, 2012.

D'Emilio, John. *Lost Prophet: The Life and Times of Bayard Rustin*. New York: Free Press, 2010.

Dittmer, John. *Local People: The Struggle for Civil Rights in Mississippi*. Chicago: University of Illinois Press, 1995.

Dulaney, W. Marvin. *Black Police in America*. Bloomington: Indiana University Press, 1996.

Edgar, Walter. *South Carolina: A History*. Columbia: University of South Carolina Press, 1998.

Ehrenhalt, Alan. *The Great Inversion and the Future of the American City*. New York: Knopf, 2012.

Ehrenreich, Barbara. *The Hearts of Men: American Dreams and the Flight from Commitment*. New York: Anchor Books, 1987.

Erem, Suzan, and E. Paul Durrenberger. *On the Global Waterfront: The Fight to Free the Charleston Five*. New York: Monthly Review Press, 2008.

Eskew, Glenn T. *But for Birmingham: The Local and National Movements in the Civil Rights Struggle*. Chapel Hill: University of North Carolina Press, 1997.

Evans, Eli N. *The Provincials: A Personal History of Jews in the South*. New York: Atheneum, 1973.

Evans, Sara. *Personal Politics: The Roots of Women's Liberation in the Civil Rights Movement and the New Left*. New York: Vintage, 1980.

Fairclough, Adam. *To Redeem the Soul of America: The Southern Christian Leadership Conference and Martin Luther King*. Athens: University of Georgia Press, 1987.

Faludi, Susan. *Stiffed: The Betrayal of the American Man*. New York: Harper Perennial, 2000.

Fields, Mamie Garvin. *Lemon Swamp and Other Places: A Carolina Memoir*. New York: Free Press, 1983.

Fink, Leon, and Brian Greenburg. *Upheaval in the Quiet Zone: A History of the Hospital Workers' Union, Local 1199*. Urbana: University of Illinois Press, 1989.

Franklin, John Hope. *The Militant South, 1800–1861*. Cambridge: Belknap Press of Harvard University Press, 1956.

Fraser, Walter J., Jr. *Charleston! Charleston! The History of a Southern City*. Columbia: University of South Carolina Press, 1989.

———. *Lowcountry Hurricanes: Three Centuries of Storms at Sea and Ashore*. Athens: University of Georgia Press, 2006.

Gaillard, J. Palmer. *Boards to Boardrooms: The Life and Memoirs of J. Palmer Gaillard, Jr*. Charleston: Self-Published, 2004.

Genovese, Eugene. *Roll Jordan Roll: The World the Slaves Made*. New York: Vintage, 1976.

Gilmore, Glenda Elizabeth. *The Radical Roots of Civil Rights, 1919–1950*. New York: W. W. Norton, 2008.

Godbold, E. Stanley, Jr., and Robert H. Woody. *Christopher Gadsden and the American Revolution*. Knoxville: University of Tennessee Press, 1983.

Goldfield, David R. *Still Fighting the Civil War: The American South and Southern History*. Baton Rouge: Louisiana State University Press, 2004.

Greenberg, Reuben. *Let's Take Back Our Streets!* New York: Contemporary Books, 1989.

Greene, Karen. *Porter-Gaud School: The Next Step*. Greeneville, S.C.: Southern Historical Press, 1982.

Heyward, DuBose. *Porgy*. New York: Grosset & Dunlap, 1925.

Holliday, J. S. *The World Rushed In: The California Gold Rush Experience*. Norman: University of Oklahoma Press, 1981, 2002.

Honey, Michael K. *Going Down Jericho Road: The Memphis Strike, Martin Luther King's Last Campaign*. New York: W. W. Norton, 2008.

Horwitz, Tony. *Confederates in the Attic: Dispatches from the Unfinished Civil War.* New York: Vintage Books, 1998.

Howard, John. *Men Like That: A Southern Queer History.* Chicago: University of Chicago Press, 1999.

Johnson, Chalmers. *The Sorrows of Empire: Militarism, Secrecy, and the End of the Republic.* New York: Verso, 2004.

Johnson, Michael P., and James L. Roark. *Black Masters: A Free Family of Color in the Old South.* New York: W. W. Norton, 1984.

———. *No Chariot Let Down: Charleston's Free People on the Eve of the Civil War.* New York: W. W. Norton, 1986.

Johnson, Patrick E. *Sweet Tea: Black Gay Men of the South.* Chapel Hill: University of North Carolina Press, 2008.

Johnson, Valerie C. *Black Power in the Suburbs: The Myth or Reality of African American Suburban Political Incorporation.* Albany: State University of New York Press, 2002.

Kantrowitz, Stephen. *Ben Tillman and the Reconstruction of White Supremacy.* Chapel Hill: University of North Carolina Press, 2000.

Klarman, Michael J. *From Jim Crow to Civil Rights: The Supreme Court and the Struggle for Black Equality.* Oxford: Oxford University Press, 2006.

Kluger, Richard. *Simple Justice.* New York, Vintage, 1977.

K'Meyer, Tracy E. *Civil Rights in the Gateway to the South: Louisville, Kentucky, 1945–1980.* Lexington: University Press of Kentucky, 2009.

Korstad, Robert. *Civil Rights Unionism: Tobacco Workers and the Struggle for Democracy in the Mid-Twentieth Century South.* Chapel Hill: University of North Carolina Press, 2003.

Kruse, Kevin. *White Flight: Atlanta and the Making of Modern Conservatism.* Princeton, N.J.: Princeton University Press, 2007.

Lamis, Alexander P., ed. *Southern Politics in the 1990s.* Baton Rouge: Louisiana State University Press, 1999.

———. *The Two-Party South.* Oxford: Oxford University Press, 1990.

Lang, Clarence. *Grassroots at the Gateway: Class Politics and Black Freedom Struggle in St. Louis, 1936–1975.* Ann Arbor: University of Michigan Press, 2009.

Lassiter, Matthew D. *The Silent Majority: Suburban Politics in the Sunbelt South.* Princeton, N.J.: Princeton University Press, 2007.

Lassiter, Matthew D., and Joseph Crespino, eds. *The Myth of Southern Exceptionalism.* Oxford: Oxford University Press, 2010.

Lester, Julius. *Lovesong: Becoming a Jew.* New York: Henry Holt, 1988.

Lipsky, David. *Absolutely American: Four Years at West Point.* Boston: Houghton Mifflin, 2003.

Lofton, John. *Denmark Vesey's Slave Revolt: The Plot That Lit a Fuse to Fort Sumter.* Kent, Ohio: Kent State University Press, 1983.

Lovell, John P. *Neither Athens nor Sparta: The American Service Academies in Transition.* Bloomington: Indiana University Press, 1979.

Macauley, Alexander. *Marching in Step: Masculinity, Citizenship, and The Citadel in Post-World War II America*. Athens: University of Georgia Press, 2009.

Manegold, Catherine S. *In Glory's Shadow: Shannon Faulkner, The Citadel, and a Changing America*. New York: Knopf, 2006.

McCurry, Stephanie. *Masters of Small Worlds: Yeoman Households, Gender Relations, and the Political Culture of the Antebellum South Carolina Low Country*. New York: Oxford University Press, 1995.

McDonough, Daniel. *Christopher Gadsden and Henry Laurens: The Parallel Lives of Two American Patriots*. Selinsgrove, Pa.: Susquehanna University Press, 2000.

McGirr, Lisa. *Suburban Warriors: The Origins of the New American Right*. Princeton, N.J.: Princeton University Press, 2002.

Mendelberg, Tali. *The Race Card: Campaign Strategy, Implicit Messages, and the Norm of Equality*. Princeton, N.J.: Princeton University Press, 2001.

Moore, John Hammond. *Carnival of Blood: Dueling, Lynching and Murder in South Carolina*. Columbia: University of South Carolina Press, 2006.

Morgan, Edmund S. *American Slavery, American Freedom*. New York: W. W. Norton, 1975.

Moye, J. Todd. *Freedom Flyers: The Tuskegee Airmen of World War II*. Oxford: Oxford University Press, 2010.

———. *Let the People Decide: Black Freedom and White Resistance Movements in Sunflower County, Mississippi, 1945–1986*. Chapel Hill: University of North Carolina Press, 2004.

Nicholson, D. D., Jr. *A History of The Citadel: The Years of Summerall and Clark*. Charleston, S.C.: The Citadel, 1994.

Orfield, Gary, Susan Eaton, et al. *Dismantling Desegregation: The Quiet Reversal of* Brown v. Board of Education. New York: New Press, 1996.

Patterson, James. Brown v. Board of Education*: A Civil Rights Milestone and Its Troubled Legacy*. Oxford: Oxford University Press, 2002.

Payne, Charles M. *I've Got the Light of Freedom: The Organizing Tradition and the Mississippi Freedom Struggle*. Berkeley: University of California Press, 1995.

Peake, Thomas R. *Keeping the Dream Alive: A History of the Southern Christian Leadership Conference from King to the Nineteen-Eighties*. New York: Peter Lang, 1987.

Pearson, Edward A. *Designs against Charleston: The Trial Record of the Denmark Vesey Slave Conspiracy of 1822*. Chapel Hill: University of North Carolina Press, 1999.

Phillips, Kevin. *The Emerging Republican Majority*. New York: Anchor Books, 1970.

Pollitzer, William S. *The Gullah People and Their African Heritage*. Athens: University of Georgia Press, 1999.

Poole, W. Scott. *Never Surrender: Confederate Memory and Conservatism in the South Carolina Upcountry*. Athens: University of Georgia Press, 2004.

Powers, Bernard. *Black Charlestonians: A Social History 1822–1885*. Fayetteville: University of Arkansas Press, 1994.

Ramsey, William L. *The Yamasee War: A Study of Culture, Economy, and Conflict in the Colonial South*. Lincoln: University of Nebraska Press, 2008.

Ritterhouse, Jennifer Lynn. *Growing Up Jim Crow: How Black and White Southerners Learned Race*. Chapel Hill: University of North Carolina Press, 2006.

Robertson, David. *Denmark Vesey*. New York: Alfred Knopf, 1999.

Robinson, Eugene. *Disintegration: The Splintering of Black America*. New York: Doubleday, 2010.

Robnett, Belinda. *How Long? How Long? African American Women in the Struggle for Civil Rights*. New York: Oxford University Press, 1997.

Rose, Willie Lee. *Rehearsal for Reconstruction: The Port Royal Experiment*. Athens: University of Georgia Press, 1999.

Rosengarten, Theodore, and Dale Rosengarten, eds. *A Portion of the People: Three Hundred Years of Southern Jewish Life*. Columbia: University of South Carolina Press, 2002.

Sass, Herbert Ravenel. *Look Back to Glory*. Indianapolis, Ind.: Bobbs Merrill, 1933.

Schulman, Bruce. *The Seventies: The Great Shift in American Culture, Society and Politics*. New York: Free Press, 2001.

Sears, James T. *Rebels, Ruby Fruit, and Rhinestones: Queering Space in the Stonewall South*. New Brunswick, N.J.: Rutgers University Press, 2001.

Self, Robert O. *American Babylon: Race and the Struggle for Postwar Oakland*. Princeton, N.J.: Princeton University Press, 2005.

Shilts, Randy. *And the Band Played On: Politics, People, and the AIDS Epidemic*. New York: St. Martin's Press, 2007.

Starobin, Robert S., ed. *Demark Vesey: The Slave Conspiracy of 1822*. Englewood Cliffs, N.J.: Prentice Hall, 1970.

Steele, Shelby. *The Content of Our Character: A New Vision of Race in America*. New York: Harper Perennial, 1991.

Sugrue, Thomas. *The Origins of the Urban Crisis: Race and Inequality in Post-War Detroit*. Princeton, N.J.: Princeton University Press, 2005.

Teaford, Jon. *The Metropolitan Revolution: The Rise of Post-Urban America*. New York: Columbia University Press, 2006.

Theoharis, Jeanne, and Komozi Woodard, *Freedom North: Black Freedom Struggles outside the South 1940–1980*. New York: Palgrave Macmillan, 2003.

Theoharis, Jeanne, Komozi Woodard, and Charles Payne. *Groundwork: Local Black Freedom Movements in America*. New York: New York University Press, 2005.

Thomas, John Peyre. *The History of the South Carolina Military Academy*. Charleston, S.C.: Walker, Evans & Cogswell, 1893.

Vito, Gennaro F., Jeffreh A. Maahs, and Ronald M. Holmes. *Criminology: Theory, Research, and Practice*. Boston: Jones & Bartlett, 2006.

Walker, Anders. *The Ghost of Jim Crow: How Southern Moderates Used* Brown v. Board of Education *to Stall Civil Rights*. Oxford: Oxford University Press, 2009.

Weir, Robert. *Colonial South Carolina: A History*. Columbia: University of South Carolina Press, 1997.

Weyeneth, Robert R. *Historic Preservation for a Living City: Historic Charleston Foundation, 1947–1997*. Columbia: University of South Carolina Press, 2000.

Wilkinson, J. Harvie, III. *From Brown to Bakke: The Supreme Court and School Integration, 1945–1978*. Oxford: Oxford University Press, 1981.

Wilson, James Q. *Thinking about Crime*. New York: Basic Books, 1983.

Wilson, James Q., and Richard J. Herrnstein. *Crime and Human Nature*. New York: Simon and Schuster, 1985.

Wolfe, Margaret Ripley. *Daughters of Canaan: A Saga of Southern Women*. Lexington: University of Kentucky Press, 1995.

Wolfe, Tom. *A Man in Full*. New York: Farrar Straus and Giroux, 1998.

Wood, Peter. *Black Majority: Negroes in Colonial South Carolina*. New York: Knopf, 1974.

Wu, Frank H. *Yellow: Race in America beyond Black and White*. New York: Basic Books, 2002.

Wyatt-Brown, Bertram. *Honor and Violence in the Old South*. New York: Oxford University Press, 1986.

Yuhl, Stephanie E. *A Golden Haze of Memory: The Making of Historic Charleston*. Chapel Hill: University of North Carolina Press, 2005.

ARTICLES AND ESSAYS

Agyepong, Tera. "In the Belly of the Beast: Black Policemen Combat Police Brutality in Chicago, 1968–1983." *Journal of African American History* 98 (Spring 2013): 253–76.

Biles, Roger. "Black Mayors: A Historical Assessment." *Journal of Negro History* 77 (Summer 1992): 109–25.

Bures, Regina M. "Historic Preservation, Gentrification, and Tourism: The Transformation of Charleston, South Carolina." *Research in Urban Sociology* 6 (2001): 195–209.

Burton, Orville Vernon. "Legislative and Congressional Districting in South Carolina." In *Race and Redistricting in the 1990s*, edited by Bernard Grofman, 290–314. New York: Agathon Press, 1998.

———. "The South as 'Other,' the Southerner as Stranger." *Journal of Southern History* 79 (Feb. 2013): 7–50.

Cantor, David, and Kenneth C. Land. "Unemployment and Crime Rates in the Post–World War II United States: A Theoretical and Empirical Analysis." *American Sociological Review* 50 (June 1985): 317–32.

Carson, Clayborne. "Black-Jewish Universalism in the Era of Identity Politics." In *Struggles in the Promised Land: Towards a History of Black Jewish Relations in the United States*, edited by Jack Salzman and Cornel West, 177–96. Oxford: Oxford University Press, 1997.

Cha-Jua, Sundiata Keita, and Clarence Lang. "The 'Long Movement' as Vampire: Temporal and Spatial Fallacies in Recent Black Freedom Studies." *Journal of African American History* 92 (March 2007): 265–88.

De Hart, Jane Sherron. "Second Wave Feminism(s) and the South: The Difference That Differences Make." In *Women of the American South: A Multicultural Reader*, edited by Christie Anne Farnham, 273–301. New York: New York University Press, 1997.

Fink, Leon. "Union Power, Soul Power." *Southern Changes* 5 (1983): 9–20.

Ford, Lacy K., and R. Phillip Stone. "Economic Development and Globalization in South Carolina." *Southern Cultures* 13 (Spring 2007): 18–52.

Gaboury, William T. "George Washington Murray and the Fight for Political Democracy in South Carolina." *Journal of Negro History* 63 (July 1977): 258–69.

Gagan, Byron J. *"Ferguson v. City of Charleston, South Carolina:* 'Fetal Abuse,' Drug Testing, and the Fourth Amendment." *Stanford Law Review* 53 (Nov. 2000): 491–518.

Greenberg, Reuben. "Less Bang-Bang for the Buck." *Policy Review* 59 (Winter 1992): 56–61.

Greene, Harlan. "Charleston, South Carolina." In *Hometowns: Gay Men Write about Where They Belong*, edited by John Preston. New York: Dutton, 1991.

Gross, Robert, ed. "The Making of a Slave Conspiracy, Part 2." *William and Mary Quarterly* 59 (Jan. 2002): 135–202.

Hale, Jon. "'The Fight Was Instilled in Us': High School Activism and the Civil Rights Movement in Charleston." *South Carolina Historical Magazine* 114 (Jan. 2013): 4–28.

Hall, Jacquelyn Dowd. "The Long Civil Rights Movement and the Political Uses of the Past." *Journal of American History* 91 (March 2005): 1233–63.

Hamer, Fritz. "Giving a Sense of Achievement: Changing Gender and Racial Roles in Wartime Charleston: 1942–1945. *Proceedings of the South Carolina Historical Association.* 1997: 61–76.

Huth, Tom. "Should Charleston Go New South?" *Historic Preservation* 31 (July–Aug. 1979): 32–38.

Johnson, Michael P. "Denmark Vesey and His Co-Conspirators." *William and Mary Quarterly* 58 (Oct. 2001): 915–76.

Jordan, Laylon Wayne. "Police and Politics: Charleston in the Gilded Age, 1880–1990." *South Carolina Historical Magazine* 81 (1980): 35–50.

Keller, Edmond J. "The Impact of Black Mayors on Urban Policy." *Annals of the American Academy of Political Science* 430 (Sept. 1978): 40–52.

Kimmel, Michael. "Saving the Males: The Sociological Implications of the Virginia Military Institute and the Citadel." *Gender & Society* 14 (Aug. 2000): 494–516.

Lacher, R. Geoffrey, and Chi-Ok Oh. "Is Tourism a Low-Income Industry? Evidence from Three Coastal Regions." *Journal of Travel Research* 51 (2012): 464–72.

Macauley, Alex. "An Oasis of Order: The Citadel, the 1960s, and the Vietnam Anti-War Movement." *Southern Cultures* 11 (Fall 2005): 35–61.

McCullough, Jane, and William V. Moore. "Exercising Dominion over Metropolitan Growth: A Case Study of Charleston, South Carolina." *Journal of Political Science* 27 (1999): 1–20.

Megget, Linda L. "Citadel of Trauma: The Untold Story of the Citadel's First Black Graduate." *Black Issues in Higher Education* 13 (Jan. 1997): 22–25.

Moore, Jamie W. "The Low Country in Economic Transition: Charleston since 1865." *South Carolina Historical Magazine* 80 (April 1979): 156–71.

Muller, Philip R. "Look Back without Anger: A Reappraisal of William A. Dunning." *Journal of American History* 61 (Sept. 1974): 325–38.

Nelson, Timothy J. "He Made a Way Out of No Way: Religious Experience in an African-American Congregation." *Review of Religious Research* 39 (Sept. 1997): 5–26.

Oldfield, John. "On the Beat: Black Policemen in Charleston, 1869–1921." *South Carolina Historical Magazine* 102 (April 2001): 153–68.

Poliakoff, Eli A. "Charleston's Longshoremen: Organized Labor in the Anti-Union Palmetto State." *The South Carolina Historical Magazine* 103 (July 2002): 247–64.

Powers, Bernard. "Community Evolution and Race Relations in Reconstruction Charleston, South Carolina." *South Carolina Historical Magazine* 101 (July 2000): 214–33.

Reardon, Sean F., and John T. Yun. "Private School Racial Enrollments and Segregation." The Civil Rights Project, Harvard University (June 2002).

Roberts, Blain, and Ethan J. Kytle. "Looking the Thing in the Face: Slavery, Race, and the Commemorative Landscape in Charleston, South Carolina, 1865–2010." *Journal of Southern History* 78 (Aug. 2012): 639–84.

Saller, Richard P. "*Pater Familias, Mater Familias,* and Gendered Semantics of the Roman Household." *Classical Philology* 94 (April 1999): 182–97.

Severens, Martha. "Charleston in the Age of Porgy and Bess." *Southern Quarterly* 28 (1989): 5–23.

Shircliffe, Barbara. "We Got the Best of That World": A Case for the Study of Nostalgia in the Oral History of School Segregation." *Oral History Review* 28 (Summer–Fall 2001): 59–84.

Smith, M. Dwayne, and Joel A. Devine. "Crime and Unemployment: Effect across Age and Race Categories." *Sociological Perspectives* 35 (Winter 1992): 551–72.

Swain, Johnnie D., Jr. "Black Mayors, Urban Decline and the Underclass." *Journal of Black Studies* 24 (Sept. 1993): 16–28.

Wiese, Andrew. "African American Suburbanization and Regionalism in the Modern South." In *The Myth of Southern Exceptionalism*, edited by Matthew D. Lassiter and Joseph Crespino, 210–33. Oxford: Oxford University Press, 2009.

Wood, Peter. "'More Like a Negro Country': Demographic Patterns in Colonial South Carolina, 1670–1740." In *Race and Slavery in the Western Hemisphere: Quantitative Studies*, edited by Stanley L. Engerman and Eugene Genovese, 131–45. Princeton, N.J.: Princeton University Press, 1975.

DISSERTATIONS

O'Neill, Steve. "From the Shadow of Slavery: The Civil Rights Years in Charleston." PhD diss., University of Virginia, 1990.

Steeley, Robert Joseph. "A History of Independent Education in South Carolina." EdD diss., University of South Carolina, 1979.

White, John. "Managed Compliance: White Resistance and Desegregation in South Carolina, 1950–1970," PhD diss., University of Florida, 2006.

Acknowledgments

Long ago, I interrupted a brilliant southern history lecture by John Boles at Rice University to correct what I saw as his mistaken notions about Charleston's history. Of course, it turned out I was the one who was wrong. John had the grace not to hold it against me and became my undergraduate advisor despite my presumptuousness. Yet that inauspicious assertion about Charleston's past was probably the moment when I first started to think about writing a history of my hometown.

When I went to graduate school, I could not let Charleston go entirely. One chapter of this book started as part of my MA thesis at the University of Georgia, and I have to thank (once again) Bob Pratt and Bryant Simon for making that project something worth returning to years later. Even though I put Charleston aside, for the most part, while getting my PhD at the University of North Carolina, my friends, mentors, and colleagues there shaped this project in less tangible ways. At the Southern Oral History Program, Jacquelyn Hall and Beth Millwood gave me the tools to interview Charlestonians and the wisdom to listen to what they had to say.

Like most history professors, I relied on assistance from three essential groups to finish this book: students, colleagues, and librarians. Student research assistants were an invaluable part of the process, helping me with everything from oral history transcription to archival research. Richard Balas, Stefanie Ramsay, and especially Amanda Kreklau and Bryan Schwartz went above and beyond the call of duty to help me. As for friends and colleagues, the following folks shared their scholarship or slogged through my work on Charleston: Chris Myers Asch, Vernon Burton, Dan Carter, Peter Coclanis, Joe Crespino, Jennifer Dixon, Marvin Dulaney, Suzan Erem, Felice Knight, Marvin Ira Lare, Alex Macauley, Peyton McCrary, Todd Moye, Steve O'Neill, William S. Poole, Blain Roberts, Christopher Schmidt, Jason Sokol, Phillip Stone, Kerry Taylor, Anders Walker, Robert Weyeneth, John White, and Stephanie Yuhl. A special thanks goes to Damon Fordham, who critiqued more of this book than he probably intended when he offhandedly agreed to read "some" of it. My colleagues at Sonoma State suffered through countless presentations and conversations on Charleston with good cheer, despite the fact that my work seemed more like journalism than real history. Finally, librarians and archivists saved me many trips to South Carolina by searching, scanning, and sending countless documents that I never would have known existed, much less found, without them. Thanks to Herb Hartsook and Kate Moore (University of South Carolina), Mary Hatfield (City of Charleston Planning Department), James Cross (Clemson University), Jabari Spruill (Porter Gaud School), Charlene Gunnells (The Citadel), Heather Woolwine (Medical University of South Carolina), Nic Butler and Dot Glover (Charleston County Library), Libby Wilder (*Post and Courier*), and especially Mary Battle, Harlan Greene, Georgette Mayo, Aaron

Spelbring, Deborah Wright, and all of the amazing folks at the College of Charleston's Avery Research Center.

Sometimes, you have to go very far away to get perspective on where you're from, and I want to thank my colleagues in Germany for giving me time and distance to think about Charleston, the South, and America in ways I never could have at home. The German-American Fulbright Commission and the Organization of American Historians funded my time in Germany, but the scholars and students I met there made all the difference. Jürgen Martschukart and Georg Schild brought me to teach about civil rights at the Universities of Erfurt and Tübingen in 2010 and 2014. They and their students helped me see U.S. race relations, culture, and politics through new eyes and with fresh perspectives.

This is my third book with the University of North Carolina Press, and I have nothing but praise for the editors and staff: Chuck Grench and his editorial assistants Rachel Berry Surles, Sara Jo Cohen, Lucas Church, and Katherine Fisher. The rest of the staff saved me from many mistakes, big and small. I could not have asked for a more supportive and intellectually rigorous publisher.

I started this book with a story about family, and I should conclude with a similar story. As I admitted up front, one of the reasons that I wrote this book was to bridge the gap between South Carolina and California. Charleston and San Francisco are surprisingly similar in many ways, but family makes them both feel like home to me. Philip, Natalie, and Lila Estes gave me all the free beer, vegan food, loud music, surfing, and love I could ever want. Judy Burges was always happy to discuss her hometown and anything else over Bessinger's barbecue. Anne and Joel Lake got me tickets to CofC basketball games and made the "House of Burgeses" a home away from home, while Howard and Marilyn Brilliant "adopted" me into their family and the Tribe. For much of my life and most of the book, there was one person who represented Charleston to me more than anyone else, and that was my mom, Gene Elizabeth Burges. She did not live to see the book finished, but she was instrumental in its completion—as with so many other aspects of my life. Dealing with the grief of her passing and finishing this book would not have been possible without Carol and Zinnia, my San Francisco family. It is to them that this book is dedicated.

Index

12/14/15